Deleted Fragments

Acquired by JOHN NICOLAY

Four score and seven years ago our fathers brought forth, upon this continent, a new nation, conceived in liberty, and dedicated to the proposition that "all men are created equal."

Now we are engaged in a great civil war, testing whether that nation, or any nation so conceived and so dedicated, can long endure. We are met on a great battle field of that war. We have come to dedicate a portion of it, as a final resting place for those who died here, that the nation might live. This we may, in all propriety do. But, in a larger sense, we can not dedicate we can not consecrate— we can not hallow, this ground— The brave men, living and dead, who struggled here have hallowed it, far above our poor power to add or detract. The world will little note, nor long remember what we say here; while it can never forget what they did here.

It is rather for us, the living, we here be dedicated to the great task remaining before us— that, from these honored dead we take increased devotion to that cause for which they here, gave the last full measure of devotion— that we here highly resolve these dead shall not have died in vain; that the nation, shall have a new birth of freedom, and that government of the people, by the people, for the people, shall not perish from the earth.

LIBRARY OF CONGRESS

B

Copyright © 1964, by LOUIS A. WARREN
All rights reserved. This book, or parts thereof,
must not be reproduced in any form
without permission of the publisher.

Privately printed for
THE LINCOLN NATIONAL LIFE FOUNDATION
By KINGSPORT PRESS, INC.,
Kingsport, Tennessee

To my son
KENNETH
born in Kentucky
reared in Indiana

Comment

THIS manuscript was the "Runner Up" in a five thousand dollar Literary Award Contest for the best monograph of at least seventy-five thousand words on a historical or non-fiction subject relating to the Civil War period. Said to be the largest prize ever offered for a historical narration, it attracted over one hundred and seventy competitors. A jury of ten historians, two Pulitzer Prize winners among them, acted as judges. An illuminated citation, dated July 1, 1963, with the caption, "For Excellence," included the following:

> "The manuscript submitted by Dr. Warren was recognized by all of the judges as an outstanding effort and the 'Runner Up' in the final selection to be worthy of special notice."

Signed by Wm. Buchanan Gold, Jr., Commander of the Pennsylvania Commandery, and Brooke M. Lessig, President of the War Library and Museum, both of the Military Order of the Loyal Legion of the United States.

Fort Wayne, Indiana
November 19, 1963

Contents

PRELIMINARIES

    Frontispiece—Statue by Schweizer
      at Gettysburg   (*faces title page*)
    Comment   vii
    Introduction   xv

COMPENDIUM

    I. BACKGROUND FOR ORATORY   1

Work of a lifetime—Home environment—Formal education—Influential books—Practice pieces—Public speaking—Political advocate—Lyceum lecture—Speech in Congress—Applauded in Massachusetts—Pronounces eulogies—Debates with Douglas—Cooper Union discourse—Stumps New England—Farewell Address—First Inaugural—July 4, appeal—Annual Message to Congress.

    II. FREEDOM MOTIF   10

Early reaction to slavery—Church influence—Observes slaves driven south—Removal to free state—Cowper on enslavement—Auction blocks at New Orleans—Protest to legislature—Resolution in Congress—"Created equal"—Great moral wrong—Cooper Union summary—Compensated emancipation—Greeley correspondence—Chicago visitors—Preliminary Emancipation Proclamation—"Vested interest in freedom"—

    III. INDEPENDENCE DAY   17

"Glorious old fourth"—Chart of liberty—Visit to Independence Hall—Union League medal—Town of Gettysburg—Omens of great battle—First contingent of Confederates—Dispatch to Washington—President announces victory—Surrender of Vicksburg—News reaches Lincoln—Dual triumphs—Added weapons—President serenaded—Speech of July 7—Proclamation of praise and prayer—Motley's communication—Significance of nation's birthday.

IV. SOLDIERS' NATIONAL CEMETERY   26
Humane disposal of dead—Mortuary reform—Care for deceased—Gigantic hospital—Volunteer helpers—Heroic lifesaving efforts—Gruesome stories—Searching for casualties—Gettysburg, huge morgue—Curtin appoints Wills—Removal of Pennsylvania dead—Disinterment prohibited—National burial grounds proposed—Evergreen Cemetery—Massachusetts burial lot—Local projects—National sepulcher—Grounds purchased—Plans presented—Removal of bodies—Identification of deceased—Proposal considered—Participating states—Cemetery register—National effort.

V. INVITATIONS EXTENDED   39
Curtin the sponsor—Dedication plans—Orator selected—Tentative date—November 19, approved—Battlefield appearance—Commissioner Carr—His memoirs—President invited—Proverbial afterthought—Personal invitation—Confirmation letter—Dignitaries included—Regrets received—General invitation.

VI. COMPOSING THE ADDRESS   48
No amanuensis—Early contributions—Other eulogies—"Glorious theme"—Adaptation begins—Permanent restoration—New race relations—Conkling letter—Correspondence received—Garibaldi's tribute—Prophetic medal—Thanksgiving proclamation—Arranging his thoughts—First draft—Defrees' approval—Cameron reads script—Brooks inquires about speech—Lamon looks over text—Two complete copies.

VII. INCIDENTS EN ROUTE   56
Traveling proposals—Arrangements approved—President's party—Personal escort—Seward's anxiety—

North Central Railroad—Governor's special—Hanover Junction pictures—Speech at Hanover—Writing on train—Nicolay denies tradition—*The Perfect Tribute*—Source of story—Mostly fiction—Wide distribution and acceptance—Summary of contents.

VIII. INFORMAL PRELIMINARIES   64

Wills' personal invitation—Accommodations for President—Evening meal—Everett's tribute to Lincoln—President serenaded—Impromptu speech—Seward responds—Other informal talks—Marshals' meeting—Writing material provided—Confers with Seward—Receives telegrams—Visits battlefield—Finishes address—Secretary Nicolay's sobriety—Extempore remarks.

IX. SOLEMN PROCESSION   74

Vehicles converge on Gettysburg—Guests from a distance—Estimates of attendance—Housing and feeding—Favorable weather—Lincoln and Lamon—Marshals' attire—Decorations—Official military escort—General Couch—Route of parade—Military units—Marshals escort President—Civic division—Injured soldiers—President appears—His mount—Lincoln's horsemanship—Chief mourner.

X. DEDICATORY PROGRAM   84

Printed instructions—Appearance of President—Arrival on platform—Distinguished guests—Seating arrangements—Ohio governors—Groups on stand—Traditional visitors—Celebrities—Dirge by Birgfeld's Band—Dr. Stockton's invocation—Reactions to prayer—Letters of regret—Marine Band selection—Poem by French—Baltimore Glee Club.

XI. ORATOR OF THE DAY   93

Lincoln and Everett—Sketch of Everett—Lincoln in contrast—Their first meeting—Springfield letters—Early reaction to Lincoln—Selection of Everett—Arrival in Gettysburg—Views battlefield—Evades parade—Desires privacy before speaking—Arrives before Lincoln—Present on time—Length of oration—Favorable reactions—Critical comments—Address inaccessible—Printed in appendix.

XII. APPROPRIATE REMARKS   103

Stenographic copy—Hale version—Fourscore—Our fathers—Brought forth—Continent—New nation—Conceived—Dedicated—Proposition—Equal—Civil War—Any nation—Endure—Battlefield—Portion—Resting place—Lives—Fitting and proper—Larger sense—Brave men—Consecrated—Say and did here—The living—Unfinished work—Great task—Honored dead—Died in vain—"Under God"—New birth—Freedom—Government—People—Shall not perish—Vast future.

XIII. PRESENTATION NOTES   119

Controversial observations—Introduction—Photographer—Lincoln's voice—Rhetoric—Reads speech—Uses references—Speaks without notes—Immediate reaction—Everett's letter—Lamon's critical comments—Reported disappointment—Carr's recollections—Mrs. Andrew's fiction—Audience reaction—Lincoln's brevity—Time element—Tired audience.

XIV. DEDICATION AFTERMATH   130

Dirge and benediction—Convalescent soldiers—Wills' letter—Commissioners' reaction—Visitors on battlefield—Gruesome souvenirs—Late dinner—Lincoln, Curtin reception—Seymour reviews troops—Burns meets the President—Pension for hero—Virginia Wade—Anderson's address—Departure for Washington—Arrival and illness.

XV. PRESS REACTION   139

Correspondents—Stenographic reports—*Chronicle* reprint—*City Document* No. 106—Holland in *Republican*—Angell in *Journal*—Scovel sends *Bulletin*—Twenty favorable reports—Three dissenters—Gettysburg *Compiler*—Politics in Adams County.

CONTENTS

XVI. PRELIMINARY HOLOGRAPHS ... 150

Five known transcripts—Secretaries' copies—Robert Lincoln's interest—John Hay's reply—His heirloom—Mrs. Hay and Miss Nicolay—Working sheet—Wilson's contradictions—Clarence Hay's information—John Nicolay copy—Ten volume history—*Century Magazine* article—Two fragments—Wills' tradition—Helen Nicolay's recollections—Robert Lincoln's inquiries—Letter discovered—Presentation to Library of Congress.

XVII. SUBSEQUENT HOLOGRAPHS ... 160

Everett, Bancroft, and Bliss copies—Jeb Stuart's pen—Chicago fair gift—Wills' requisition—Nicolay's memory—No "lost copy"—Everett's request—Revised address—Everett acknowledges receipt—Sold for $1,000—Acquired by Keys family—Purchased by school children—Bancroft requests transcript—Not suitable for reproduction—Bancroft's personal property—Given to Cornell University—Baltimore copy to Bliss—Reproduced in book—Standard version—Painstaking copy—Robert Lincoln's preference—Bliss family to Cintas—Willed to White House.

XVIII. INCREASING RESPECT ... 171

Lord Curzon's tribute—Prize to Lincoln—Lamon's claim—Tributes; — Adams — Arnold — Austin — Boutwell — Brooks — Browne — Bryan — Brice — Caine — Charnwood — Conway — Curtis — Eliot — Emerson — Fisk — Graham — Greeley — Green — Hanley — Higginson — Hillis — Hoover — Hayes — Ingersoll — Irelan — Lambros — Longfellow — Ludlow — McCulloch — Newton — Nicolay — Parker —Purvis—F. D. Roosevelt—T. Roosevelt—Smith— Sumner — Tumulty — Watterson — Wheeler — Wilson—Acropolis recitation—Curzon's query.

XIX. IN MEMORIAM ... 177

Stanton's comment—Diversified mementoes—Congress acquires land—Speech memorials—Tablets in national parks—Location of exedra—Bust by Brown—Statue by Schweizer—Reproduction of address—Description of Soldiers' Monument—Cornerstone—Dedication—Site of speakers' stand—Statements of Carmichael, Bullard, Melegakes—Adams *Sentinel* report—Impossible site—Selleck memorandum—Location of platform—Unimpressive memorial—Colossal statue—Landscaped field—"New birth of Freedom,"

APPENDIX—EDWARD EVERETT'S ORATION 185

Introduction—Law of Athens—Tokens of respect—Governor's invitation—Auspicious day—Significance of victory—Army of Potomac—Train of events—Presidential election—Cotton-growing states—Northern thrust—Confederate plan, part one—Part two—Penetration of Pennsylvania—Pursuit by Union Army—Converging on Gettysburg—The encounter—July 1, attack—July 2, engagements—July 3, hostilities—Retreat of Confederates—Tremendous loss of life—Mournful spectacle—Women's contribution—Responsibility for war—Precedents considered—Properly called a rebellion—The "sovereign" theory—Agency of the states—Wretched sophistries—Two hostile governments—National suicide—Vigorous prosecution of war—Confiscation and emancipation—Injuries inflicted and retaliated—England—Germany—Italy—France—No bitterness among masses—Heart of the people for union—Honored graves—"The whole earth a sepulchre of illustrious men."

SOURCES 215

INDEX 223

Introduction

THE YEAR 1863 brought Abraham Lincoln more distinction at home and abroad than any other period of twelve months. The phenomenal Proclamation of Emancipation, issued on January 1, set in motion enactments that freed a race from bondage, and kindled the flame of freedom around the world. The victories of two Union armies, 1,000 miles apart, culminating on July 4, gave the commander-in-chief of the Union forces the most significant dual victory ever achieved. The political letter of August 26, prepared for the mass meeting of unconditional Union men at Springfield, Illinois, caused the London *Star* to comment: "It is the manifesto of a truly great man in the exigency of almost unequaled moment." The Proclamation of Thanksgiving, signed on October 3, prefaced the establishment of the November festival as an annual Federal holiday. Crowning the spirit of these contributions to enslaved humanity, military science, political acumen, and religious progression, on November 19, the President concentrated into a literary classic the essence of all these accomplishments which has influenced the destiny of the human race. A sequel to these pronouncements of the memorable year is found in the message to Congress on December 8, commending the armed forces "to whom, more than to others, the world must stand indebted for the home of freedom disenthralled, regenerated, enlarged, and perpetuated."

Surely, during the centennial observance of the Civil War,

events which occurred in 1863 will be highly regarded. From the northern viewpoint, the most dramatic engagement of the entire contest took place at Gettysburg, where a supposedly invincible southern army of invasion was repulsed, never again to occupy northern soil. The close of the hostilities on "The glorious fourth," has contributed much to memorializing the spectacular contest and given emphasis to the historical importance of the furious struggle.

John Richard Green, famous English historian, considered that Gettysburg was, "The most momentous battle in history." Yet, a contributor to the Brooklyn *Daily Eagle* in 1913, wrote with reference to Lincoln's speech at the site of the conflict, he was "expressing something vaster than the battle of Gettysburg, and more far reaching than even the Civil War."

On the sixty-fourth anniversary of the Lincoln speech, the Philadelphia *Bulletin* prophesied that the address would be "fresh and inspiring in its lines, when the very story of the battlefield itself will be as hazy as the siege of Troy." In almost parallel terms Charles Sumner prophesied, "The address will live when the battle of Gettysburg is forgotten, or remembered only on account of the speech which it inspired." Herbert Hoover expressed this same sentiment: "Every American's thought of this great battlefield of Gettysburg flashes with the instant vision of the lonely figure of Lincoln, whose immortal words dominate the scene." These comments recall Edward Bulwer Lytton's famous adage: "The pen is mightier than the sword."

One of the objectives of the Civil War Centennial Commission is to encourage people "to derive inspiration from the notable events occurring in the fraternal struggle." It would be difficult to discover an episode providing a creative impulse equal to Lincoln's address at Gettysburg. The brilliant French editor, M. E. Dusergier, responded almost immediately upon reading the address: "I do not believe that modern speech has ever produced anything that will excel his eloquent discourse over the graves of the dead soldiers." A chancellor of Oxford University, Lord

Curzon, after choosing Lincoln's Second Inaugural Address and the speech at Gettyburg, as two of the three greatest orations delivered in the mother tongue, pondered: "It sets one to inquiring with nothing short of wonder: 'How knoweth this man his letters, having never learned.'" The prominent New Jersey lawyer, Honorable Courtland Parker, reasoned: "The day must come when the pure English which he uttered and in which he clothed his noble sentences, will make all men wonder, as many already do, how it came about that one so little educated should be so proficient!"

Most of the dissertations about the address have made no attempt to create a literary, rhetorical or historical background for the masterpiece. One of the earliest news releases pretending to convey information about the delivery of the speech and especially Lincoln's own reaction to it, was an open letter to the Chicago *Tribune* in 1886 by Ward H. Lamon. After an interval of twenty-three years, he attempted to repeat conversation verbatim relating to the President's address. Immediately afterwards he is said to have discussed with Edward Everett and William H. Seward the effectiveness of the discourse and also talked with Lincoln about it. Lamon's conclusions ended in a tirade against those who spoke in a complimentary manner of the brief Gettysburg remarks.

The *Century Magazine* for 1894, with an article by John G. Nicolay, was the earliest periodical to feature the story of Lincoln's writing the address. Like Lamon's it was in the form of memoirs, relating incidents in some detail which had occurred many years before. The fact that Nicolay was the President's private secretary gave much weight to the argument and it was widely accepted. Its chief contributions were two facsimile copies of the speech, one written before and the other after its delivery. Both of the Lamon and Nicolay articles greatly influenced subsequent writings.

The year 1906 brought three publications from the press, a pamphlet, a brochure, and a book featuring the dedicatory remarks. The pamphlet, *Lincoln at Gettysburg*, contained an address delivered by Clark E. Carr before the Illinois State Historical Society at Springfield on January 25. Although forty-three years had now passed, Mr. Carr, in preparing his copy, did not hesitate to rely upon his rather defective memory. He was prompted by the Lamon-Nicolay statements and the report of the Commissioners of the National Cemetery at Gettysburg of which body he was a member. His monograph was later put in book form and it added much to the confusion about the activities of the commission, their reaction to Mr. Lincoln and incidents relating to the dedication. A brochure entitled *The Perfect Tribute* by Mrs. Mary Raymond Shipman Andrews, because of its excellent literary qualities, reached the highest total sales ever achieved by a Lincoln publication. It was widely distributed in the high schools of the nation. For over fifty years the youth of the country have read and believed the fictitious story that Lincoln wrote the famous address on an old scrap of paper while on the train en route to Gettysburg. The same year 1906, under the title *Gettysburg and Lincoln*, Henry Sweetser Burrage, a brevet Major, United States Volunteers, brought out the first objective study of the Gettysburg Cemetery, its dedication, Lincoln's speech, and the National Park. Although somewhat influenced by prevailing traditions it was by far the best historical account of the proceedings which had appeared up to that time.

There followed after 1906, at intervals of about a decade, these cloth bound books: *Lincoln's Gettysburg Address* by Orton H. Carmichael, 1917; *Lincoln at Gettysburg* by William E. Barton, 1930; *A Few Appropriate Remarks* by F. Lauriston Bullard, 1944. After a period of two decades has elapsed, since the appearance of the last volume, there has been discovered enough little known early information and associated data to warrant another Gettysburg volume. Its use of many quotations with their sources and references should constitute reliable authority for those who may decide to delve still further into the preparation, delivery and reception of the address.

Information gathered in Kentucky and Indiana for his two

books, *Lincoln's Parentage and Childhood* and *Lincoln's Youth*, has greatly helped the author in creating the literary and political background for this study. The vast collection of Lincolniana brought together during twenty-eight years as director of the Lincoln National Life Foundation, further supplemented by important acquisitions under the present director, R. Gerald McMurtry, provided the primary—and almost exclusive—source for this treatise.

CHAPTER 1

Background for Oratory

AFTER some individual achievement of exceptional merit has been observed, the comment is often heard that it was the work of a lifetime. Daniel Webster admitted that in the preparation of his memorable reply to Hayne, such was the case. Upon hearing Abraham Lincoln speak at Gettysburg, one listener in a meditative mood concluded: "It seems as though he must have been preparing it all his life." An understanding of Lincoln's remarkable use of words, either spoken or written, cannot be acquired without a knowledge of his surroundings in early youth, and his subsequent development.

During Abraham's childhood he was greatly influenced by a worthy home environment, as well as the cultivation of estimable innate tendencies, and instruction by helpful teachers in subscription schools. The fortunate possession of informative and inspirational books provided for him an adequate foundation for his remarkable advancement. We may observe with some degree of accuracy his steady progression through the subsequent decades until finally, on the battle field of Gettysburg, he delivered his renowned oration.

The parents of Abraham, ardent church members, while deprived of educational advantages themselves, had great respect for learning. At the earliest opportunity their children were sent to school, and by the time Abraham was seven years of age, he had received two terms of instruction from different school masters. Upon moving to Indiana, three more sessions under three other teachers brought to a close his formal education. Thus providing him with as much schooling as was usually received by the average pioneer boy. A contemporary biographer made this statement which Mr. Lincoln must have read: "For writing he manifested a great fondness. It was his custom to form letters, to write words and sentences wherever he found suitable materials. He scrawled them with charcoal, he scored them in the dust, in the sand, in the snow, anywhere and everywhere that lines could be drawn there he improved the capacity for writing."

Over and over again the boy went through the few books that he was able to acquire or borrow. The family *Bible*, ever present, was the one most often read and excerpts were repeated. Of second importance was Weems' *Washington* which, almost in its entirety, he was able to quote from memory. Elias Nason, New England editor, in commenting about its influence on Abraham, said: "The patriotic Weems, by the vivacity, and glowing fervor of his style, inspiring as no other man a love for country in the breast of youth." These two books, the *Bible* and Weems' *Washington*, not only fixed the simplicity of his diction and his unique way of "putting things," but also proved to be the most inspirational sources of his boyhood days.

When Abraham was about twelve, a copy of Scott's *Lessons in Elocution* became available to him. It was a four-hundred-page book containing a compilation of the world's best literature for reading and reciting in public. Within these covers he was learning how to articulate distinctly and deliberately, to pronounce words forcibly, using the proper accent, to distinguish the significant words in a sentence; also to observe pause, to note

170. p. 16 / *193, 131.* p. 11

cadence and to reveal his emotions by facial expressions and gestures.

While still attending the log cabin schools in Indiana, he began to show some proficiency in reading and in speaking practice pieces. A little later, according to his stepmother, he would come home from a church service and repeat, almost verbatim, the preacher's sermon. Returning from sessions of the county courts, he often reviewed the cases tried and presented the arguments of the lawyers. However, up to this time, although he spoke well in public, his reputation as a declaimer was purely local.

Upon reaching Illinois, at twenty-one years of age, he soon became an impressive speaker. The earliest political meeting he attended in the state was at Decatur, where two candidates for the legislature were appearing. Abraham was invited to speak at the meeting and his presentation was acknowledged to be the best talk of the day. Encouraged by the reaction to his effort, he later announced his candidacy for a seat in the Illinois House of Representatives. When he was twenty-five years of age he was elected and subsequently became the spokesman for his party. Soon he was considered to be the best stump speaker in the state.

When Abraham was twenty-eight years old, while living in Springfield, he made a speech before the Young Men's Lyceum. This was the first patriotic declamation which gave evidence of his unusual ability and great promise in the art of public speaking. He had occasion to mention the passing of the fathers of the Revolution in this figurative language: "They *were* a forest of giant oaks; but the all-resistless hurricane has swept over them, and left only, here and there, a lonely trunk, despoiled of its verdure, shorn of its foliage; unshading and unshaded, to murmur in a few more gentle breezes. And to combat with its mutilated limbs, a few more ruder storms, then to sink, and be no more.

168, 189. pp. 76–80 / *189.* pp. 121, 197 / *109.* No. 152, *1.* I, 5

They *were* the pillars of the temple of liberty." This address was ordered published by the Lyceum and it marked an early milestone in his progress as a rhetorician.

Four years after his marriage, in 1842, he was elected to the United States House of Representatives and while he did not distinguish himself by sponsoring any important legislation, no one who heard him would soon forget his humorous speech on "Military Coattails." At the close of the first session in 1848, on his way back to Springfield, he filled some speaking engagements in Massachusetts. This hurriedly arranged itinerary allows one to learn from the press what the intellectuals of the Bay State thought of him. He had received the approval of the people with whom he grew up, but it was problematical how university and college trained men would accept his quaint manner of expression.

At Worcester on September 12, 1848, he spoke: "in a clear, and cool, and very eloquent manner, for an hour and a half, carrying the audience with him in his able arguments and brilliant illustrations, . . . At the close of this truly masterly and convincing speech, the audience gave three enthusiastic cheers for Illinois, and three more for the eloquent Whig member from that state." Three days later, he addressed the Boston Whig Club at Washington Hall "in a speech of an hour and a half, which, for sound reasoning, cogent argument and keen satire, we have seldom heard equalled." The press at Lowell stated his address was "replete with good sense, sound reasoning, and irresistible argument, and spoken with that perfect command of manner and matter which so eminently distinguishes the Western Orators. "At Chelsea the conclusion was that his speech "for aptness of illustration, solidity of argument, and genuine eloquence is hard to beat." Again back in Boston, on September 22, he appeared on the same platform with William H. Seward. A reporter stated that Lincoln "spoke about an hour and made a forcible and

1. I, 108–115 / 1. II, 1, 5; 1. II, 5

convincing speech." By this time, the Westerner must have sensed that the stamp of approval had been placed on his oratory by the discerning and critical Easterners.

Two eulogies, one on Zachary Taylor in 1850 and the other on Henry Clay in 1852, indicate how well Lincoln was able to express himself appropriately on occasions which called for dignity and solemnity. He observed that the late President Taylor: "indulged in no recreations, he visited no public places seeking applause; but quietly, as the earth in its orbit, he was always at his post."

About Clay's oratory, he admired: "that deeply earnest and impassioned tone, and manner, which can proceed only from great sincerity . . . Mr. Clay's predominant sentiment, from first to last, was a deep devotion to the cause of human liberty—a strong sympathy with the depressed every where, and an ardent wish for their elevation."

The "Lost Speech," so named because Lincoln's eloquence stayed the pens of the reporters, was but one of over fifty speeches delivered in the year 1856. By the time of the first Republican convention, held at Philadelphia on June 19, his fame as a political speaker had reached that body and on the first ballot he received 110 votes for the vice presidential nomination, although unaware that his name was to be presented. That same year at Kalamazoo, Michigan, he used this characteristic language: "We are a great empire, we are eighty years old. We stand at once the wonder and admiration of the whole world, . . . It has been said that such a race of prosperity has been run nowhere else."

Then in 1858, came the "House Divided" speech and the debates with Stephen A. Douglas. This series of seven contests, in as many Illinois cities, received wide publicity and made Lincoln a national figure. The fact that he received 5,000 more popular votes than Douglas in the statewide balloting, reveals Lincoln's remarkable personal appeal to the masses. The following year, his

103. pp. 10, 11 / *1.* II, 89 / *1.* II, 126 / *1.* II, 364

fame as an orator was accentuated by speeches in Cincinnati, Columbus, and Dayton, Ohio; Milwaukee, Beloit, and Janesville, Wisconsin; and Elwood, Troy, Doniphan, Atchison, and Leavenworth, Kansas.

Moncure D. Conway, famous author and one-time editor of the Boston *Commonwealth,* first heard Lincoln speak before an outdoor political meeting at Cincinnati in 1859, and commented: "I perceived that there was a certain artistic ability in him as a public speaker," and later observed: "For terse, well-pronounced, clear speech, . . . for perfect tones; for quiet, chaste, and dignified manner; it would be hard to find his superior."

While Lincoln captured the West with his unique and impressive manner of speaking, it was not until 1860 that he won equally wide fame in the East. He was invited to speak in New York City at Cooper Union which boasted of having the most beautiful auditorium in the nation. After his speech The New York *Tribune* reported: "Since the days of Clay and Webster, no man has spoken to a larger assemblage of the intellectual and mental culture of our city . . . no man ever before made such an impression on his first appeal to a New York audience," L. E. Chittenden wrote: "The most competent critics promptly pronounced it, the most powerful contribution ever made to the literature of the slave question."

Moving on from New York to New England, where more than two hundred years before his ancestors had settled, Lincoln was greeted with great acclaim, the news of his triumph at Cooper Union having preceded him. At Providence, a representative of the press noted that he attempted to show "by plain, simple and cogent reasoning that his position is impregnable and he carries his audience with him." The *Statesman* at Concord asserted: "A political speech of greater power has rarely if ever been uttered in the capital of New Hampshire." At Dover, the scribe noted: "Mr. Lincoln spoke nearly two hours and we believe he would have held his audience, had he spoken all night." At Hartford, the reporter

1. II, 461–469 / 72. May 12, 1865 / *139.* Feb. 28, 1960

Background for Oratory 7

listened to: "The most convincing and clearest speech we have ever heard made."

In New Haven: "As Mr. Lincoln concluded his address there was witnessed the wildest scenes of enthusiasm and excitement." While Meridian reported: "His clear statements, irresistible logic, perfectly candid, courteous and honest manner, carried conviction." In 1860, these were reactions to his oratory in New York and New England.

Judge Logan of Springfield, who had been a law partner of Lincoln and an observer of Lincoln's advancement as a public speaker, from his first appearance in Illinois up to the time of his election to the presidency, made this significant comparison between his earlier and later manners of expression: "He had the same peculiarity in presenting his ideas. He had the same individuality that he kept through all his life."

On February 11, 1861, the day before the fifty-second anniversary of his birth, Lincoln delivered this "Farewell Address," at Springfield.

> My friends; no one, not in my situation, can appreciate my feeling of sadness at this parting.
>
> To this place, and the kindness of these people, I owe everything.
>
> Here I have lived a quarter of a century, and have passed from a young to an old man.
>
> Here my children have been born, and one is buried.
>
> I now leave, not knowing when, or whether ever, I may return, with a task before me greater than that which rested upon Washington.
>
> Without the assistance of that Divine Being, who ever attended him, I cannot succeed.
>
> With that assistance I cannot fail.
>
> Trusting in Him, who can go with me, and remain with you and be everywhere for good, let us confidently hope that all will yet be well.
>
> To His care commending you, as I hope in your prayers you will commend me, I bid you an affectionate farewell.

103. pp. 22, 23, *149.* pp. 36–41 / *103.* p. 27 / *189.* p. 268, *1.* IV, 190, 191 / *1.* IV, 190

If anyone had any doubts as to Lincoln's ability to choose the proper words, when every sentiment expressed was to be put under microscopic observation, the fears were dispelled with the reading of the First Inaugural Address. It was as eloquent an appeal for peace as ever came from the lips of any statesman and concluded with this final entreaty: "I am loath to close. We are not enemies, but friends. We must not be enemies. Though passion may have strained, it must not break our bonds of affection. The mystic chords of memory, stretching from every battle-field, and patriot grave, to every living heart and hearthstone all over this broad land, will yet swell the chorus of the Union, when again touched, as surely they will be, by the better angels of our nature."

However, his eloquence failed to penetrate the barrier of misunderstanding already constructed, and a special session of congress was called to convene on the birthday of the nation. All hopes for averting hostilities now relinquished, the paramount question before the nation, he put in these words: "Our popular government has often been called an experiment. Two points in it, our people have already settled—the successful *establishing* and the successful *administering* of it. One still remains—its successful *maintenance* against a forminable (internal) attempt to overthrow it."

The annual message to Congress on December 3, 1861, closed with another of those farseeing inspirational assurances that breathed the very essence of a benediction: "The struggle of today, is not altogether for today—it is for a vast future also. With a reliance on Providence, all the more firm and earnest, let us proceed in the great task which events have devolved upon us."

This last statement, like so many of the other similar sentiments expressed through the years, was put in a condensed form and became simply, "the great task remaining before us," in his remarks at Gettysburg.

1. IV, 271 / 1. IV, 439 / 1. V, 53 / 1. VII, 23

After observing Lincoln's gradual progression in the art of public speaking, from a reciter of practice pieces in a log cabin school, to a presidential expositor on problems of state, one will not be astonished at his ability to speak as eloquently and intelligently as he did on November 19, 1863, at the dedication of a cemetery.

109. No. 908

CHAPTER 2

Freedom Motif

THE EVOLUTION of Abraham Lincoln's concepts about civil-liberty can be traced with the same precision as his development in the field of oratory. His lifelong passion for the freedom of mankind contributed as much to the universal acceptance of the Gettysburg remarks as his proficiency in oratory. Joseph Fort Newton, prominent clergyman and author, attempting to account for the essence of Lincoln's remarks, concluded: "Into those few brief words was distilled, drop by drop, the very life of the man."

It is not difficult to learn of Abraham's earliest reaction to slavery, as he tells in his own words about the very beginnings of his feelings with respect to the institution. His attitude towards keeping men in bondage is clearly set forth in these words he wrote to Albert G. Hodges of Frankfort, Kentucky on April 4, 1864: "I am naturally anti-slavery. If slavery is not wrong, nothing is wrong. I cannot remember when I did not so think, and feel." This clear-cut statement should leave no doubt about Abraham's lifelong abhorrence of serfdom. Anti-slavery by nature, implies at least, that he looked upon this sentiment as something for which his parents were partly responsible. Keeping men in bondage was considered by him, even in childhood, as a

136. V, 18

stupendous evil. His earliest thoughts and sensations rebelled against the very idea of enslavement.

A church historian states: "Slavery was by far the most fruitful of mischief of all the questions that agitated the Baptist churches of Kentucky from 1788 until 1820." The Lincolns lived in the very geographical center of this slavery controversy. In 1808, a church within two miles of the Lincoln home was closed because the members could not meet in peace. Abraham was born in the midst of this neighborhood feud over the moral issue involved. The pastor of the church had declared himself an "Amansapator" (sic) and fifteen members finally withdrew because they refused to have fellowship with slave owners. A church in the county was named "The Emancipation Church." Possibly one of the first five-syllable words Abraham learned to pronounce was emancipation. His parents affiliated with the Little Mount group, an anti-slavery organization. The two ministers serving the congregation during the Lincolns' residence near by, were both ardent emancipationists of considerable oratorical ability. The first sermons the boy ever heard were on the wrongs of enslaving one's fellow man.

Between Abraham's second and seventh years, the Lincoln cabin home faced the old pioneer trail running from Louisville to Nashville. Over this much traveled turnpike, slaves were driven on foot to the southern markets. Possibly Abraham may have observed some such a scene as another boy witnessed who lived on that same road: "One evening a gang of slaves was driven up to my father's house at dusk. We had a big haystack out doors and the men, women and children were chained together and slept on it that night. Some of the women had babies in their arms. I have never forgotten that sight." Close by the school Abraham attended lived Peter Atherton, who had at least twenty slaves. Another citizen owned fifty-eight, and in Hardin County where the Lincolns lived, in 1813 there were 1,007 listed on the tax commissioner's book.

1. VII, 281 / *175.* I, 163 / *190.* p. 9

When Abraham was seven years of age, a significant and far-reaching event occurred in his life. The Lincoln family moved from Kentucky, a slave state, to Indiana, a free state. This change of residence according to Abraham, was "partly on account of slavery." Thomas and his wife wanted to bring up their children in the atmosphere of freedom. In later years, Lincoln put this question to an Illinois audience: "How many Democrats are there about here (a thousand) who have left slave states and come into the free State of Illinois to get rid of the institution of slavery? Another voice answered "a thousand and one." Lincoln responded: "I reckon there are a thousand and one."

Abraham is said to have told one of his associates: *"Murray's English Reader* was the best school-book ever put into the hands of an American youth." Therein, he must have observed in the copy he used this excerpt from Cowper:

> I would not have a slave to till my ground,
> To carry me, to fan me while I sleep,
> To tremble when I wake, for all the wealth
> That sinews bought and sold have ever earn'd,
> No: dear as freedom is, and in my heart's
> Just estimate, prized above all price:
> I had much rather be myself the slave,
> And wear the bonds, than fasten them on him.

When Abraham was nineteen years old, he made his first trip on a flat boat to New Orleans. Here he observed the shocking and revolting scenes of the auction blocks, where men, women, and children, were sold with as much abandon as were cattle. When Abraham was twenty-one, the family again moved still farther from slavery territory into central Illinois. A year later, for the second time, he observed the New Orleans slave markets. He wrote to a Kentucky friend after making a short trip on an Ohio River steamer: "There were, on board, ten or a dozen slaves, shackled together with irons. That sight was a continual torment to me; . . . It is hardly fair for you to assume, that I have no

1. III, 312 / *130.* p. 34, *189.* p. 239

interest in a thing which has, and continually exercises, the power of making me miserable."

As a public servant, Lincoln made his earliest protest against enslavement when he was but twenty-eight years old. He joined with one other member of the Illinois House of Representatives in drawing up this remonstrance against the passage of a resolution on keeping men in bondage: "They believe that the institution of slavery is founded on both injustice and bad policy." They also believed that the Congress of the United States: "has the power, under the constitution, to abolish slavery in the District of Columbia; but that that power ought not to be exercised unless at the request of the people of said district." It was not until Lincoln became a member of Congress that he had an opportunity to take more positive action about this last affirmation. On January 10, 1849, he introduced in the House of Representatives, a series of resolutions, "concerning abolition of slavery in the District of Columbia." Nothing ever came of his effort, but it does indicate that he followed through on the proposal he had made in the Illinois legislature a decade before.

An autobiographical sketch Lincoln prepared in the third person contains this notation: "In 1854, his profession had almost superceeded the thought of politics in his mind, when the repeal of the Missouri compromise aroused him as he had never been before." Later, in correspondence with his old friend Joshua Speed, he stated: "Our progress in degeneracy appears to me to be pretty rapid. As a nation, we began by declaring that *'all men are created equal.'* We now practically read it 'all men are created equal except negroes.'"

At Peoria, on October 16, Lincoln made one of his longest and most exhaustive addresses on the Missouri Compromise, in answer to a speech made that same day by Stephen A. Douglas. In his closing observations Lincoln said: "The great mass of mankind . . . consider slavery a great moral wrong; and their feelings against it, is not evanescent, but eternal. It lies at the very

_{189. p. 182, 1. II, 320 / 1. I, 75, 1. II, 20 / 1. IV, 67, 1. II, 323}

foundation of their sense of justice, and it cannot be trifled with." The moral issue in slavery became the crux of the series of seven debates in 1858 with Douglas. At Alton, Illinois, Lincoln drew this conclusion which might serve as a final summary of his arguments: "That is the real issue. That is the issue that will continue in this country when these poor tongues of Judge Douglas and myself shall be silent. It is the eternal struggle between these two principles—right and wrong—throughout the world. . . . The one is the common right of humanity and the other the divine right of kings. It is the same principle in whatever shape it developes itself. . . . No matter in what shape it comes, whether from the mouth of a king who seeks to bestride the people of his own nation and live by the fruit of their labor, or from one race of men as an apology for enslaving another race, it is the same tyrannical principle." Possibly a fragment penned by Lincoln at this time sets forth in a concise form the basic concept of his philosophy respecting equality. "I believe the declaration that 'all men are created equal' is the great fundamental principle upon which our free institutions rest."

The debates with Douglas, however, did not present the grand climax of his discussions on equality. His most impressive presentation was at Cooper Union in New York City, where, according to William O. Stoddard, his address was "a masterly review of the history of the slavery question, from the foundation of the government."

Lincoln's message to the special session of Congress on July 4, 1861, with half a dozen states already in rebellion, contained this query: "Is there, in all republics, this inherent and fatal weakness? Must a government, of necessity, be too *strong* for the liberties of its own people, or too *weak* to maintain its own existence?"

Lincoln states in his correspondence, that he made unsuccessful appeals to the border states to favor compensated emancipation. The conclusion of a proclamation issued on May 19, 1862 illustrates the urgency of the proposal: "The change it contem-

1. II, 281, 282, 1. III, 315, *143.* I, 369 / *178.* p. 412 / 1. IV, 426

plates would come gently as the dews of heaven, not rending or wrecking anything. Will you not embrace it? So much good has not been done, by one effort, in all past time, as, in the providence of God, it is now your high privilege to do. May the vast future not have to lament that you have neglected it."

As the adjournment of Congress drew near, Lincoln invited to the White House on July 12, the representatives and senators of the Border States and made his final appeal for compensated emancipation: "Our common country is in great peril, demanding the loftiest views, and boldest action to bring it speedy relief. Once relieved, its form of government is saved to the world; its beloved history, and cherished memories, are vindicated; and its happy future fully assured, and rendered inconceivably grand." Twenty members rejected the President's proposal and it drew the approval of but eight. A bill embodying his plan was read to the House and Senate on July 14, 1862, but Congress adjourned before action was taken.

Lincoln's letter to Horace Greeley on August 22, 1862, in reply to an article appearing in the *Tribune*, under the caption, "The Prayer of Twenty Million," is one of the President's most famous writings. The editor accused Lincoln of many failures, one of the grievances enumerated: "We think you are strangely and disastrously remiss . . . with regard to the emancipation provisions in the Confiscation Act." Mr. Lincoln replied that his paramount object was to save the union regardless of the part slavery might play in it. In quoting Lincoln, however, this last paragraph in the reply is invariably omitted: "I have here stated my purpose according to my view of *official* duty; and I intend no modification of my oft-expressed *personal* wish that all men everywhere could be free."

On September 15, 1862, the President stated in the conclusion of a reply to an emancipation memorial submitted by a delegation of Chicago Christians from all denominations: "I have not decided against a proclamation of liberty to the slaves, but hold the matter

1. V, 223 / 1. V, 319 / 1. V, 389

under advisement. And I can assure you that the subject is on my mind, by day and night, more than any other." Nine days after this memorial, the preliminary proclamation was issued and on January 1, 1863, Abraham Lincoln signed the official Emancipation Proclamation, which contained this clause: "I do order and declare that all persons held as slaves within said designated states, and parts of states, (In rebellion against the United States) are, and henceforth shall be free."

Just a month previous to the signing of this significant proclamation on the first day of December 1862, the President had submitted to Congress a further appeal for compensated emancipation. In reviewing its advantages he used in the last paragraph of the message this statement: "In *giving* freedom to the *slave*, we *assure* freedom to the *free*—honorable alike in what we give and what we preserve. We shall nobly save, or meanly lose, the last best, hope of earth."

On the last day of July 1863, he wrote to General Hurlbut with respect to the Emancipation Proclamation: "Those who shall have tasted actual freedom I believe can never be slaves, or quasi slaves again." Considering gradual emancipation for those not coming under the proclamation he said: "It should begin at once, giving at least the newborn, a vested interest in freedom, which cannot be taken away." The idea of the "new birth," which is to be declared so emphatically, at Gettysburg, already seems to be taking form in his thinking.

1. V, 425, *1.* VI, 29, 30 / *1.* V, 537 / *1.* VI, 358

CHAPTER 3

Independence Day

ONE FACTOR which contributed to the preparation, presentation and reception of the President's address on the battlefield, was its association with the "glorious old 4th," as referred to by Lincoln, in a letter written the day after the arrival of marvelous news from Vicksburg. From his boyhood, his patriotism had made him time conscious and the anniversary of the nation's birth was an occasion for oration and meditation. Even in his own day he lamented the lack of appreciation for the work of the founding fathers and wrote derisively: "The fourth of July has not quite dwindled away; it is still a great day—*for burning firecrackers!!!*"

An excerpt from a speech that Lincoln made in 1858 illustrates very well the tone of his patriotism and serves as a good introduction to an account of the episode which is to follow: "My countrymen, if you have been taught doctrines conflicting with the great landmarks of the Declaration of Independence; if you have listened to suggestions which would take away from its grandeur, and mutilate the fair symmetry of its proportions; if you have been inclined to believe that all men are *not* created equal in those inalienable rights enumerated by our chart of liberty, let me

1. VI, 321, 1. II, 318

entreat you to come back. Return to the fountain whose waters spring close by the blood of the Revolution."

A visit to Philadelphia on Washington's Birthday, 1861, provided one of the most inspirational experiences in Abraham Lincoln's entire life. Entering Independence Hall for the first time, he commented: "I am filled with deep emotion at finding myself standing here in the place where were collected together the wisdom, the patriotism, the devotion to principle, from which sprang the institutions under which we live." He then made this significant avowal: "All the political sentiments I entertain have been drawn, so far as I have been able to draw them, from the sentiments which originated, and were given to the world from this hall in which we stand. I have never had a feeling politically that did not spring from the sentiments embodied in the Declaration of Independence." Later in the day at Harrisburg, in recalling the kindled emotions of the morning, he lamented that he did not have: "more time to express something of my own feelings excited by the occasion."

While Lincoln's place consciousness was awakened by his visit to the "Cradle of Liberty," his awareness of the time element was also aroused. This likewise contributed to the patriotic atmosphere of the occasion. He referred to "the birthday of the Father of his Country," as "that beloved anniversary." However, it was the annual observance of the nation's birth so forcibly called to his attention at Independence Hall, that always had been, to him, the most significant annual patriotic festival.

Two years after his stimulating experience at Philadelphia, Lincoln was invited to spend Independence Day, 1863, in that city. The Union League Club, to show their approval of "his conduct of the war and national affairs," had arranged to present him with a medal. However, important military movements in another section of Pennsylvania prevented his attendance. The medallion prepared for the occasion, which later he received in Washington, bore on its obverse side: "E PLURIBUS UNUM,"

1. II, 547 / *1.* IV, 240, 244 / *1.* IV, 244

engraved on a shield. On its left, appeared: "1776," on its right: "1863," and, between these two dates: "JULY 4 TH." Under the shield there was inscribed the name: "PHILADELPHIA." Military operations which were coming to a climax on Independence Day, 1863, must have made the striking of this medal almost prophetic. For the first time in the annals of military combat, successful major military engagements by detachments of the same army were taking place contemporaneously in war theaters a thousand miles apart. One was fought on northern ground in the eastern part of the country, and the other on southern soil in the area of the west. The former resulted in the dispersing of what had been considered an invincible army and the other the capture of a presumably impregnable stronghold.

The town of Gettysburg, the center of one of these strategic battles, was founded by James Getty in 1780, and upon the establishment of Adams County, in 1800, it became its seat of government. By 1863, it was the hub of at least eleven roads leading to the town; one from Carlisle, directly north, then others approaching clockwise from; Harrisburg, Hunterstown, York, Hanover, Baltimore, Taneytown, Emmitsburg, Hagerstown, Chambersburg and Mummasburg. The main thoroughfare was the Baltimore-Pittsburg pike, passing through York and Chambersburg. The mileage to eastern and southern cities helps to orient the town: Philadelphia, 114; Washington, 70, Baltimore, 52, and Harrisburg, 36. Gettysburg was only eight miles north of the Mason and Dixon's line.

With the many highways leading to the town, it is not surprising that the chief industry was carriage making, with ten small plants in operation. Also, the community had become a center of education, including: Pennsylvania College, Lutheran Theological Seminary, and a school for young ladies conducted by Miss Carrie Shead. The usual number of churches, business houses and offices of professional men which one finds in a town of about 2,500 population, were located there.

109. No. 1088 / *102.* / ibid

Gettysburg, as a focal point with so many approaches, became uneasy in the latter part of June upon learning the Confederates were entering Pennsylvania. The Adams *Sentinel* in its issue of June 23 under the caption "Invasion of the North" stated: "There has been much excitement here all week owing to the presence of the Confederates in the neighboring counties." The press noted that after General Milroy was obliged to evacuate Winchester, large Rebel forces were moved across the Potomac at Williamsport and Hancock. The editor concluded the story with the statement: "It is possible a great battle will be fought before they will be allowed to return to Virginia."

Three days later, the first contingent of gray-clad soldiers arrived in Gettysburg and made demands on the citizens for supplies and cash, but the order was not rigidly enforced. Soon there was a concentration of Confederates at Cashtown, nine miles to the west. By the morning of July 30, the blue-suited men had reached Marsh Creek, five miles to the south. At nightfall, it is estimated that over 10,000 troops of the two armies were in camp a few miles from Gettysburg. The *Sentinel* gives the story of the positions of the two armies as viewed by the citizens of Gettysburg on the eve of the battle: "Lee's main army appeared on Seminary Hill from the direction of Chambersburg, at the same time Gen. Buford of the Potomac Army appeared on the opposite side of the town with a body of cavalry. It now became evident that our beautiful village was to be the scene of a terrible conflict." On July 1, the three-day holocaust began, with approximately 150,000 men locked in mortal combat before the contest was over.

One would surmise that information about any important Union land engagement would reach the President through the Secretary of War. But while Lincoln was at the War Department, a telegram arrived dated July 3, addressed by a news corrrespondent to the Secretary of the Navy. This dispatch stated that: "The most terrible battle of the war was being fought at or near Gettysburg, that he had left the field at 6 p.m. with tidings and

2. June 23, 1863 / 2. July 7, 1863

that everything looked hopeful." This information reached Washington at 11:30 p.m. on July 3. Other reports confirming the victory caused Mr. Lincoln to prepare this announcement for publication at 10:00 a.m. on July 4.

"The President announces to the country that news from the Army of the Potomac, up to 10:00 p.m. of the 3rd is such as to cover that Army with the highest honor, to promise a great success to the cause of the Union, and to claim the condolence of all for the many gallant fallen. And that for this, he especially desires that on this day, He whose will, not ours, should ever be done, be everywhere remembered and reverenced with profoundest gratitude."

The President also made some comments about both Gettysburg and Vicksburg prior to the battle, which indicates he had a good understanding of the situation in both areas. On June 30, he wrote to Governor Parker of New Jersey: "I really think the attitude of the enemies' army in Pennsylvania, presents us the best opportunity we have had since the war began." As early as May 26, he had written to Isaac N. Arnold: "Whether General Grant shall or shall not consummate the capture of Vicksburg, his campaign from the beginning of this month up to the twenty-second day of it, is one of the most brilliant in the world." At the very hour Lincoln was announcing to the country the triumph at Gettysburg, the Union soldiers standing on the ramparts at Vicksburg, Mississippi: "Witnessed with deep emotion the Confederates stacking their arms in front of the works they had defended so long." Even while Lee was withdrawing his troops from the Gettysburg battle line, Pemberton was negotiating with Grant for the surrender of Vicksburg.

Once again it was Secretary Welles who became the harbinger of the good news, this time about the Vicksburg triumph. This message was directed to Welles by Acting Rear Admiral D. D. Porter: "Sir: I have the honor to inform you that Vicksburg has surrendered to the United States on this 4th of July." Although

194. I, 357 / *1.* VI, 314 / *1.* VI, 230, 311, *142.* VII, 302, 303

the telegram did not arrive until July 7, Welles immediately took it to the President. After reading it, Mr. Lincoln threw his arms about Welles and said: "What can we do for the Secretary of the Navy for this glorious intelligence. He is always giving us good news. I cannot, in words, tell you of my joy over this result. It is great, Mr. Welles, it is great."

The Gettysburg and Vicksburg triumphs, so closely associated in point of time with the annual festival, electrified the nation. Welles, in referring to the report on Vicksburg stated that it "excited a degree of enthusiasm not excelled during the war." The President wrote to Hon. F. F. Low at San Francisco: "There is no doubt that Gen. Meade, now commanding the Army of the Potomac, beat Lee at Gettysburg, Pa. at the end of a three days battle . . . We also have dispatches rendering it entirely certain that Vicksburg surrendered to Gen. Grant on the glorious old 4th." That both contests had been won in the highly emotional atmosphere of Independence Day deeply impressed Lincoln.

Possibly not enough attention has been paid by historians to the spirit of aggressiveness and determination aroused among the soldiers of both contesting northern armies by the approach of the fourth day of July. It is apparent that Lee did not choose to extend hostilities into that day which, psychologically, would contribute an added weapon to each Union soldier. Pemberton, at Vicksburg, also was trying to avoid combat on July 4. The Vicksburg *Daily Citizen* in its issue of July 2, printed on wall paper, stated cynically: "The great Ulysses—the Yankee Generalissimo—surnamed Grant—has expressed his intention of dining in Vicksburg on Saturday next and celebrate 4th of July by a grand dinner and so forth. . . . Ulysses must get the city before he dines in it. The way to cook a rabbit, is, to first catch the rabbit."

It was General Grant's conviction that "Gen. Pemberton commenced his correspondence looking toward capitulation on the 3rd with a twofold purpose; first to avoid an assault which he knew would be successful, and second to prevent the capture

194. I, 364 / 194. I, 356, 1. VI, 321 / 186. July 2, 1863

Independence Day

taking place on the great national holiday." He failed in this last objective by holding out for better terms, so the surrender actually occurred on the morning of Independence Day. It would have been indeed, a tactless Union officer, either at Gettysburg or Vicksburg, who did not sense the opportunity of driving home to the soldiers in the ranks, at this season, the truism expressed by Lincoln in his first message to Congress: "Surely each man has as strong a motive *now* to *preserve* our liberties, as each had *then* to *establish* them."

After receiving the dispatch about Vicksburg on July 7, the President must have anticipated there would be a series of public demonstrations in the evening and that one of them would take place at the executive residence. According to Benjamin B. French, Commissioner of Public Buildings, he arranged for Colonel J. A. Peck to confer with Mr. Lincoln on the afternoon of July 7, for the purpose of asking him "to remain at the Presidential mansion that evening and receive the serenade."

With the arrival of the band, cheering and music brought Lincoln to the central window under the portico where he addressed the jubilant throng in these words:

Fellow-citizens: I am very glad indeed to see you to-night, and yet I will not say I thank you for this call, but I do most sincerely thank Almighty God for the occasion on which you have called. (Cheers) How long ago is it?—eighty odd years—since on the Fourth of July for the first time in the history of the world a nation by its representatives, assembled and declared as a self-evident truth that "all men are created equal." That was the birthday of the United States of America. Since then the Fourth of July has had several peculiar recognitions. The two most distinguished men in the framing and support of the Declaration were Thomas Jefferson and John Adams—the one having penned it and the other sustained it the most forcibly in debate—the only two of the fifty-five who signed it being elected President of the United States. Precisely fifty years after they put their hands to the paper it pleased Almighty God to take both from the stage of action. This was indeed

185. XXIV (I) 283, 1. IV, 432 / 111. French to Lincoln, July 7, 1863

an extraordinary and remarkable event in our history. Another President, five years after, was called from this stage of existence on the same day and month of the year; and now, on this last Fourth of July just passed, when we have a gigantic Rebellion, at the bottom of which is an effort to overthrow the principle that all men were created equal, we have the surrender of a most powerful position and army on that very day, (Cheers) and not only so, but in a succession of battles in Pennsylvania, near to us, through three days, so rapidly fought that they might be called one great battle on the 1st, 2nd and 3rd of the month of July; and on the 4th the cohorts of those who opposed the declaration that all men are created equal, 'turned tail' and run. (long and continued cheers) Gentlemen, this is a glorious theme, and the occasion for a speech, but I am not prepared to make one worthy of the occasion. I would like to speak in terms of praise due to the many brave officers and soldiers who have fought in the cause of the Union and liberties of the country from the beginning of the war. There are trying occasions, not only in success, but for want of success. I dislike to mention the name of one single officer lest I might do wrong to those I might forget. Recent events bring up glorious names, and particularly prominent ones, but these I will not mention. Having said this much, I will now take the music.

The events of July 4 were kept prominently before the people by the President. On July 15, he issued a Proclamation of Thanksgiving: "for victories on land and on the sea," concluding: "It is meet and right to recognize and confess the presence of the Almighty Father and the power of His Hand equally in these triumphs and in these sorrows."

Communications received by Lincoln also kept freshly in mind the events of early July. J. Lothrop Motley, famous historian whom Lincoln had appointed United States minister to Austria, wrote to the President on July 25, with reference to the Confederate withdrawals at Gettysburg and Vicksburg: "Their retreat upon the Fourth of July, and that the great western stronghold towards which the attention of the world has so long been directed, should have surrendered on the same day, are events which must strike the fullest imagination. . . . In all coming time, the loyal

---

1. VI, 319, 320 / *1.* VI, 332

American will have additional reason to cherish this most august of national holidays."

Lincoln made a patriotic speech in Chicago in 1858 in which he emphasized the value of our national holidays and especially the contributions made by the annual observance of the Fourth of July. A few excerpts from the address seem to offer an appropriate conclusion for this chapter: "We run our memory back over the pages of history for about eighty-two years. . . . We find a race of men living in that day whom we claim as our fathers and grandfathers; they were iron men . . . we understand that by what they then did it has followed that the degree of prosperity that we now enjoy has come to us." Speaking in a community where half the population was of European descent, Lincoln endeavored to show how they became a part of this heritage by the assertion of the founding fathers that: "All men are created equal." He then declared: "That is the electric cord in that Declaration that links the hearts of patriotic and liberty loving men together . . . as long as the love of freedom exists in the minds of men throughout the world."

These historical facts and principles which Lincoln discussed, not only reveal his own attitude toward the glorious fourth, but this concluding note stresses the need for the periodically observed day on which our history should be reviewed: "We hold this annual celebration to remind ourselves of all the good done in this process of time of how it was done and who did it, and how we are historically connected with it; . . . in every way we are better men in the age, and race, and country in which we live for these celebrations."

111. Motley to Lincoln, July 15, 1863 / *1.* II, 499, 500 / ibid

CHAPTER 4

Soldiers' National Cemetery

A SIGNIFICANT BY-PRODUCT of the Gettysburg battle was the nation's more humane consideration for the soldier dead. The rank and file of the men killed in the Revolution, the War of 1812, Indian skirmishes, and the Mexican War usually were buried where they fell. The practice also was followed during the first two years of the Civil War. This was a universal custom, little attention having been paid to the disposal of fallen patriots who died for creed or country. There was one exception; Athens prescribed by law, that the obsequies of all citizens who fell in battle: "should be performed at public expense and in the most honorable manner."

The Secretary of War of the United States, in September, 1861, ordered that: "records be kept of deceased soldiers and their places of burial." This was a basic step in a much needed reform. Two years later, a law was put in force requiring mortuary records be filed in the Adjutant General's office; also, the Quarter-Master's Department was charged to provide proper means for "a registered head board" to be secured for each grave. The burial of soldiers was likewise put under the jurisdiction of the department.

Congress approved an act on July 17, 1862, authorizing: "That

83. July, 1866, p. 310 / *182.* 1861, No. 75, *183.* 1863, p. 159

the President of the United States shall have power, whenever in his opinion it shall be expedient, to purchase cemetery grounds and to cause them to be securely enclosed, to be used as a national cemetery for the soldiers who shall die in the service of the country." This law was interpreted as limiting the acquisition to but one area for the purpose. Someone suggested that Congress should provide additional legislation to authorize the President to acquire any number of tracts that should be needed to bury the dead, at or near the place where the casualties occurred. It was not until the scenes of hostilities changed from the southern fields to the northern soil, and the increasing number of dead were laid at the very doors of the Union homes, that the first general movement was inaugurated to give proper attention to the burial of fallen heroes.

General Meade sent a dispatch to General Halleck on July 5, stating: "My wounded and those of the enemy are in my hand." A correspondent of the New York *Herald* wrote: "The fields about Gettysburg are strewn with dead and the dying. . . . Our ambulances brought in the wounded of both armies alike." During the first four days of July, 1863, Gettysburg, Pennsylvania, had emerged from a quiet county seat town to a gigantic hospital. One observer summarized the expansive institution as occupying the "College, Seminary, Courthouse, Public School House, Lutheran, Presbyterian, Catholic, and United Presbyterian churches, hotels, warehouses, private houses, depots and tents almost everywhere, in twenty to thirty Confederate hospitals, in barns, stables, sheds, dwelling houses, taverns, mills, in woods and in tents." Even during the battle, young ladies in Miss Carrie Shead's school for girls cared for as many as sixty of the wounded men who had been moved there. The Lutheran Seminary was primarily utilized for Confederate wounded and Pennsylvania College was the sanitarium where mostly Union injured were gathered. Yet, it was noted that: "in almost every tent the Union soldiers and the rebels lie side by side, friendly as brothers."

83. July, 1866, p. 312 / *184.* p. 82, *137.* July 6, 1863, *59.* p. 67, *174.* p. 36

Within three days after the battle, the Christian Commission of Philadelphia established headquarters in a store on the public square and began their ministrations. The Sanitary Commission soon had tents erected and with volunteer physicians and nurses supplemented the medical units of the army. The Sisters of Charity were also present and the Baltimore Fire Department and Adams Express Company each sent a group of men to aid in the great emergency. Volunteer helpers from the churches of the large cities of the East arrived and rendered invaluable service. One of these ladies, Mrs. Edmund A. Souder of Philadelphia, recorded some of her experiences from day to day. She states: "The groans, cries, and shrieks of anguish are awful indeed to hear . . . ghastly suffering stares you in the face. . . . Death is very busy with these poor fellows on both sides— There are hundreds of men who will never leave the battlefield alive." A large percentage of the injured were amputees and one surgeon estimated: "Two-thirds of all the cases must die." The heroic effort to save the lives of wounded men is a story of great personal sacrifice on the part of surgeons, nurses, and volunteer helpers, and especially the unselfish services rendered by the citizens of Gettysburg of which one case is illustrative: The home of Solomon Powers: "had been a hospital for wounded Union soldiers. . . . More than twenty had been provided for (four of whom died) and all without charge to relative or friend." It was not until July 28, that there was established on elevated grounds east of town, a general sanitarium to which the wounded, by the hundreds, were being removed daily.

However, it is the burial of the dead and the dedication of the grounds where they were interred, that calls for emphasis in this Gettysburg story. On July 7, three days after the battle, this notice appeared in the Adams *Sentinel:* "Men, horses and wagons wanted immediately to bury the dead and to cleanse our streets in such a way as to guard against pestilence." At noon on July fourth, and continuing for several hours, a severe storm swept

174. p. 15–23, 26, 42, 25. pp. 8, 9

over the stricken area. While the downpour may have helped sanitary conditions, it caused considerable damage to the newly-made mounds. The rain washed off the thin layer of earth thrown over the bodies, hurriedly deposited in shallow graves, on the spots where they had fallen.

Shortly after the battle ceased, the relatives of the deceased soldiers came to Gettysburg—singly and in groups—in search of the bodies of their loved ones. One observer described them: "strangers looking for their dead, on every farm and under every tree." Such identification writings, inscribed on make-shift grave markers, were temporary and would soon be erased by inclement weather. Gettysburg might be described as a huge morgue where people from many states had come to claim their own. The burial of these dead—those killed in battle, others who died on the field, and the great numbers who succumbed in hospitals—presented a tremendous task.

As early as February 28, 1862, the Pennsylvania Legislature had passed a joint resolution with provisions for taking care of her wounded and the burial of her soldiers who fell in battle. Apparently, with this act in mind, Governor Curtin visited Gettysburg shortly after the battle to make arrangements to carry out the purpose of the law. He secured a young lawyer, David Wills, who resided there, to act as his local representative in the task. Wills was born in 1831, graduated from Pennsylvania College in 1851, entered the law office of Thad Stevens at Lancaster, was licensed to practice in 1854, and opened an office at Gettysburg the same year. Mr. Wills' name will appear very often in the proceedings which follow, not only in the arrangements for the burial of the dead, but also in the preparations for the dedication of the cemetery. Governor Curtin in his annual message on January 7, 1864, paid him this compliment: "Mr. Wills has discharged his delicate and important duties with fidelity and to my entire satisfaction."

The first duty of Mr. Wills is set forth in the Adams *Sentinel* of

2. July 7, 1863 / *174.* p. 63 / *136.* V, 14, *173.* p. 2

July 28: "Governor Curtin has made arrangements with David Wills, esq. of this place for the removal of all Pennsylvanians killed in the late battles, furnishing transportation for the body and one attendant at the expense of the State." About this time, the same paper stated that one of the undertakers had estimated that within three weeks after the battle, between six and seven hundred coffins had been used for the sending of deceased soldiers to their former homes. However, Mr. Wills plans, as well as those of representatives from other states, were suddenly curtailed by a military enjoiner.

Colonel H. C. Allerman, in command at Gettysburg, on July 30 issued Order No. 2, which prohibited the further removal of the bodies. The citizens of Gettysburg sent a letter of appreciation to Colonel Allerman for correcting substantially the prevailing conditions: "The extensive and careless disinterment of the dead from our battle-fields had become a great nuisance, and very great fears were entertained universally for the health of our people, and by many, strong apprehension of pestilence. The intense heat which prevailed ever since the issuance of your order, must, if the practice of disinterment had continued, have produced widespread sickness and distress. Our atmosphere was that of a charnel house." Even two weeks after the hostilities, visitors claimed that long before reaching the town, "the odors of the battle-field were plainly perceptible." One woman wrote from Gettysburg: "The atmosphere is truly horrible and camphor and smelling salts are prime necessities for most persons, certainly for ladies."

The concept of a national cemetery at Gettysburg was not the original idea of any one person or group. An early exponent of the plan was Andrew B. Cross of the Christian Commission then at work there. On July 25, he prepared an appeal to be distributed through the press which he urged the papers in the large cities to print: "It must be known to the nation that not less that 3,000 men lie in and about Gettysburg, in corn fields, in wheat fields, in

2. July 27, 1863 / 2. Aug. 25, 1863

gardens, by the way-side and in the public road, buried hastily where they fell, and others in long rows with a piece of box-lid or board of any kind, with the name of the person and when he died, written with lead pencil, ink, or whatever they had to make a mark."

Mr. Cross states that after consulting with several others: "We looked around for a burial place, none seemed so appropriate as Cemetery Hill the spot which controlled and secured to us this battle." It was the place where General Meade said to his men: "You must hold it if it costs every man of you." The piece of ground is further described by Mr. Cross: "There are about eight acres of ground on the opposite side of the turnpike from the cemetery to the town . . . from it you see almost the entire field for miles." The acquisition of this land was urged and the erection of a monument proposed. David Wills was named as one who had taken an interest in the project and to whom one might write for information. Mrs. Souder of Philadelphia, already mentioned, wrote to her brother on July 29: "I have said to several who proposed removal, 'The cemetery at Gettysburg is the most honorable burying-place a soldier can have, like Mt. Vernon it will be a place of pilgrimage for the nation.' . . . Evergreen Cemetery is a lovely spot—a noble resting place for the dead." She also said it was being proposed that "the different states acquire ground near the cemetery, where their dead might be buried."

Evergreen Cemetery was located on an elevation which had been named Cemetery Hill. The annual meeting of the board of managers was held on June 9, 1863, and D. McConaughy was reelected president. The *Sentinel* published on July 21, this item about the appearance of the grounds: "The once beautiful Evergreen Cemetery now presents a sad appearance. From its commanding site, it was found necessary to post a number of batteries on the summit of the eminence, on which the city of the dead is located. It was one of the best positions we occupied and the fire of the enemy artillery was constantly directed upon it, with the view

59 p. 60 / *59.* p. 60, *174.* 63, 64

of driving us back of the crest, tombstones were broken and graves turned up by plowing shot."

The mayor of Boston, F. W. Lincoln, presented a written recommendation to the city council on July 23, 1863, containing the following paragraph: "I would respectfully suggest for your consideration the propriety of purchasing a lot in the Cemetery (Gettysburg) and having the bodies of our dead removed to it." The council, that very day, approved the suggestion and a committee was appointed to carry out the mayor's recommendation. Before departing, the sub-committee advised the governor of Massachusetts of the proposal and received his approval. After carefully marking the graves of all Massachusetts men, and having "secured the privilege of a burying-lot" for the state, they returned and recommended to the governor the proposal of a national cemetery.

In the same issue of the *Sentinel* announcing Mr. Wills' employment, it was reported that the Evergreen Cemetery Association: "Proposes to the American people the erection of a noble monument upon the grounds of the cemetery, at the center and apex of the battlefield," commemorating the battle and "the glorious dead who fell and consecrated the spot with their blood."

Mr. Wills, in his official report covering these preliminary measures states: "A persistent effort was made by persons here, to have the soldiers buried in grounds controlled by the local cemetery association of this place. The plan proposed having the burials made at a stipulated price, to be paid to the cemetery association. Failing in this project, these persons endeavored to connect the two cemeteries, so that they should both be in one enclosure, and all under the control, supervision and management of the local cemetery association."

The governor seems to have taken a hand in the cemetery situation about this time and announced that Mr. Wills had been made official agent of Pennsylvania with authority to purchase

2. July 21, 1863 / *25.* pp. 3, 10, 11 / 2. July 28, 1863 / *173.* p. 5

Soldiers' National Cemetery

land "and make available such tracts as were needed." A brother of Governor Seymour was already on the grounds looking out for New York's interest in the project.

When the Massachusetts agents returned to Gettysburg, they were confronted with a decision that almost caused their withdrawal from the united effort by the states. Mr. Wills, who by this time had been appointed to promote the national character of the project, was insistent that "the burials should be promiscuous," irrespective of states. To this proposal the Boston committee strenuously objected. They alleged that for three weeks Mr. Wills demanded that his plans should be adopted. Apparently he wrote to Governor Curtin on August 16 about the situation and while the letter is not available, the reply on August 21, in part, is presented: "It is of course probable that our sister States joining with us in this hallowed undertaking may desire to make some alterations and modifications of your proposed plan of purchasing and managing these sacred grounds, and it is my wish that you give to their views the most careful and respectful consideration. . . . It becomes her (Pennsylvania's duty, as it is her melancholly pleasure, to yield in every reasonable way to the wishes and suggestions of the States, who join with her in dedicating a portion of her territory to the solemn uses of a national sepulcher."

It is extremely fortunate that Mr. Wills' plan for the indiscriminate burials of all soldiers did not prevail. The various states were invited to accept a burial lot and cooperate in the united effort. The acquisition of the land was described in a letter to the governor on August 17: "It is the ground which formed the apex of our triangular line of battle and the key to our line of defenses. It embraces the highest point on Cemetery Hill and overlooks the whole battlefield. It is the spot which should be especially consecrated to this sacred purpose. It was here that such immense quantities of our artillery were massed, and during Thursday and Friday of the battle, from this most important point on the field, dealt out death and destruction to the Rebel army in every

173. p. 5 / *27.* Nov. 19, 1863, *33.* p. 6, *171.* pp. 15, 16

direction of their advance." Mr. Wills reported that there were five separate tracts in the area and the costs per acre were approximately: two at $225 each, one at $200, one at $150 and the other at $135. The total cost of the land which comprised about seventeen acres was $2,475.87. The ground faced on the Baltimore Turnpike on the north, the eastern line followed the boundary of the Evergreen Cemetery, the western survey ran along the Taneytown Road, then in a straight line northeast back to the Baltimore Turnpike. It was located about one-half mile south of the town.

William Saunders, for many years associated with the propogating gardens of the Department of Agriculture, kept a journal in which information about the planning of the cemetery is recorded. He received a letter from Mr. Wills in the latter part of August, requesting that he come to Gettysburg "for the purpose of consulting upon the selection of the site and land for the cemetery." When he reached Gettysburg, he found that Mr. Wills had already chosen the location and purchased the land, part of which had formerly been in the possession of the local cemetery company. This may not have been the site Saunders would have selected if he had been consulted earlier but his only choice was to do the best he could with the acquisition. While he was pleased with the land, he observed that: "it was angular, and its front on the Baltimore Turnpike was only about 150 feet." Mr. Wills was advised: "to get more ground, extending the front line and straighening out other lines, which was speedily done, adding about five acres more to the cemetery and simplifying its outlines."

This recommendation was made by Mr. Saunders on the first visit after studying the ground thoroughly: "The remains of the soldiers from each state should be laid together in a group," thereby silencing Mr. Wills' promiscuous burial project. Saunders also observed that the surface was undulating "some high or elevated points, but others low and inferior in comparison." So,

171. p. 14, *173.* p. 6 / *136.* I, 19

that in the allotment of plots an unjust discrimination might be inferred. He came to the decision that: "A central point on the highest reach of the ground be designated for a monument, and a semicircular arrangement made so that the appropriation of each state would be a part of a common center, and the position of each lot would be relatively of equal importance." The spot selected for a monument coincided with the idea of the local cemetery group which would contribute to their interest in the national aspect of the project.

When the general plans were blocked out, Mr. Saunders acquired the services of a surveyor, J. S. Townsend of Washington, to go to Gettysburg and secure a list of the dead including the states they came from. With this information available Mr. Saunders was able to provide the surveyor with a definite state by state arrangement. The ground was marked off in semi-circular parallels twelve feet in width, allowing seven feet for the burials and five feet for a walk between the parallels. The coffins were to be placed side by side. The radius from the site of the monument to the circumference of the burial area was approximately three hundred feet.

At the request of the President, Mr. Saunders laid before him the plan for the cemetery and noted: "He took much interest in it asked about its surroundings, about Culp's Hill, Round Top, etc. and seemed familiar with the topography of the place . . . . he was much pleased with the method of the graves, said it differed from the ordinary cemetery, and after I had explained the reasons, said it was an admirable and befitting arrangement." In his report to the commission, Mr. Saunders stated: "The headstones form a continuous line of granite blocks, rising nine inches above the ground, showing a face or width of ten inches on their upper surface. The name, company and regiment being carved in the granite."

The whole country was now aroused and The Washington *Chronicle* for November 5, summarized the effort with this item:

136. I, 19 / *173.* pp. 156, 159, 165 / *136.* I, 19 / ibid, *173.* pp. 158–160

"This is, and must be, a national institution and the whole country has an interest in its being laid out and ornamented in a way, worthy of a people who so truly honor the memories of their brave dead. We are glad therefore to announce that the whole design and embellishment of this cemetery has been confined to Mr. William Saunders, one of the best and most tasteful landscape gardeners of the present day. . . . Mr. Saunders left this city yesterday morning with his plans completed for the interesting work he has undertaken. . . . No state will be permitted to embellish its own lot, but what is done for one will be done for all. . . . We congratulate the country, and especially the friends of those who fell and now sleep at Gettysburg, upon the taste that will be displayed upon this national cenetery."

The major task which confronted the commissioners from the eighteen states cooperating in the effort, was the removal of the bodies from their temporary resting places to their permanent locations of repose. On October 6, the *Sentinel* reported that Mr. William Saunders from Washington was at Gettysburg plotting and laying out the cemetery grounds. The following week, the paper printed a notice requesting all who intended to remove bodies from the battlefield to notify the committee before interments began. On October 27, the press announced: "The work of removing the dead will begin immediately, the grounds have been laid out."

Identification of the bodies was one of the most difficult tasks confronting those who were engaged in making the final interments. Soldiers killed on the first day were mostly left unburied until the following Monday, as the Confederates soon occupied the grounds where they fell. The soldiers who were killed in battle on the second and third days had their burial places marked with temporary boards. The bodies in unmarked graves were identified by letters, papers, receipts, certificates, diaries, memorandum books, photographs, etcetera, found in the pockets of their cloth-

191. Nov. 5, 1863 / 2. October 6, 27, 1863

ing. Other identification aids were marks on belts, cartridge boxes and wearing apparel.

Massachusetts elected to care for its own dead. The fact that a committee arrived early on the field and spent a week remarking head boards and using every means to discover where their men were engaged, made the task much easier when the bodies were placed in their final resting places. They were further assisted by securing the services of a Gettysburg man, Mr. Solomon Powers, who worked with them and was made their agent to continue the search for bodies throughout the summer months. They received much help by visiting the hospitals and securing first-hand information from comrades of the deceased. They also prepared a memorandum verifying every discovered burial. During the week they were there, they located and marked 135 graves and later Mr. Powers found twenty-four more bodies. All the fallen except two, at some distance away, were interred before the dedication.

Two separate proposals for the task of removal were submitted by the commissioners on October 15, 1863, with all bids to be presented by the 22nd of the month. The first called: "For the exhuming and removal, to the Soldiers' National Cemetery, of the dead of the Union Army, buried on the Gettysburg battlefield and at the several hospitals in the vicinity." The second proposal provided: "For the digging of the graves in the cemetery, putting in the bodies, building a stone foundation for the headstone, and burying the bodies." Detailed specifications were included in the contracts, the work to begin between the dates of October 26 and November 1. Thirty-four bids were received varying from $1.59 to $8.00 per body. With both proposals united into one, the lowest bidder, F. W. Biesecker, was awarded the contract.

Samuel Weaver was designated by the cemetery commission to supervise the work, and he affirmed that not a grave was opened, unless he was there to personally examine the remains and check

173. pp. 149–151 / *27.* Nov. 19, 1863, *25.* pp. 7–15 / *173.* pp. 14–16, 149–151

the contents. The name, company, regiment and the number of the space where the body was to be interred, were inscribed on the coffin. This entry was also copied in the cemetery register. Mr. Weaver also made a supplemental recording of all items of value found on the person or in the graves. These could be claimed by relatives. It must be remembered that large numbers of the Union dead were sent to their home towns for burial.

The work was not entirely completed by the specified time and Mr. Weaver's report includes all interments up to March 19, 1864. The 159 Massachusetts soldiers buried by private contract are included in the totals. There were 3,355 interments divided by states as follows: Maine, 104; New Hampshire, 49; Vermont, 61; Massachusetts, 159; Rhode Island, 12; Connecticut, 22; New York, 866; New Jersey, 78; Pennsylvania, 526; Delaware, 15; Maryland, 22; West Virginia, 11; Ohio, 131; Indiana, 80; Illinois, 6; Michigan, 171; Wisconsin, 73; Minnesota, 52; U. S. Regulars, 138; Unknown, 979.

Mr. Weaver made this statement about the Confederate dead: "In searching for the remains of our fallen heroes, we examined more than three thousand rebel graves. They were frequently buried in trenches, and there were instances of more than one hundred and fifty in one trench. In one place it is asserted by a reliable farmer who saw them buried that there are over two hundred in one trench. I have made a careful estimate . . . of the Rebel bodies buried on that battlefield and at the hospitals and I place the number at not less than seven thousand bodies."

The Washington *Chronicle* published this prophecy: "The name of Gettysburg will be lost in the prouder grander title of 'The National Cemetery.' It will be the latter and not the former that the patriotic pilgrim will visit, leading hither his wondering sons and in the presence of that grand but silent 'Congress' with tears of grateful appreciation will tell them what the sleeping soldiers achieved."

173. pp. 149–151 / ibid / ibid / *191.* Nov. 19, 1863

CHAPTER 5

Invitations Extended

ANDREW G. CURTIN might be called the sponsor for the program of dedication at the Soldiers' National Cemetery since the proceedings were authorized over his signature. He was born in Bellefonte, Pennsylvania, on April 22, 1815. After studying law at Dickinson College, he was admitted to the bar in 1839. A Whig in politics, he canvassed for both Harrison and Clay in their efforts to gain the presidency. In 1854, he was appointed Secretary of Pennsylvania and ex-officio superintendent of public schools. He was elected governor on the Republican ticket in 1860.

During the political campaign of that year, the Republicans of Pennsylvania were divided into two rival groups; the followers of Curtin, led by Alexander K. McClure, and the friends of Simon Cameron. When Lincoln's attention was called to the controversy, he replied in a letter to John M. Pomeroy on August 31, 1860: "I am slow to listen to criminations among friends, and never espouse their quarrels on either side." After the election, the President-elect received a letter from Curtin asking some advice as to how he should proceed with the writing of his inaugural address. Mr. Lincoln replied: "I think you would do well to express, without passion, threat, or appearance of boasting, but

10. II, 34

nevertheless, with firmness, the purpose of yourself, and your state to maintain the Union at all hazards."

Later on, Curtin was informed that Lincoln had received an impression unfavorable to him. This caused Lincoln to deny any such feeling in a letter written on February 4, 1861. Furthermore, he wrote he would be pleased to meet him on the way to Washington. This opportunity occurred at Harrisburg on February 22. Governor Curtin made an acceptable address upon introducing Mr. Lincoln, who highly complimented Curtin on his patriotic and eloquent speech. The President-elect closed his remarks by commenting: "With my consent, or without my great displeasure, this country shall never witness the shedding of one drop of blood in fraternal strife." With the site where the battle of Gettysburg was to be fought but a few miles away, possibly both Lincoln and Curtin recalled this statement nearly three years later when they met at the cemetery dedication.

On the last day of August, 1863, Governor Curtin wrote to David Wills: "The proper consecration of the grounds should have early attention." For two weeks or more Wills had already been making plans for the exercises, even before there was any final decision as to what form the ground complex would take, or how the interments were to be arranged.

Mayor F. W. Lincoln of Boston, on September 23, 1863, called on Edward Everett to inquire if he would be in a position to "deliver an address on the consecration of the ground where the slain were buried at Gettysburg. Mr. Everett replied that he thought he could not refuse." On the same day, Mr. Wills sent this letter to Mr. Everett: "The several states having soldiers in the Army of the Potomac, who fell in the battle of Gettysburg in July last, gallantly fighting for the Union, have arrangements here for the exhuming of all their dead, and their removal and decent burial in a cemetery selected for that purpose on a prominent part of the battlefield. The design is to bury all in common marking the headstones, with the proper inscription, the

1. IV, 103, 158 / 1. IV, 184, 244 / 173. p. 182

known dead, and to create a suitable monument in memory of all these brave men, who have there sacrificed their lives on the altar of the Country. This burial ground will be consecrated to this sacred purpose on Thursday, the 23d day of October next, with appropriate ceremonies, and the several states interested have united in the selection of you to deliver the oration on that solemn occasion. I am therefore instructed by the governors of the different states interested in the project to invite you cordially to join with them in the ceremonies, and to deliver the oration for the occasion."

Mr. Everett replied on September 26 and after a few words of appreciation stated: "The occasion is one of great importance, not to be dismissed with a few sentimental or patriotic commonplaces. It will demand as full a narrative of the events of the three important days as the limits of the hour will permit, and some appropriate discussion of the political character of the great struggle, of which the battle of Gettysburg is one of the most momentous incidents. As it will take me two days to reach Gettysburg, and it will be highly desirable that I have at least one day to survey the battlefield, I cannot safely name an earlier time then the 19th of November. Should such a postponement of the day first proposed be admissable it will give me great pleasure to accept the invitation."

The date suggested by Mr. Wills would have provided but three weeks for preparation. Mr. Everett felt that this was not sufficient time to do the necessary research, the laborious writing and memorizing, as well as allowing for a day to visit the scene of the military conflict. The new date he proposed, November 19, would make available nearly five additional weeks for preparation. There was a second letter from Mr. Everett, or possibly a deleted portion of the original one, in which Mr. Everett raised a second objection to the earlier date. Not much thought had been given to how the grounds would appear at that time. In a subsequent letter to the governor, Mr. Wills wrote: "Mr. Everett suggests that the

121. p. (1), *173*. p. 183, *171*. p. 16 / *171*. p. 17

ceremonies would be rendered more interesting if deferred till after the removal of the soldiers. All references to their self sacrificing bravery in the cause of their country would be far more effective if uttered over their remains, than if only pronounced on a spot to which they are hereafter to be removed."

The impressive contribution which the Boston committee made to the appearance of the cemetery, by holding out for interments by states rather than "promiscuous" burials, was supplemented by Everett in changing the date of the dedication. If October 23, selected by Mr. Wills, had been retained, the thousands of guests at Gettysburg would have witnessed a shocking and revolting spectacle with poorly marked and thinly-covered graves scattered over the entire battlefield.

An authentic word picture of how the area appeared on the October date first selected, allows one to visualize the scene: "The battlefield had been over run by thousands of sorrowing friends in search of lost ones, and many of the graves opened and but partially or carelessly closed. Many of the undertakers who were removing bodies, also performed their work in the most careless manner, invariably leaving the graves open, and often leaving particles of the bones and hairs lying scattered around. These things are frequently to be seen in every part of the battlefield."

While the arrangements of Mr. Everett's appearance at Gettysburg are clearly set forth by Mr. Wills, the preliminaries associated with the President's invitation to be present are vague and confusing. Primarily responsible for many untenable and contradictory statements is the faulty memory of Clark E. Carr, the commissioner from Illinois. His brochure entitled *Lincoln at Gettysburg*, first published in pamphlet form and also in *Transactions*, Illinois State Historical Society, 1906, has been so widely accepted as a dependable account of the proceedings leading up to Lincoln's address, that its authenticity seems not to have been questioned. Dr. W. E. Barton, in his Gettysburg story published in 1930, refers to Mr. Carr's work as a "charming and reliable

171. p. 17 / *25.* Nov. 19, 1863 / *173.* p. 162

little book . . . whose testimony I rank highest of all among those with whom I have conversed on the subject." A eulogy on Mr. Carr pays this tribute: "To him, perhaps more than any other man we are indebted to the universal knowledge and appreciation of it (Gettysburg Address) the world possesses today."

From thirty-five to fifty years is a long time to remember the details of incidents which occurred so long before. The Chicago *Tribune* of February 12, 1900, published a story, "Lincoln at Gettysburg," contributed by Clark E. Carr. Among the comments he said: "In considering the program of exercises it was suggested that Mr. Lincoln be especially asked to speak." There seemed to be no objection but some of the members wondered about his ability to grace such an occasion. However, it was decided to invite him. Six years later, Mr. Carr gave an address before the Illinois State Historical Society in which he said: "It did not seem to occur to anyone that he (Lincoln) could speak on such an occasion. . . . The proposition to ask Mr. Lincoln to speak at the Gettysburg ceremonies was an afterthought." This "afterthought" statement, although in contradiction to Carr's earlier comments, struck the popular fancy and has been given a major emphasis in telling the story. Several years later, the Chicago *Journal* reported an interview with Mr. Carr in which he stated there was much opposition to having the President speak but "they finally yielded to my demands." The *Journal* concluded the article with the comment: "Colonel Carr is the man directly responsible for that classic." (Gettysburg Address). Albert H. Gilmer talked with Mr. Carr at Galesburg in 1906 and from his notes, prepared for the Galesburg *Register-Mail* for November 19, 1949, a brief monograph. He reports Mr. Carr as stating that the committee had no intention of having Lincoln take any part in the dedicatory services. When it was proposed that he speak "there was immediate and vigorous objection." There is no record of any called meeting of the committee prior to the dedication.

20. p. 145, *96*. No. 11, pp. 138–152, No. 26, p. 88 / *49*. Feb. 12, 1900, *38*. pp. 21, 22, *44*. Nov. 19, 1913, *136*. II, 6

Still another variation of the procedure of the committee is presented by Mr. Carr in this affirmation: "A formal invitation to be present was sent to the President of the United States and his cabinet" and several other dignitaries mentioned, but, Mr. Carr continues: "Mr. Lincoln was not at that time invited to speak." There is no evidence available to support the statement that Mr. Lincoln, or any of the other persons named, received such formal invitations previous to November 2. One tradition, however, observes that the President answered his invitation, stating he would attend, which greatly disturbed the committee and forced them to ask him to speak. How early the President, Commander-in-Chief of the army, may have considered visiting Gettysburg is not known, although some of his friends said that soon after the battle he expressed a desire to go over the scene of the conflict. As soon as the Governors of the various states were advised about the plans for a National Cemetery, he must have heard about the project. He may have considered attending the ceremonies even before the invitation arrived.

Governor Curtin visited Washington on August 28, for a conference with Mr. Lincoln. That very day the President had written to General Samuel W. Crawford: "I regret that I cannot be present to witness the presentation of a Sword by the gallant Pennsylvania Reserve Corps, to one so worthy to receive it as General Meade." With the subject of the presentation to Meade, of Gettysburg fame, introduced, it is not unlikely that Curtin and Lincoln would talk about the plans for the dedication. One story notes that his presence was solicited by Curtin.

When it was proposed to invite the President to speak, one committee man claimed: "Senator Alexander Ramsay of Minnesota, a member of the commission. . . . expressed a willingness to see the President and suggest it to him. . . . which he and Thomas F. Ferry, also a member of the commission, did; and it was arranged." This would confirm the supposition that Lincoln

38. pp. 19-21 / *1.* VI, 418

was personally invited to speak and accepted the assignment. Certainly, Mr. David Wills of the commission would not usurp the authority vested in the two members delegated to present a personal invitation to the President, by forwarding a written invitation before the two authorized members had contacted him. Just when the oral invitation was extended is not known.

Mr. Wills sent to the President this letter dated November 2, 1863, which was in confirmation of the oral invitation.

Gettysburg, Nov. 2nd, 1863

To His Excellency,
A. Lincoln
President of the United States
Sir:

    The several states having soldiers in the Army of the Potomac, who were killed at the battle of Gettysburg, or have since died at the various hospitals which were established in the vicinity, have procured grounds on a prominent part of the Battle Field for a Cemetery, and are having the dead removed to these and properly buried.

    These Grounds will be Consecrated and set apart to this Sacred purpose by Appropriate Ceremonies on Thursday the 19th instant. Hon. Edward Everett will deliver the Oration.

    I am authorized by the Governors of the different States to invite you to be present, and participate in these ceremonies, which will doubtless be very imposing and solemnly impressive. It is the desire that, after the Oration, You as Chief Executive of the Nation formally set apart these grounds to their Sacred use by a few appropriate remarks.

    It will be a source of great gratification to the many widows and orphans that have been made almost friendless by the Great Battle here, to have you here personally and it will kindle anew in the breasts of the Comrades of these brave dead, who are now in the tented field or nobly meeting the foe in the front, a confidence that they who sleep in death on the Battle Field are not forgotten by those highest in authority: and they will feel that, should their fate be the same their remains will not be uncared for.

49. Feb. 12, 1900

We hope you will be able to be present to perform this solemn act to the Soldier dead on this Battle Field.

> I am with Great Respect
> Your Excellency's Obedient Servant
> David Wills
> agent for

A. G. Curtin, Gov. of Penna. and acting for all the states.

No answer to this letter has ever been discovered, which supports the suggestion that an oral invitation was extended and an oral acceptance received. The printed report of the proceedings states that: "Special invitations were sent to the President and Vice President of the United States, and the members of the Cabinet, to Major-General George G. Meade, Commanding the Army of the Potomac, and through him, to the officers and privates who had fought so valiantly and to Lieutenant-General Winfield Scott and Admiral Charles Stuart." The one sent to the Secretary of the Navy, Gideon Wells—in his papers at the Library of Congress—bears the date of November 4, 1863, the same date as the one sent to the President. In fact, the first two paragraphs and a part of the third, are alike in both the Wells and Lincoln letters. The closing salutations are also similar.

A regret directed to Mr. Wills was received November 13, from General George G. Meade, who answered for himself and on behalf of the soldiers "who stood side by side in the struggle, shared the peril, and the vacant places in those ranks, bear sad testimony to the loss they have sustained." He explained however: "This army has duties to perform which will not permit of being represented on the occasion."

The public was invited to be present through this release in the press:

"The loyal citizens generally, of all the States and the charitable and benevolent associations are most cordially invited to be present at the consecration of the Soldiers' Cemetery, at Gettys-

111. Wills to Lincoln, Nov. 2, 1863 / *173.* p. 179, 110, *136.* II, 5 / *173.* pp. 187–189

burg, Pennsylvania, on Thursday, the 19th inst. and participate in the solemn exercises on the occasion."

By order of the governor of the several states interested
David Wills
agent for A. G. Curtin, Gov. of Pennsylvania
and acting especially for the other states.
Gettysburg, Nov. 7, 1863

191. Nov. 13, 1863

CHAPTER 6

Composing the Address

When Abraham Lincoln was elected to the presidency, one of the opposition newspapers submitted this query: "Who will write this ignorant man's state papers?" Possibly the fact that William H. Seward offered to take over some of the President's responsibilities caused one author to conclude that the Gettysburg Address was written by the Secretary of State, and "put into every collection of great speeches, and attributed to Lincoln not Seward." Lincoln needed no amanuensis. Even in boyhood he had been the neighborhood's scribe, and a maker of speeches. As an adult he had earned his livelihood by practicing law, which called for the preparation and presentation of arguments. His political advancement was greatly enhanced by his ability as a speaker and it is doubtful if he would have gained the presidency, had he not been an orator of much ability.

At some length, there have been presented in the early chapters of this book three factors that contributed directly to the task of preparing his remarks for the Gettysburg dedication: his lifelong practice of preparing speeches; his belief in the equality of men, so recently climaxed by the Emancipation Proclamation; and the spirit of patriotism, so greatly stimulated by the July 4 memories associated with the place where he was to speak.

96. 1927, p. 121, *136*. II, 41

Composing the Address

Granted that these underlying influences were helpful in the composition of his discourse, there must have been some specific nucleus around which he could marshal his thoughts for the dedication.

Upon being invited to speak at a burial place, Lincoln may have recalled other occasions when he had delivered eulogies. The most important one was his Chicago address on the passing of Henry Clay, which he began in this fashion: "On the fourth day of July, 1776, the people of a few feeble and oppressed colonies of Great Britain, inhabiting a portion of the Atlantic coast of North America, publicly declared their national independence. . . ." More likely, the request brought to his mind the speech made a few months before, partly inspired by events which had taken place at this same town of Gettysburg. The striking similarity of his opening remarks on July 7, and the opening sentences he prepared for the speech on November 19, have caused students of Lincoln to refer to the former impromptu talk as the "Preliminary Gettysburg Address."

In this short tribute from the balcony of the Executive Mansion, already reported in full, Lincoln not only referred to the Union victories of July 4, but also mentioned other incidents which had occurred on previous anniversaries of the nation's birth. Then followed the significant statement: "This is a glorious theme, and the occasion for a speech, but I am not prepared to make one worthy of the occasion." Now, an opportunity does present itself where he could prepare something worth while on that "glorious theme." There is no evidence that he made any notes for the July 7 speech, but it was widely printed in the press, which not only provided the President, but posterity as well, with copies of what he had said.

As he worked over the opening rhetorical question of July 7, "How long ago is it?—eighty odd years," it was translated into the classical expression, "Four score and seven years ago". "A nation by its representatives," became simply, "our fathers". "Assembled

1. II, 121, 1. VI, 320 / ibid

and declared as a self evident truth," was expressed by "conceived" and "dedicated." Then came the all-important pronouncement, alike in both speeches, "that all men are created equal." On two more instances in the July talk the President used the above expression. If repetition, in this case, can be considered a means of emphasis, Lincoln stressed the "equality" theme in the July 7 address.

In addition to the serenade speech, other sources which may have contributed suggestions and created atmosphere for the dedicatory composition, are found in Lincoln's significant jottings preliminary to the November writing. One week after the Executive Mansion celebration, he issued a Thanksgiving Proclamation setting apart August 6, as a day of national praise and prayer. He referred to the recent military victories which gave "reasonable grounds for augmented confidence that the Union of these States will be maintained, their constitution preserved, and their peace and prosperity, permanently restored."

General Banks, then stationed at New Orleans, received a letter from the President written on August 5, 1863, expressing the hope that Louisiana would: "Adopt some practical system by which the two races could gradually live themselves out of their old relation to each other, and both come out better prepared for the new. Education for young blacks should be included in the plan." This suggestion was made a hundred years ago and similar sentiments have encouraged many reflective observers to wish that Lincoln had lived to direct the reconstruction period.

A letter sent to James C. Conkling on August 26, was prepared for reading at a mass meeting of unconditioned Union men at Springfield, Illinois. Many of them disliked the Emancipation Proclamation and urged that the war was being waged to free negroes. The President wrote: "I thought that whatever negroes can be got to do as soldiers, leaves just so much less for white soldiers to do, in saving the Union. . . . . But negroes, like

1. VI, 320 / 1. VI, 332 / 1. VI, 364, 365

other people, act upon motives. . . . If they stake their lives for us, they must be prompted by the strongest motive—even the promise of freedom. And the promise being made, must be kept." Here again Lincoln's thoughts seem to be directed towards the freedom emphasis.

A clipping from the London *Star* commenting on the Conkling letter states: "It is a masterpiece of cogent argument, as an appeal to the spirit of the nation it is sublime in the dignified simplicity of its eloquence. . . . It is worthy of a Cromwell or a Washington." Such assurance as this, of Lincoln's ability to express himself eloquently, must have made him conscious of the reputation he was building in the field of literature and inspired a desire to enhance the prestige he enjoyed.

Not only his own writings and the comments of others about them, but letters written to him, furnish important exhibits which provided valuable direct and indirect sources for the preparation of his famous address. J. Lothrop Motley, whom Lincoln appointed minister to Austria, wrote at Vienna, a letter which must have reached the President the latter part of September, 1863. Among other complimentary statements about military victories, he expressed: "heartfelt gratitude to the skillful generals and brave soldiers, whose breasts have been the living ramparts of republican liberty, and whose life blood, also, has been so freely poured forth that the nation should live. . . . They who believed in the capacity of the people to govern themselves, will find their belief strengthened." This letter abounded in comments such as found expression in the conclusion of Lincoln's brief speech, with special emphasis on the "government of the people."

About this same time, a letter arrived from Garibaldi, the Italian patriot, in which he wrote: "You will pass down to posterity under the name, the Emancipator! more enviable than any crown and any human treasure. . . . America, teacher of liberty to our fathers now opens the most solemn era of human

1. VI, 409 / *115*. Sept. 19, 1863 / *111*. Motley to Lincoln, July 25, 1863

progress. . . . Greeting to you Abraham Lincoln, great pilot of freedom: Greeting to all who for two years have fought and bled around your regenerating standard."

There was also received by Lincoln about September 30, the prophetic medal from the Union League at Philadelphia. Originally, it was hoped that it could be presented to him in person at Philadelphia on July 4. Its arrival at this time must have been an occasion for Lincoln to again recall his 1861 visit to Independence Hall and the successful military achievements of the last July 4.

Lincoln's next writing of importance was the epochal First National Annual Thanksgiving Proclamation. Little attention has been paid to his contribution in the nationalizing of our significant American religious festival. On October 3, the same day of the month in which Washington had issued his 1789 call for the observance of the day of praise and prayer, Abraham Lincoln put his signature to the Proclamation of Thanksgiving which was to supplement the acts of the governors of the various states and make the celebration national. Not only was it of consequence in the creation of a new American holiday, but it was beautiful in its literary expression. One can almost feel the very sentiment of the Gettysburg lines while reading it. Although it seems a sacrilege to disturb its contents, one excerpt appears to almost paraphrase the Gettysburg conclusion. In the proclamation, Lincoln observes: "The country, rejoicing in the consciousness of augmented strength and vigor, is permitted to expect continuation of years with large increase of freedom." Coming to the conclusion of his remarks at Gettysburg, the President uses the phrase, "A new birth of freedom." The "continuance of years" becomes "shall not perish from the earth."

With all these patriotic sentiments finding expression in his thinking, the speech of July 7 providing the nucleus, with

---

111. Garibaldi to Lincoln, Aug. 1863 / 1. VI, 533 / 109. No. 972, 1. VI, 496, 497

"freedom" the inspiration, it would be but a matter of selection and arrangement as he prepared to put in writing his few remarks for the commemoration.

Lincoln's first mention in his correspondence about the dedication appears in a letter of November 9, to Stephen T. Logan of Springfield, Illinois, inviting him to attend what he thought would be, an interesting ceremony. This note makes it very clear that he was keeping the Gettysburg obligation before him. John G. Nicolay, twenty years after the dedication, made this comment in an article for *Century Magazine:* "There is no decisive record of when Mr. Lincoln wrote the first sentences of his proposed address. He probably followed his usual habit in such matters, using great deliberation in arranging his thoughts, and moulding his phrases mentally, waiting to reduce them to writing until they had taken satisfactory form."

In the maze of traditions collected referring to the time of the actual writing of the speech, a descriptive note appearing in an exhibit at the Chicago Historical Society, presents the earliest suggested date. On November 19, 1950, there were on display all five holograph copies of the address. The citation on the exhibit marked "First Draft" stated: "Written in Washington ten days or two weeks before the dedication ceremonies. The fact that the conclusion is in pencil may indicate that Lincoln worked on the draft at two different times." If the maximum time of "two weeks" is considered, it places this writing as early as November 5.

One important but little known testimony associated with the composition of the address was recalled by John D. Defrees of Indiana, whom Lincoln had appointed government printer. On October 24, 1863, Lincoln visited his department and made a short speech to the employees. A young lady who worked there was encouraged to tell, or write to, the President about her brother who had been made a prisoner. On November 12, Mr. Lincoln wrote to Defrees: "Please see this girl who works in your office,

1. VI, 319, 320 / 1. VII, 7, 41. Feb. 1894 / 136. V, 81

and find out about her brother, and come and see me." This meeting likely was responsible for the story Defrees' son-in-law, J. O. Smith, has preserved: "John D. Defrees was sent for one night and asked into a room where Mr. Lincoln awaited him. After locking the door the President took a paper out of his pocket and said: 'John, I want you to read this carefully and make any changes your judgment dictates.' That paper was the famous Gettysburg speech. After reading it, Mr. Defrees handed it back with the injunction, 'Don't change a word of it—it is perfect.' " No mention was made of their conversation about the girl and her brother.

Simon Cameron, Lincoln's first Secretary of War, stated: "Mr. Lincoln wrote that speech in the White House several days before he went to Gettysburg. He took great pains in writing it. On a visit to him he showed it to me. It was written with a lead pencil on commercial note paper. Receiving it from his own hand he asked me to read it and tell him what I thought of it. I did both. . . ." This reminiscence was told to Colonel Yingling who released it to the press in 1901.

One of the President's assistant secretaries, Noah Brooks, who noticed a printed proof sheet of Mr. Everett's long Gettysburg oration, quoted the President as commenting with respect to his own address: "What he had ready to say was very short or as he emphatically expressed it: 'short, short, short.' " In reply to a question as to the speech having already been written, the President said it was, "written but not finished." On another occasion Brooks claimed: "The speech was written and rewritten a great many times."

While there are some variations in Lamon's report of the interview with Lincoln on the morning of November 18, the most condensed form states: "that the President took from his tall hat a sheet of foolscap, handed it to me with the remark: 'Hill, there is what I have written for Gettysburg tomorrow. It does not suit me,

1. VII, 12, *136.* II, 35 / *136.* II, 34 / *31.* p. 286, *30.* pp. 394, 395

but I have not time for anything more.' This was the address substantially as delivered."

The affirmations by Defrees, Cameron, and Lamon, that they read the document, and the positive statement of assistant secretary Brooks that Mr. Lincoln told him it was written, should cause no doubt about the address having been prepared in Washington before the President left for the dedication. Evidence which can be more conveniently and convincingly presented in a subsequent chapter, will reveal that at least one, and probably two, complete copies of the address were written by the President at the Executive Mansion in preparation for delivery at Gettysburg.

136. III, 73

CHAPTER 7

Incidents en Route

LINCOLN's first political communication to appear in the press, published in 1832, states: "No other improvement that reason will justify us in hoping for, can equal in utility the railroad. It is a never failing source of communication, between places of business remotely situated from each other." Yet, as he prepared for the visit to Gettysburg over thirty years later, he realized that one could not depend absolutely on railroad time tables. He had approached Secretary Stanton with respect to transportation facilities to Gettysburg and had received this prospectus:

War Department, November 17, 1863
Mr. President: It is proposed by the Baltimore and Ohio road—
First, to leave Washington Thursday morning at 6 a.m.; and
Second, to leave Baltimore at 8 a.m., arriving at Gettysburg at 12 noon, thus giving two hours to view the ground before the dedication ceremonies commence.
Third, to leave Gettysburg at 6 p.m. and arrive in Washington, midnight; thus doing all in one day.
Mr. Smith says the North Central road agrees to this arrangement.
Please consider it and if any change is desired, let me know, so that it can be made.
Yours truly
Edwin M. Stanton

1. I, 5 / *1.* VII, 16

On the back of the note appears this endorsement by the President:

> "I do not like the arrangement. I do not wish to so go that by the slightest accident we fail entirely, and, at the best, the whole to be a breathless running of the gauntlet. But, any way."
> A. Lincoln

Stanton immediately conferred with the railroad officials suggesting a less crowded schedule, with the result that he received at 3:30 p.m. on November 17, this reply from J. W. Garrett of Baltimore: "We will take great pleasure in making the arrangements as you propose. This program furnishes abundant margin and will be less fatiguing. I have ordered the special train as desired to leave Washington at 12 o'clock tomorrow (Wednesday) and will notify and arrange with the other roads for it to proceed directly through to Gettysburg. Mr. Smith's suggestions were designed to effect economy of time if that were essential."

It was Mr. J. Preston Smith, master of transportation for the Baltimore and Ohio Railroad, instead of Stanton, who had suggested the early unfavorable schedule. The latter immediately sent this note to the President: "The arrangement I proposed has been made. The train will leave the depot at 12 o'clock. I will assign the Adjutant General or Col. Fry to accompany you as personal escort and to control the train. A carriage will call for you at 12. Please furnish me with the names of those whom you may invite that they may be furnished with ticket and unauthorized intrusion prevented."

A complete roster of those who accompanied Lincoln does not seem to be available. John Hay in his wartime diary, listed these celebrities who were in the party: The President, Secretary Seward, Secretary Usher, Secretary Blair, Private Secretary John Nicolay and Assistant Private Secretary John Hay, Henri Mercier, the French Minister and Admiral Reynaud, Joseph Bertinatti, the Italian Minister, Captain Isola, and Lieutenants Martinez and Cora, Captain and Mrs. H. A. Wise, son-in-law and

---

1. VII, 16 / *111.* Garrett to Stanton, Nov. 17, 1863 / *1.* VII, 16

daughter of Edward Everett, Wayne MacVeagh and Honorable William McDougall of Canada.

On the morning of November 17, McDougall was visiting with the President who told him about the contemplated trip to Gettysburg and stated that it was "an important event perhaps you would like to be my guest and accompany my party."

On the same train with the President were: his personal escort, General James B. Fry, a bodyguard from the First Regiment of the Invalid Corps under Lieutenant Ford, the Washington Marine Band and members of the press. General Fry recalled that on the day of departure he went to the White House at the time appointed and found the carriage there waiting for the President. As it was getting late, Fry commented to Mr. Lincoln that there was no time to lose, whereupon the President told his well known story about the man sentenced to be executed, who while being taken to the gallows, called out to those who hurried past him: "You needn't be in such a hurry to get ahead, there won't be any fun until I get there." On November 19, the Washington *Chronicle* printed this notice: "The President left the city yesterday to take part in the dedication of the National Cemetery at Gettysburg. He did so at considerable personal inconvenience but he could not deny himself the opportunity to be present on an occasion of such melancholy interest. His presence will help to deepen the impressiveness of the scene. . . ."

Henry Clay Cochrane, on writing about the first part of the trip, claimed that Secretary Seward, who was in charge of the party, "began to get uneasy as we approached Baltimore." It was Lincoln's first visit there since the memorable journey to Washington for his Inaugural, when it was reported that an attempt would be made to assassinate him as he passed through the city. Although the locomotive, as usual, was detached upon reaching Bolton station at the outskirts of Baltimore, and the cars, "dragged by tandem teams of horses to Calvert St. Station," the terminal of the Northern Central Railroad, no incident occurred to mar their

88. I, 20 / 147. July 19, 1947 / *165.* p. 403, *191.* Nov. 19, 1863

Incidents en Route

passage through the city. Here another large contingent was taken aboard the presidential train, among them General Schenck and his staff.

The train now consisted of four coaches, as well as a baggage car which was utilized as an improvised diner. The last coach, in which the President traveled, was frequently used by the directors of the railroad company. One-third of the car had been partitioned off into a separate compartment with the seats arranged along the walls. It was a fifty-mile run from Baltimore to Gettysburg over the Western Maryland Railroad. John Eckert was the conductor on the train. The news and candy boy, Andrew B. Staley of Baltimore, in later years recalled details of the trip. Wayne MacVeagh stated: "Whenever the train stopped, Mr. Lincoln was required to address, from the rear platform, some words to the few people who had gathered" but MacVeagh did not remember anything of importance that he said. At one of the towns a little girl presented Mr. Lincoln with some flowers saying: "Flowerth for the Prethident." Whereupon Lincoln kissed the child and remarked: "You'er a sweet little rosebud yourself. I hope your life will open into perpetual goodness and beauty."

The governor's special excursion train from Harrisburg numbered among its principal dignitaries: Governors: Curtin, Seymour, Pierpont, Brough, Tod, Dennison, Boureman and their respective staffs. Generals: Vanderpoel, Doubleday, Stahel, Stoneman, Colonel Anderson, ex-Secretary Cameron, and Clement C. Barclay of Philadelphia. The following officers of the Governor's staff were also included; Adjutant General Russell, Commissary General Irwin, Surgeon General King, Quartermaster General Reynolds, Colonel J. H. Raleston, Colonel Roberts, Lieutenant Colonel Thomas, Lieutenant Colonel J. A. Wright, Colonel Quay and private secretary George H. T. Morgan. Birgfeld's Band of Philadelphia was also aboard. The misgivings of the President about the uncertainty of railroad schedules were supported by the difficulties confronting the Governor's special. It was supposed to

126. Feb. 13, 1907 / *146.* June 13, 1925, *41.* Nov. 1919, *157.* Feb. 7, 1931

connect with the train from Baltimore at Hanover Junction, "where the President will be received with becoming honors." The train from Harrisburg was six hours late and did not reach Gettysburg until 11:00 p.m.

Some photographs discovered a few years ago taken at Hanover Junction, were supposed to show Lincoln walking on the platform. According to Secretary Nicolay, the President did not leave the train at the Junction but he did appear for a brief talk at Hanover, thirteen miles to the west, where the train was detained for eight minutes and, at this point, the Hanover and Gettysburg Railroad took the train on the last lap of the journey. This gave the people who had come to the depot hoping to see the President, an opportunity to cheer and call for him. Eventually, Reverend M. J. Alleman, pastor of the St. Mark's Lutheran Church, stepped into the coach and said: "Father Abraham, your children want to see you!" The local paper reported the following week that the President; "delivered one of the brief quaint speeches for which he is celebrated, commenting: 'I understand the enemy was in your town and was driven out the day before the battle of Gettysburg. Did you help do it?' Pastor Alleman answered: 'It was here Kilpatrick commanding a division of Union Cavalry defeated the forces of Jeb Stuart and drove him from the town.' " The ladies then presented the President with flowers and also a beautiful flag they had made. At Hanover, he was introduced to the telegraph operator, Daniel Trone, who had sent the telegram to Secretary Wells on July 3, announcing the success of the Union troops at Gettysburg.

One of the most controversial episodes relating to the Gettysburg proceedings, is the traditional story about the President writing his dedicatory address while en route. Possibly the earliest printed version is found in Isaac N. Arnold's *The History of Abraham Lincoln*, published in 1866. This account states that it was not until he was on his way that he was notified: "he would be expected to make some remarks. Retiring a short time, he prepared

136. I, 40, *88.* II, 120 / *136.* II, 18–21, 26–30, *156.* Feb. 1929

the following address. . . ." One observer, many years later stated: that after entering the train, as soon as he made himself comfortable, he prepared "the first draft of his speech by the time he reached Baltimore." The running time between the two cities was one hour and fifteen minutes. Mr. Cochrane recalled that it was not until the train was approaching Hanover Junction that Mr. Lincoln mentioned that the people would expect him to say something at the dedication; "And I must give the matter some thought." Such newspaper celebrities as Ben Perley Poore and Henry Watterson gave publicity to the story. Andrew Carnegie was mentioned as having loaned the pencil with which Lincoln did the writing, although Carnegie's associates seem to have successfully refuted the story. Even before the turn of the century, the train tradition was so generally credited that Robert Lincoln accepted it and wrote to Miss Bell F. Keyes on December 15, 1885: "My father's Gettysburg address was jotted down in pencil, in part at least on his way to the place." However, in later years he changed his mind about the train writing.

What appears to be the most important testimony from a non-traveler came from Lincoln's assistant secretary, W. O. Stoddard, who stated in 1884 that the address was written "while on the way." It probably brought John Nicolay to say in his *Century Magazine* article ten years later, but thirty-one years after he had accompanied the President: "There is neither record, evidence, nor well-founded tradition that Mr. Lincoln did any writing or made any notes on the train between Washington and Gettysburg." One fact is certain, that there is not extant today a single line that Lincoln wrote while the train was in motion, as Nicolay reasoned: "the rockings and joltings of the train, rendering writing virtually impossible."

The train tradition receiving the widest circulation and attracting the largest group of proponents was presented by Mary Raymond Shipman Andrews, in *Scribner's Magazine* for July,

12. p. 328, *165.* p. 228, *162.* June 30, 1909, *55.* Feb. 12, 1920 / *178.* p. 412, *41.* Feb. 5, 1896

1906, under the caption: "The Perfect Tribute." Later in the year, it was published in a book of forty-seven pages by Charles Scribner's Sons. A school edition in limp cloth was printed in 1910. Thirty years later, half a million copies of the book had been sold. It continued to come from the press periodically and on its fiftieth anniversary it came out in a new format. No comment by author or publisher appeared about the authenticity of the story until 1956, when on the jacket of the edition there was printed the statement: "A short moving tale of Abraham Lincoln." The reviews of the book were very complimentary and the New York *Times* referred to it as one of the "greatest stories" that had appeared in recent years. Metro-Goldwyn-Mayer reproduced the essay as a one-reel film in 1935, with Charles (Chic) Sales as Lincoln.

Mrs. Andrews' son, Paul, when about fourteen years old, had a history teacher named Walter Burlingame. One day the teacher told of a reminiscence of his boyhood that related to a conversation he recalled between his father, Anson Burlingame, and Edward Everett. Walter remembered that Mr. Everett was telling about the preparation of his own oration and then mentioned how: "Lincoln wrote his address on a piece of brown paper on the train going up to Gettysburg," and other details about the program the following day. Paul was thrilled with this story and told it to his mother as it was related by the teacher. Mrs. Andrews also was captivated by the narrative and it formed the basis of her essay.

In later years, Paul prepared a brief account of the composition, telling of his mother's birth in Mobile, Alabama, her residence in Lexington, Kentucky, and her removal to Syracuse, New York, where the story was written. Although southern born, Mrs. Andrews had a deep reverence for Lincoln and felt, "some tribute to him ought to be written by a Southerner." *The Perfect Tribute* was the result. Paul Andrews also stated that his mother added the fiction part, "about the young Southern boy and the dying

8. 1–47, *109*. No. 408 / *136*. VI, 50, *109*. Nos. 408, 1400

Southern soldier, his brother." Mrs. Andrews did not expect the entire essay would be accepted as a historical narrative. Walter Burlingame related this story to his class forty years after the incident occurred and thirty-five years after his father's death. Everett, who is represented as having witnessed the writing on the train, was already in Gettysburg.

The Perfect Tribute, as a highly regarded essay in the field of literature, has been widely introduced into the high schools across the nation. Placed on the required or elective reading lists for courses in English, because of its brevity, it has had a phenomenal number of readers. One young lady student was asked how she happened to elect to read it and she frankly replied, "It was the shortest book in the list." Mrs. Andrews made this prophetic observation when commenting on the address: "Fifty years from now American school boys will be learning it as a part of their education."

Here are some of the conclusions one draws upon reading Mrs. Andrews' book. The Gettysburg Address, the day before it was delivered, was written on a railroad train with a stub of a pencil on a zigzag piece of brown wrapping paper. After Lincoln finished writing, he read it, dropped it on the floor, and called it a failure. He retrieved, folded, and placed it in his pocket and concluded it was a bad thing. When he delivered the address, his "squeaking falsetto" voice caused an unmistakable titter through the crowd, which he detected, but as he proceeded, the people were hushed and upon his conclusion: "not a hand was lifted in applause." There was "no sound of approval" from the audience. The President was sure he had failed.

It is to be regretted that American Youth for over half a century have received the impression that the finest oration in our language, was belatedly, hurriedly, and even slovenly written on a railroad train. The story is a travesty on how masterpieces are created.

109. Nos. 408, 1400 / *136.* VI, 50 / *8.* pp. 13, 17, 43 / *109.* No. 1400

CHAPTER 8

Informal Preliminaries

THE SAME DAY that David Wills sent the letter to the President confirming the commissioners' desire to have him make the short dedicatory speech, he also wrote this personal note:

> To his excellency A. Lincoln
> President U.S
> Sir:
>   As the hotels in our town will be crowded and in confusion at the time referred to in the extended invitation, I write to invite you to stop with me. I hope you will feel it your duty to lay aside pressing business for a day, to come here to perform this last rite to our brave soldier dead on this 19th instant.
>   Governor Curtin and Hon. Edward Everett will be my guests at the time and if you come you will please join them at my house. You will confer a favor if you will advise me early of your intentions.
>
> > With great respect
> > Your obedient servant
> > David Wills.

Obviously, the President would first wish to inquire about his host, a total stranger, and what accommodations could be provided. It is likely that questions regarding the visit would be answered by Governor Curtin. Inasmuch as no written reply to

111. Wills to Lincoln, Nov. 2, 1863

Informal Preliminaries

Mr. Wills' invitation has been discovered, it seems likely the acceptance was relayed through the Governor who wrote to Mr. Lincoln on November 4 that he would see him shortly.

Marshal Lamon and several of his aides met the train from Washington and the President was conducted to the home of Mr. Wills where he was to spend the night. It was but a block from the depot but far enough for a large crowd to fall in line and gather about the residence, which stood on the public square facing York Street. Mr. Lincoln was conducted to the guest room on the second floor, immediately over Mr. Wills' law office, and adjacent to the large corner apartment used as the family living room. John Hay wrote in his diary that when the President's group reached Gettysburg, "our party broke like a drop of quicksilver spilled." Cornelius Cole, a member of Congress, stated: "There was no hotel in Gettysburg. Mr. Lincoln was assigned for the night to sleep with the mayor, or chief man, of Gettysburg." The Senator was in error about many details relating to the President's visit.

There seems to have been some possibility, when arrangements were first considered, that Mrs. Lincoln and Tad had contemplated accompanying the President. One paper mentions Mr. and Mrs. Lincoln and their youngest son as having arrived at Gettysburg. Another account erroneously states that Robert Lincoln was with his father and occupied the same room. Tad had been taken ill a day or two before and Mr. Lincoln left Washington deeply concerned about his condition. There is some evidence that the President took William Johnston, his negro servant with him, at least that was his intention as a brief memorandum suggests and Mr. Wills states that the servant accompanied him.

According to one of the college students present, a serenade of Mr. Lincoln began immediately after he reached the Wills' home and "did not allow time enough for the President and his party to partake of supper," before he was called out. Another student

111. Curtin to Lincoln, Nov. 4, 1863 / *88.* I, 121, *136.* II, 53 / *191.* Nov. 20, 1863, *1.* VIII, 562

states that in response to the call: "The President appeared in the doorway standing for a few minutes but not speaking."

The evening meal in honor of the President and special guests, served at the home of Mr. Wills, lacked the presence of Governor Curtin and several other celebrities, due to the late arrival of their train. Nevertheless, among the twenty-five persons invited were: the President, Mr. Everett, three cabinet members, three former governors, one governor-elect, five major generals, three foreign ministers, and other notables. The only glimpse of these famous guests at mealtime comes to us through Edward Everett. He attended a dinner at the Revere House in Boston on November 15, 1864, honoring Captain Winslow and the officers of the *Kearsarge*. Asked to respond to the toast, "Our President," Mr. Everett commented: "It may seem hardly worth while to notice the descriptions which represent the President as a person of uncouth appearance and manners. . . . I will take the liberty to say that the only social occasion on which I ever had the honor to be in the President's company, namely the commemoration of Gettysburg, he sat at the table at the home of my friend David Wills, Esq. by the side of several distinguished persons, ladies and gentlemen, foreigners and Americans . . . in gentlemanly appearance, manners and conversation he (the President) was the peer of any man at the table."

During the dinner period, people continued to congregate in the public square and the New York *Tribune* reporter gives this account of the proceedings: "After supper the President was serenaded by the excellent band of the 5th New York Artillery. A group of young women sang, 'We are coming Father Abraham, Three Hundred Thousand Strong.' Also, a male quartette rendered several numbers. A great crowd had gathered by this time and called continually and vociferously for the President.

The press noted two different appearances of Mr. Lincoln and it was before this larger gathering that he made a few comments. There are several versions of what he said, but this one published

201. Nov. 19, 1914, *86*. Feb. 12, 1929 / *136*. I, 38 / *139*. Nov. 20, 1863

in the *Tribune* the next day has been accepted, generally, as the authentic evening speech: "I appear before you, fellow-citizens, merely to thank you for this compliment. The inference is a very fair one that you would hear me for a little while at least, were I to commence to make a speech. I do not appear before you for the purpose of doing so, and for several substantial reasons. The most substantial of these is that I have no speech to make. (Laughter.) In my position it is somewhat important that I should not say any foolish things. (A voice—If you can help it.) It very often happens that the only way to help it is to say nothing at all. (Laughter.) Believing that is my present condition this evening, I must beg of you to excuse me from addressing you further." One reporter who commented on the remarks observed: "He had said nothing, but he had said it well."

The serenaders with a band, singers, and the town full of celebrities, planned to make an evening of it. Just around the corner from the Wills' home lived Robert G. Harper, who was entertaining William H. Seward as his guest. The Secretary was loudly called for and he responded with what was probably the longest speech of the evening. It was printed in full by the Albany *Evening Journal* on the following day. Only the opening and concluding paragraphs are presented:

"Fellow-Citizens—I am now sixty years old and upward; I have been in public life practically forty years of that time, and yet this is the first time that ever any people or community so near the border of Maryland was found willing to listen to my voice; and the reason for that, I said fifty years ago that Slavery was opening before this people a grave yard that was to be filled with brothers falling in mutual political combat. . . .

"When we part tomorrow night, let us remember that we owe it to our country and to mankind that this war shall have for its conclusion the establishing of the principle of democratic government;—the simple principle that whatever party, whatever portion

139. Nov. 20, 1863, *1.* VII, 16, 17 / *136.* II, 44 / *4.* Nov. 20, 1863

of the community, prevails by constitutional suffrage in an election, that part is to be respected and maintained in power, until it shall give place, on another trial and another verdict, to a different portion of the people. (Good.) If you do not do this you are drifting at once and irresistibly to the very verge of universal, cheerless, and hopeless anarchy. But with that principle this government of ours—the purest, the best, the wisest, and the happiest in the world—must be, and, so far as we are concerned, practically will be immortal."

The correspondent of the New York *Tribune* was not favorably impressed with the speech and pointed out that he used the personal pronoun "I" ten times, and thought the speech too long. Another observer chided the speaker for bungling his introduction by implying that Gettysburg was in Maryland. John Hay wrote in his diary that Seward "spoke so indistinctly that I did not hear a word of what he was saying." One youth who stated that he spoke very slowly was impressed by the weight of his arguments.

After the speech of Seward, the crowd moved in succession to the places where Representative McPherson, Representative McKnight, Judge Shannon, Colonel John W. Forney and Wayne MacVeagh were staying. Forney according to John Hay: "had been drinking a good deal during the day and was getting to feel a little ugly and dangerous." He made a speech in which he referred to Douglas' service to the Union. He eulogized the President and spoke of him as one that: "would live in history, as the savior of the country." According to Hay: "In tipsy fashion he mingled drollery and gravity, quite Shakesperian, in this low comedy presentation." The Gettysburg *Compiler* commented: "The renegades Forney and Shannon were on hand and came out 'too.' Their speeches were low political tirades out of time and out of place." MacVeagh recalled: "When my time came I confined myself to some words of praise of General Reynolds, who had been killed in the first clash of the battle, with his back to his birthplace at Lancaster and his face, as always, to the fire." The

4. Nov. 30, 1863 / 136. II, 9, *88.* I, 121–122

Informal Preliminaries

crowd is said to have become disorderly by this time and General Sedgwick promised to lead them to the home where Governor Curtin was staying and eventually a dispersion of the group was effected.

Ward H. Lamon, who had been appointed as Marshal in Chief, had come to Gettysburg the day before the President's arrival to make arrangements for his reception and organize the group of assistants in preparation for the parade and program. He called a meeting for 8:00 p.m. in the courthouse and Honorable Joseph Casey was made chairman and Honorable S. Newton Pettis and Mr. B. S. Hendricks were appointed secretaries. The roll of the aides to the Marshal was called: Joseph Casey, A. B. Olin, S. N. Pettis, P. C. Shannon, W. A. Newell, B. B. French, G. B. Lincoln, C. B. Boteler, Robert Lammon, Colonels: S. P. Hanscom, A. P. Chipman, John Hay, Major George B. Brastow, Captains: H. A. Scheetz, A. S. H. White, Thos. Lloyd, B. B. French, Jr., John Mattingly, Nathan B. Barrett, W. M. Behan, Levi Scorey, Major John F. Tobias, B. P. Snyder, Hugh B. McCanby, W. L. Church, W. Y. Selleck, B. S. Hendricks, John Van Resworth, M. E. Flanagan, William Brooks, Colonel J. G. Stevenson, General E. C. Carrington, Colonel Henry O. Kent, Alex Stevens, Master Percey Gordon, John M. Barclay, Judge M. W. Tappan.

Aide B. B. French wrote in his diary this account of a matter of business at the Marshal's meeting: "A contribution of one hundred and sixty dollars was raised to purchase food for soldiers in Libby Prison at Richmond. Mr. Seward said that the Confederate government would not allow the money to be given to the prisoners. Mr. French replied to Mr. Seward: 'They will if it is given by individuals.'" It was then recorded in the French diary: "Thereupon, Seward gave ten dollars saying 'Put that down for Marshal Seward, an individual.'"

Possibly the most widely circulated tradition associated with

41. Feb. 1894, *88*. I, 121, 122, *76*. Nov. 23, *41*. Nov. 1909 / *191*. Nov. 20, 1863 / *128*. p. 15

the writing of the address claims that the President wrote it either in full or in part, at the home of Mr. Wills, either the night before or the morning of the exercises. This statement signed by Mr. Wills for Charles M. McCurdy, twenty years after the occasion, presents this traditional background for the account of the evening writing: "Between nine and ten o'clock the President sent his servant to request me to come to his room. I went and found him with paper prepared to write, and he said he had just seated himself to put upon paper a few thoughts for tomorrow's exercises, and had sent for me to ascertain what part he was to take in them, and what was expected of him. After a full talk on the subject I left him. About eleven o'clock he sent for me again and when I went to his room he had the same paper in his hand, and asked me if he could see Mr. Seward. I told him Mr. Seward was staying with my neighbor, next door and I would go and bring him over. He said 'No, I'll go and see him.' He went, and I went with him, and Mr. Lincoln carried the paper on which he had written his speech with him, and we found Mr. Seward and I left the President with him. In less than half an hour, Mr. Lincoln returned with the same paper in his hand. The next day I sat by him on the platform when he delivered his address, which has become immortal, and he read it from the same paper on which I had seen him writing it the night before."

Mr. Wills' version of the writing of the address affirms that it was completed by the time of his visit to Mr. Seward. But The New York *Evening Post*, on May 3, 1865, stated that it was written, "in the small hours of the morning" on the very day it was delivered.

This same Mr. McCurdy who secured the Wills' testimony also recorded a statement from H. P. Bingham, who had been detailed to guard the door to the room Mr. Lincoln occupied. He stated that while on duty "A telegram was handed me for Mr. Lincoln. . . . In a few minutes he opened the door and said: 'The telegram is from home, my little boy was very sick but is better.' It

136. II, 48 / 136. II, 50

Informal Preliminaries

seemed to do him good to tell me." Bingham states that later in the evening the President requested him to show him the way to the home where Mr. Seward was staying. Upon returning Mr. Lincoln said: "You clear the way and I will hold on to your coat tails."

Apparently, after leaving Washington, every time the President held either pen or pencil in his hand along with a piece of paper, onlookers concluded he was writing the address. There were other notations made during his absence from Washington. Very naturally, he would be kept informed by the Secretary of War about the military situation. A message received at Gettysburg from Stanton dated November 18, advised Lincoln about Burnside's position and the lack of information from Chattanooga, also the encouraging information about the improvement of his sick child, Tad. Two more notes dated the 18, were received telling about movements of troops and dispatches from Burnside. On the 19, a telegram was sent from Washington noting reports from Grant, another "no news of special importance," and a further encouraging word about the condition of his boy.

Possibly it has been overlooked that his annual message to Congress was less than three weeks away. It must not be assumed that every passing hour was given to meditating on his short speech. There is evidence that one of the expressions used in the subsequent message came out of the Gettysburg meditation. Some of the most significant thoughts in the document may have evolved during the moments when he appeared to be composing his few remarks for the ceremonies.

On the day of the dedication, Governor Tod while in conversation with Mr. Seward, mentioned that he had called upon him that morning and did not find him at home. Seward replied: "Yes, sir, I visited the ground around the Seminary this morning, and Mr. Lincoln joined me." We do know that Lincoln had a conference with Mr. Seward late the evening before, when the trip may have been arranged. Honorable William McDougall, Lincoln's

156. Feb. 1929 / *111.* Stanton to Lincoln, Nov. 18, 19, 1863 / *1.* VII, 22, 23

Canadian guest, stated that when he was invited to make the trip, the President said: "We will drive to the battlefield in the morning." McDougall also recalled that: "after breakfast the party mounted buckboards and were driven to the battlefield. On the drive Mr. Lincoln was solemn and absorbed." Charles W. Schenck also remembered having seen the President riding in a carriage with three or four other persons. One of the incentives which prompted the President to visit Gettysburg, was to see with his own eyes the terrain over which the battle had been fought. The first prepared travel arrangements submitted to him, provided "two hours to view the ground before the dedication ceremonies commence," possibly included in the schedule at Mr. Lincoln's request. The revised plans, although providing for the arrival eighteen hours earlier, made no mention of any sightseeing period. The only time available for a field trip was during the early morning hours of November 19.

It was thirty years after these events occurred at Gettysburg that Mr. Nicolay contributed to the *Century Magazine* this account of his observations: "It was after the breakfast hour on the morning of the 19th that the writer, Mr. Lincoln's private secretary, went to the upper room in the house of Mr. Wills which Mr. Lincoln occupied, to report for duty, and remained with the President while he finished writing the Gettysburg Address, during the short leisure he could utilize for this purpose before being called to take his place in the procession. . . ."

Mr. Wills heard about the contribution that Mr. Nicolay was preparing for the *Century Magazine* and, apparently, had not forgotten his former correspondence with Mr. Nicolay and Mr. Gilder about the address. Wills and Nicolay got into a controversy over whether it was written Wednesday night or Thursday morning, and Mr. Nicolay smoothed it over in this fashion: "Perhaps Mr. Lincoln in the evening only made hasty notes for the closing portion of his address, which he copied more deliberately in the morning."

191. Nov. 21, 1863, *147.* July 19, 1947, *136.* I, 22, 23, *1.* VII, 16 / *41.* Feb. 1894, p. 601 / *109.* No, 1437, *88.* II, 122, 123, 8

It is doubtful if Nicolay remembered with any detail the activities of Mr. Lincoln during the entire hour he was with the President, but the secretary should not be accused of having imbibed so much liquor the night before that he was incapacitated for observing anything of importance the next morning. The fact that he may have taken a social glass on Wednesday evening and also sang, "his little song of the three thieves" has been greatly misinterpreted. Upon Hay's retirement as secretary, he wrote to Nicolay, after observing the actions of some drunken friends: "You and I have kept drinking company, all our lives, and yet have never felt for an instance the claws of temptation." This statement should cease the gossip about Nicolay being on a binge, which does a great injustice to his memory and to his loyalty to the President.

If we grant that Lincoln had made at least one and probably two preliminary writings of the complete address at Washington, looked over the manuscript on the train, made some pencil notations, and then put the finishing touches on it at the Wills' home either in the evening or the next morning, or perhaps both, we might have a plausible story of the evolution of the address that would account for the varied observations. It is known that he included in the address when it was delivered, two additional words, "Under God," and made some other minor changes that did not appear in the earlier writings.

The most fantastic suggestion associated with the traditional preparation of the address, appears in the remarks credited to Senator Cornelieus Cole, who said in a speech before Wesleyan College students in 1922: "Mr. Lincoln probably made not a word or a note in preparation for that address . . . I have no doubt whatever but what it was extempore, and called forth by the circumstances of the occasion." One historian moves the extemporaneous theory right up to Lincoln's opening remarks when he has the President say in his salutation: "It is intimated to me that this assemblage expects me to say something on this occasion."

109. No. 1437, *88.* II, 8 / *109.* No. 1314 / *195.* July, 1922, *151.* Oct. **1909**

CHAPTER 9

Solemn Procession

THE CEREMONIES of Gettysburg's long anticipated day began at 7:00 a.m. on Cemetery Hill when "salvos of artillery rolled through the air thundering away over the battlefield a stern and mighty requiem of the brave." Long before this military awakening, in some instances shortly after midnight, citizens of Adams County and the adjacent countryside began to wind their way towards the town in every conceivable type of vehicle, on horseback and on foot. One reporter observed that "old-fashioned Pennsylvania wagons with canvas covers, large enough to carry a cargo, came in drawn by four and six horses and loaded with people." Some sections of the county had been depleted of horses (driven off in July) by the Confederates, which caused many, thus deprived of their mounts, to walk to the ceremonies. Another reporter wrote: "The roads leading to Gettysburg were crowded with citizens from every quarter thronging into the village in every kind of vehicle, old Connestogia wagons, spring wagons, carts, carriages, buggies, and more fashionable modern vehicles, all crowded with citizens."

For more than a week, guests from a distance had been arriving by rail and the number of passengers increased to such an extent that by Thursday, the schedules became very irregular. According

2. Nov. 24, 1863, *136*. I, 30, *191*. Nov. 21, 1863

to a local observer: "Heavy trains of cars began to pour in laden with masses of human beings; train after train came." One news correspondent who left Cincinnati at 6:00 a.m. on Monday did not arrive at Gettysburg until 11:00 p.m. on Wednesday.

There have been many divergent estimates of the number present. The Washington *Chronicle* calculated that at least twelve thousand strangers were in town during the day. Including the local population, the Albany *Journal* estimated at fifteen thousand the number present. These figures probably are not far from correct. However, Clark E. Carr placed the total attendance at 100,000. There can be no doubt that it was the largest group of people ever assembled in Adams County—with the exception of the visiting armies in July.

The entertainment of this unusual influx of people presented a housing and feeding problem. A meeting of the citizens was held on Monday evening, November 9, to make plans for the coming of the visitors, with Robert J. Harper as chairman and Dr. Charles Horner, secretary. A reception committee of nine was appointed. Accommodations at the American House, Eagle and McClellan Hotels and all boarding houses had been reserved for weeks in advance. Every available room in the town was utilized; in many public houses there were several guests sitting up all night for lack of beds or cots. Halls of fraternal organizations, churches, and the colleges that had served as hospitals, were thrown open so that all might have shelter.

Favorable weather conditions contributed tremendously to the increasing of the attendance; the expediting of the movement of the parade and especially the presentation of the outdoor program, with no adequate facilities for holding the exercises indoors, in case of severe storms. The earlier October date, selected primarily for better prospects of a pleasant day during that month, could not have excelled this nineteenth day of November. In the early morning it was hazy and the atmosphere was cool and brisk, but it

2. Nov. 24, 1863, *136*. I, 30 / *191*. Nov. 20, 1863, *4*. Nov. 20, 1863, *38*. p. 35 / 2. Nov. 10, 1863

began to clear, and one reporter wrote: "The sun never broke to life and warmth on a fairer fall day than this . . . one of the most beautiful Indian summer days ever enjoyed."

At 9:00 a.m. James A. Rebert, Company B. 21st. Pennsylvania Cavalry, who had been detailed as an orderly to the President, reported to his room. He was requested to wait until the President wrote an order to be delivered to Marshal Lamon at the Eagle Hotel. At this hour, however, probably he was found in the public square where his aides had been ordered to assemble. As early as 1832, Ward H. Lamon and Lincoln, had been associated in trying law cases before the circuit court at Danville, Illinois, where Lamon then lived. He was a member of the Presidential party which accompanied Lincoln to Washington in 1861. On April 6, he was appointed Marshal of the District of Columbia and on May 28, 1862, the President recommended him for scouting purposes and referred to him as "my particular friend, born and raised at Bunker Hill (Virginia), an excellent horseman." Lamon married a daughter of Judge Stephen T. Logan, law partner of Lincoln at Springfield.

Sometime before November 9, Lamon was called on to act as Marshal at the dedication of the cemetery. According to the President: "He came to me, and I told him I thought that in view of his relation to the Government and to me that he could not well decline." Possibly Lamon may not have recalled that November 19 was an anniversary occasion for him. On that day in 1861, after some pressure had been brought against him, he resigned as Marshal of the District of Columbia but Lincoln refused to accept his resignation.

On November 12, as already noted, Lamon went to Gettysburg to make preliminary arrangements for the event. The publicity value of a parade must not have been considered in that day, or this carriage-making town would have provided for the principal guests to be seated in the finest phaetons it could produce. What

191. Nov. 21, 1863 / *136.* V, 14, *76.* Nov. 26, 1863, *1.* IV, 323, *1.* V, 247, *1.* VII, 7 / *1.* V, 247, *112.* III, 77

an opportunity to display before many thousand people the products of their leading industry! The fact that Lamon was "an excellent horseman" may have had something to do with putting the celebrities in the saddle. We have already observed that a special meeting of the marshal's aides was held the evening before, to receive their final instructions. They had previously been advised in press notices about the uniformity of dress:

1. Plain black suit, black hat, white gloves.
2. White satin scarf, five inches wide to be worn over right shoulder and carried across the breast and back to left hip, and there fastened with a rosette, the ends to be fringed and to extend to the knee. At the center on the shoulder the scarf should be gathered and mounted with a rosette.
3. Rosette four inches and raised in center to be made of black and white ribbon, the outer circle only to be white.
4. Rosette of red, white and blue ribbon on left breast. The initials of state in center for identification. The saddle cloths on their horses, of white cambric bordered with black.

The marshal's aides furnished the mounted escort for the President and in their black and white costumes, with the blending of the national colors, they must have made a striking appearance.

Gettysburg was well decorated for the parade with numerous flags draped in mourning. The ladies of Valley Forge had presented to the ladies of the town an impressive streamer which bore the inscription: "Valley Forge and Gettysburg, 1776–1863." On November 16, two tall flag poles were raised, one in the public square 100 feet high at the occasion, Professor Muhlenburg gave an address, another pole was placed near the speakers' stand at the cemetery.

Four days prior to the dedication, the War Department had ordered to Gettysburg the Fifth New York Artillery, a full regiment stationed at Baltimore. Major General Darius Nash Couch, commanding this department of the Susquehanna, was in charge and reviewed the troops on Wednesday afternoon. Suffi-

191. Nov. 13, 1863 / 2. Nov. 17, 1863

cient emphasis has not been given to the fact that there was present an official military escort similar to those which participate in the burial rites of the highest officer in military service. The detachment consisted of a regiment of infantry, one squadron of calvary, and two batteries of artillery.

The program for the occasion stated: "The military will form in Gettysburg at nine o'clock a.m. on Carlisle Street, north of the square, its right resting on the square, opposite McClellan's Hotel." General Couch was born in Putnam County, New York, July 23, 1822, and was graduated from the United States Military Academy in 1846. Serving in the Mexican War, he gained the brevet of First Lieutenant. He retired from the service in 1855, but on June 15, 1861, he became a colonel of Massachusetts volunteers. In August he advanced to a brigadier general and was promoted to major general on July 4, 1862. Beginning June 11, 1863, General Couch was engaged in organizing the Pennsylvania militia to resist the invasion of the Confederates.

The route of the parade covered about half a mile: "Baltimore Street to the Emmitsburg road; thence to the junction of the Taneytown road; thence by the latter road to the cemetery." The head of the column was supposed to move "at precisely 10:00 a.m." The various military units were assigned places in this order:

Marine Band
Second United States Artillery
United States Regular Cavalry
Major General Couch and staff
General Stahel and staff
Twentieth Pennsylvania Cavalry under Command of Colonel Stickney
Colonel Provost of Philadelphia and staff
Battery A. Fifth United States Regulars
Major General Schenck and staff
Band of the Fifth New York Heavy Artillery Regiment under command of Colonel Murray.

27. Nov. 23, 1863, *144.* Nov. 23, 1863 / *171.* p. 24, *10.* I, 753 / *171.* p. 24.

The marshal's division which followed, included: the President of the United States, attended by Secretary Seward of the State Department, Secretary Usher of the Department of the Interior and Postmaster General Blair, escorted by Chief Marshal Lamon and aides. Next in order, came Brigadier General Wright, General Doubleday and General Gibbon attended by their staffs. Then followed the governors and commissioners of the participating states, and other guests of honor.

Henry Clay Cochrane presented his reminiscences of the parade for the Military Order of the Loyal Legion at their meeting of February 13, 1907. He said: "Mr. Seward and Mr. Blair rode on his (Mr. Lincoln's) right and Judge Usher and Marshal Lamon on his left. In the next rank were six horses ridden by General Fry, Colonel Burton, John G. Nicolay, John Hay, Captain Ramsay and myself." Many prominent government officials in Washington who were expected to attend, were not present.

The civic division of the parade did not measure up to advance notices. Many who had come found the lure of the battlefield to be a greater attraction than the prospect of marching in a procession. Some of the ranks of the various organizations were so depleted that the forming of their units was discouraged. Nevertheless, one Gettysburg young man wrote a letter to his brother the following day commenting on the parade: "This was a grand and impressive sight. I have no language to depict it and though the mighty mass rolled on as the waves of the ocean, everything was in perfect order."

    These units made up the civic division:
        United States Sanitary Commission under command of Dr. W. F. Sewall
        Odd Fellows Lodge of Gettysburg, Number 124 with 250 men
        Hanover Lodge I.O.O.F., Number 334 with 100 men
        Councils of Baltimore and civic officials
        Faculty and students of the college and seminary
        Several hundred citizens from many states

171. p. 24 / *126.* 1907, p. 11 / *97.* VI, No. 1, Spring 1968

Carriages containing visitors from different sections of the country

As the military section of the parade prepared to move, there were several vacancies in the originally proposed personnel. The absence of General Meade and his staff and a considerable number of his army was disappointing.

A letter of invitation had been sent to Major General George G. Meade, commanding the Army of the Potomac, and through him, "to the officers and privates of that army, which had fought so valiantly and gained such a memorable victory on the Gettysburg battlefield." Easily, the feature of the parade was a detachment of forty soldiers who had been injured in the battle and who had been removed to the military hospital at York, thirty miles to the east. They were sent to represent their comrades, every one bearing the marks of the fearful struggle, many of them on crutches. They carried a large white banner draped in mourning which bore this inscription on one side: "Army of the Potomac, Gettysburg, July 1, 2, 3, 1863." and on the other side appeared the likeness of a funeral urn and the tribute: "Honor to our brave soldiers."

At 10:00 a.m. the President made his appearance at the York Street entrance of the Wills home. As usual, on public appearances, he was dressed in a black suit with a frock coat. On this occasion he wore a wide mourning band around his tall silk hat, and on his hands were white gauntlets. He passed between two files of soldiers to the spot where the parade was forming. His presence caused the usual rush of citizens to shake hands with him.

Even after Mr. Lincoln was astride his horse, the people still surged about him until Chief Marshal Lamon himself was obliged to break up the unscheduled reception. These prolonged greetings plus the added difficulty in organizing so many units, delayed the start of the parade nearly an hour.

The traditions preserved relating to the mount provided for the

2. Nov. 24, 1863 / ibid / *171.* p. 12, *191.* Nov. 20, 1863 / ibid / *174.* p. 140

President, and his appearance in the parade, have contributed about the only amusing incidents of the day. With the many somber recitals presented, it might serve as an easement, to give some attention to the folklore gathered about an otherwise trivial narrative. Mrs. Rosenburg, then Lena Wolf, eighteen years of age, recalled: "Horses stamped about, big horses, but for Lincoln they brought out a small one. He smiled as he straddled it. His feet hung down and touched the ground. Everyone laughed and so did he. They then let him know it was all a joke and brought him a larger horse." This was literally, "horse play," and one wag commented: "Say Father Abraham if she goes to run away with yer, you just stand up and let her go." One observer thought the animal was of medium size, but that Lincoln's exceedingly long legs made it look smaller. Another citizen who watched the proceedings recalled that the parade was delayed until a larger horse could be provided. The second mount secured seemed to be a beast of varying sizes and many colors. Rev. J. B. Remensynder, then a student at Pennsylvania College, stated that it was "a diminutive pony." John A. Sprengle described the animal as a "squat fat steed known as a 'dutch horse.' " But H. B. Crawford appraised the animal as the "largest in the Cumberland Valley. . . . It was gaily caparisoned in honor of its illustrious rider and the saddle blanket was a work of art." Presumably, the committee had selected an animal of fine style for the President. However, this request Lincoln signed on November 19, implies his mount may have been provided by the army: "Captain Blood furnish one horse for bearer. A. Lincoln."

Even so, the descriptions written at the time are at variance about its color. The following day, an observer of the parade wrote that the President was mounted on a "beautiful bay charger"; the reporter for the Ohio *State Journal* described it as a "splendid black steed"; others called it "chestnut," "light bay,"

136. III, 45, 201. Nov. 19, 1914, 136. I, 75, 81, 20. 180, 1. VI, 23

and "chestnut bay." Clara McCrea, fifty years later, was quite sure that when Lincoln reached the speakers' platform, he dismounted from a "white" horse.

Following the traditional pattern in after years, many writers described the President in the parade, with his feet almost touching the ground and presenting a most grotesque figure in the saddle. Seward probably drew more smiles than Lincoln, as one who rode behind him stated that Seward was not much of a rider, and "as he went along his trousers gradually worked up revealing the tops of his homemade grey socks, of which he was entirely unconscious." Although the parade route was but half a mile, Clark E. Carr states that at first the President sat erect in a dignified manner, but "Before we reached the grounds he was bent forward, his arms swinging, his body limp and his whole frame swaying from side to side . . . riding just as we did over the circuit in Illinois."

Lincoln on horseback, described by Mr. Carr, presents an entirely different picture than one drawn by an associate who observed the President on his visit to the Army of the Potomac: "A splendid spirited large black horse was selected for the President to ride, when the time came he walked up to the animal and the instant he seized the bridle to mount, it was evident to horsemen that he knew his business. He had the animal in hand at once. No sooner in the saddle than the coal black steed began to prance and whirl and dance, as if he was proud of his burden. But the President sat as undisturbed and fixed to the saddle as if he and the horse were one . . . Lincoln was at home in the saddle, everybody saw it. Finally the riding down the lines was performed amidst the flaunting of standards, beating of drums, loud cheering of the men, and rapid discharge of artillery every now and then, startled the best trained horses. . . . The President went on his graceful charger, fired by the tumultous scene, snorted and pawed the earth as if he would like to tear it to pieces, Lincoln sat easy

144. Nov. 23, 1863, *36*. p. 52, *126*. p. 11, *136*. I, 81, *126*. p. 11 / *126*. 1907, p. 11, *38*. p. 39

to the end, when he wheeled his horse into position to witness the vast columns march in review. . . ."

While there was no such exhibition of horsemanship at Gettysburg, a reporter of the *Boston Journal* wrote for his paper: "I must do the President justice to say, his awkwardness, which is so often remarked, does not extend to his horsemanship." One rider in the procession noted that the President "rode easily, bowing to the right and left." That Lincoln was the most striking figure in the procession was the concensus. One viewer of the parade wrote at the time this impression: "Like Saul of old he towered, a head taller than any other man." Fifty years later, one who attended the anniversary ceremonies recalled, that the most vivid impression of all the dedicatory services was: "Lincoln on horseback towering above his fellows."

The parade became virtually a funeral procession, moving slowly in step with the solemn dirges played by the different bands. The mourning symbols worn and the heavily draped banners, contributed to the realization that its destination was a cemetery. One woman wrote: "Then came the President, easily distinguished from all others. He seemed the chief mourner."

120. Ex. no. 129, 1917 / *27.* Nov. 23, 1863, *126.* 1907, p. 11, *36.* p. 56 / *174.* p. 139

CHAPTER 10

Dedicatory Program

THE PROGRAM of arrangements specified that when the parade reached the cemetery: "The military will form a line, as the general in command may order, for the purpose of saluting the President of the United States. The military will then close up and occupy the space on the left of the stand. The civic procession will advance and occupy the area in front of the stand, and the military leaving sufficient space between them and the line of graves for the civic procession to pass. The ladies will occupy the right of the stand, and it is desirable that they be upon the ground as early as 10 o'clock a.m."

The President came forward from the parade between the columns of soldiers and reached the platform at 11:20. Upon his appearance he received an ovation, cheer after cheer announcing his arrival. Members of the cabinet and other dignitaries, especially the governors of the various states, were welcomed with applause.

The seating arrangements on the platform are not very clearly noted, with the exception of a few of the principal guests and participants on the program. Marshal Lamon, who directed the proceedings of the day, took his position on the left side of the stand. The central seats in the front row were occupied by Mr. Lincoln and Mr. Everett who sat on his right. The clergymen,

171. pp. 24, 25 / *191.* Nov. 21, 1863

Dedicatory Program

Reverend Doctor Baugher, President of Gettysburg College and Reverend Doctor Stockton, Chaplain of the Senate, sat next to Mr. Everett in the order named. On Mr. Lincoln's left was Secretary of State, William H. Seward. Members of the President's party, also Simon Cameron, John Forney, Benjamin French and William Saunders, occupied prominent places. Others who were given preferential seats, were the governors of the states participating in the project: Arthur I. Boreman, West Virginia; Augustus W. Bradford, Maryland; Abner Coburn, Maine; Andrew J. Curtin, Pennsylvania; William Dennison, Ohio; Oliver P. Morton, Indiana; Joel Parker, New Jersey; and Horatio Seymour of New York; Ex-Governors David Tod, Ohio; and Joseph A. Wright, Indiana; also Governor-elect John Brough, Ohio.

Shortly after the President reached the platform, Governor Tod and Governor Brough approached him, and after Governor Brough had been introduced, Mr. Lincoln stated: "Why I have just seen Governor Dennison of Ohio, and here are two more Governors of Ohio—how many more Governors has Ohio?" Governor Brough replied: "She has only one more, sir, and he's across the water." He might have replied: "But Lieutenant Governor-elect Anderson is here, sir." If the President had cared to continue this pleasantry he might have told Governor Tod that his wife spelt her maiden name "Todd" belonging to the double "d" branch of the family, and concluding, as he often did, with respect to the spelling of the name: "One 'd' was enough for God, but not for the Kentucky Todds."

On the front row, to the left of Secretary Seward, sat the host executive, Curtin, and next to him Seymour and Tod. The other governors were grouped near them. Several of the chief executives serving the eighteen states joining in the enterprise were unable to be present. Maine was the only New England state to send its governor, and from the West, Illinois, Michigan, Minnesota and Wisconsin failed to respond.

Among the military personnel on the stand, aside from the

26. Nov. 20, 1863, 52. Nov. 23, 1863 / *191.* Nov. 21, 1863 / *173.* p. 13

President's escort already mentioned, there were; Major General D. N. Couch, Brigadier Generals, Abner Doubleday, Robert C. Schenck, George Stoneman, and Colonel John Gibbon.

The commissioners associated with David Wills were; B. W. Norris, Maine, L. B. Mason, New Hampshire, Henry Edwards of Massachusetts, Alfred Coit of Connecticut, Levi Scorey of New Jersey, James Worrall of Pennsylvania, John S. Berry of Maryland, L. W. Brown of Ohio, Gordon Lofland of Ohio, John G. Stephenson of Indiana, Clark E. Carr of Illinois, and W. Y. Selleck of Wisconsin.

The Chief Marshal's nine aides, some of whom have been mentioned before, were; Silas Casey, Chief Justice of the United States Court of Claims, Judge George P. Fisher, Doctor Hanscomb, John Hay, Judge James Hughes, Charles Kent, Judge Abarim Olin, W. Yates Selleck and Benjamin Schnyder. Among those at the table reserved for the newsmen were; John Russell Young of the Philadelphia *Press*, the noted correspondent, Ben Perly Poore, Charles Hale of Boston, four reporters for the Washington *Chronicle* who arrived on Wednesday, and representatives from the following papers; Chicago *Tribune*, Cincinnati *Gazette*, Columbus *State Journal*, Hanover (Penn.) *Spectator*, New York *World*, *Forney's War Press* and other large city papers.

There was also a group with political interests headed by Wayne MacVeagh, chairman of the Republican Central Committee, Edward McPherson, Arthur B. Farquhar and Harvey W. McKnight. Other individuals on the platform, included; Captain H. A. Wise, U.S.N. and his wife, a daughter of Edward Everett, and William McDougall of Canada. The Misses Gilbert of Philadelphia must not be left out or two other sisters Sarah and Elenora Cook who sat on the steps leading to the stand. An eight-year-old boy named H. Peters, wearing red top boots, settled on the edge of the platform and should be included.

136. I, 40 / *127.* Feb. 2, 1909 / ibid / *136.* I, 41, *136.* I, 55, *138.* Feb. 13, 1931

An extension would have to be made to the 12 x 20-foot platform if all those who claim to have occupied reserved seats were accommodated. And strange to say, nearly all of them were "seated beside," "directly behind," or "very near" the President.

The purely fictitious engravings and lithographs by professional artists have done much to increase the number of celebrities who were supposed to have occupied the special seats. A painting by Albion H. Bicknell entitled: "Lincoln at Gettysburg," depicts the likenesses of twenty-one famous men who were supposed to have been on the stage. A key for identification, noting seating arrangements, was published in a book containing biographical sketches of the persons portrayed. At least fourteen of the men mentioned were not present, leaving but seven actually in attendance. Because the missing men were famous citizens associated with the administration, officers in the army, or persons of prominence, it was thought the sale of the prints might be increased by noting their presence—whether they were there or not. Among Mr. Bicknell's selections were: John A. Andrew, Benj. F. Butler, Salmon P. Chase, Frederick Douglass, William P. Fessenden, U. S. Grant, Horace Greeley, Andrew Johnson, George B. McClellan, George G. Meade, Charles Sumner, Edwin M. Stanton, Gideon Wells, and Henry Wilson. Vice President Hamlin is also listed but his presence has not been confirmed.

The seating accommodations for the President have been described as a bench, a settee, a straight back chair and a rocking chair. He is said to have relinquished the comfortable rocker to a woman who had fainted, and an interesting bit of folklore, told by Wayne Whipple, has grown up around the tradition about Jacob and Lydia of Ephrata, Pennsylvania.

The Gettysburg *Sentinel* reported on November 7: "The final preparations are now being made which will make the consecration services the most interesting and solemn ever witnessed in this country." Now that all participants were present, a reporter for the Cincinnati *Daily Commercial*, looking over the number of

136. I, 42, 67 / 22. pp. 1–48 / 201. Nov. 19, 1914

celebrities, sent this message to his paper: "Perhaps upon no other American stage has there been such a conjunction of all that is distinguished by official position, statesmanship, learning and eloquence." Possibly many of the presidential inaugural ceremonies should have been made exceptions to this conclusion.

The stated program began with a dirge by Birgfeld's Band of Philadelphia, sponsored by the Union League. A prayer was then offered by Reverend T. H. Stockton, D.D., Chaplain of the United States Senate. He was born in Philadelphia, where at one time he was the pastor of the church of the New Testament. He was a magazine editor and a pioneer in the anti-slavery movement. The entire program had taken the form of funeral solemnities, and an extended prayer in memory of so many thousand fallen, very appropriately would be given a significant place in the obsequies. Doctor Stockton referred to the deceased soldiers impressively, in these words:

"In the freshness and fullness of their young and manly life, with such sweet memories of father and mother, brother and sister, wife and children, maiden and friends, they died for us. From the coasts beneath the Eastern star, from the shores of the Northern lakes and rivers, from the flowers of Western prairies and from the homes of the Midway and the Border, they came here to die for us and for mankind. Alas, how little we can do for them: we come with the humility of prayer, with the prophetic eloquence of venerable wisdom, with the tender beauty of poetry, with the plaintive harmony of music, with the honest tribute of our Chief Magistrate, and with this honorable attendance; but our best hope is in thy blessing, O Lord our God."

The closing petition is likewise couched in the language such as the people of that day expected to hear in an emotional entreaty: "As the trees are not dead though their foliage is gone, so our heroes are not dead though their forms have fallen. In their proper personality they are with Thee. And the spirit of their example is with Thee. It fills the air; it fills our hearts. And, as long as time

2. Nov. 7, 1963, *52.* Nov. 23, 1863 / *171.* pp. 26–29 / ibid

Dedicatory Program

shall last, it will hover on these skies and rest on this landscape, and the pilgrims of our own land and of all lands, will thrill with its inspiration, and increase, and confirm their devotion to liberty, religion, and God." These fervent words closed with The Lord's Prayer.

The petition, consisting of about a thousand words, was not out of proportion to the length of the extended oration which was to follow. A dedicatory prayer at the laying of the cornerstone of the Soldiers' Monument two years later, given by Reverend Stephen H. Tyng, D.D., followed his reading of fifteen passages from the Bible and contained approximately forty-five hundred words.

The local paper reported that Doctor Stockton "offered a most impressive prayer. The most profound silence prevailed and many were affected to tears." The Illinois *Journal* in Lincoln's home town, commented: "Never was a man selected for any service so fit in every respect to perform it." However, Wayne MacVeagh stated: "Mr. Hay (John Hay) who was seated by my side said after the prayer had been made: 'that he regarded it as the finest invocation ever addressed to an American audience,' which was the first of many delightful and illuminating witticisms that I was privileged to hear from him in our long and friendly interview." Hay's comment on the prayer offered by the Chaplain of the United States Senate during the sacred solemnities honoring the dead heroes at Gettysburg, is confirmed in Hay's diary, where he entered this notation: "Mr. Stockton made a prayer which thought it was an oration." The New York *Times* commented: "The opening prayer by Rev. Stockton was touching and beautiful and produced quite as much effect upon the audience as the classic sentences of the orator of the day." Everett called it: "A highly rhetorical but otherwise extremely well written prayer."

Following the prayer, came the reading of regrets from those who were unable to attend the ceremonies. An excerpt of the one read from General Meade is of special interest: "It seems almost

171. pp. 26–29 / *173.* pp. 244–251 / *2.* Nov. 24, 1863, *97.* Nov. 23, 1863, *41.* Nov. 1909, *88.* p. 125, *138.* Nov. 20, 1863, *121.* pp. 12, 13

unnecessary for me to say that none can have a deeper interest in your good work than the comrades in arms, bound in close ties of long association and mutual confidence and support with those to whom you are paying this last tribute of respect; nor could the presence of any be more appropriate than that of those who stood side by side in the struggle, shared the peril and the vacant places in whose ranks bear sad testimony to the loss they have sustained. But this army has duties to perform which will not admit of its being represented on the occasion: and it only remains for me in its name with deep and grateful feelings, to thank you and those you represent, for your tender care of the heroic dead, and for your patriotic zeal, which in honoring the martyrs, gives a fresh incentive to all who do battle for the maintenance of the integrity of the government."

Secretary Chase expressed his regrets in this manner:

Dear Sir: "It disappoints me greatly to find that imperative public duties make it impossible for me to be present at the consecration of the grounds, selected as the last resting place of the soldiers who fell in battle for their country at Gettysburg. It consoles me to think what tears of mingled grief and triumph will fall upon their graves, and what benedictions of the country, saved by their heroism will make their memories sacred among men."

Winfield Scott's regrets were received also and he explained that: "Besides the determination, on account of infirmities, never again to participate in any public meeting or entertainment I was too sick at the time to write more than a short telegram to His Excellency Governor Curtin."

It is fortunate that Edward Everett's "Programme of Arrangements and Order of Exercises for the Inauguration" has been preserved and reproduced in a publication of the Massachusetts Historical Society. He crossed out the word "Inauguration" and supplied "Consecration," although the proceedings are usually termed a "Dedication." The most striking omission in the "Order

171. p. 18 / 171. p. 20 / 171. pp. 18, 19

of Exercises" was the failure to name Mr. Everett as the speaker of the day, the only citation being "Oration." This whole line is used to note Mr. Lincoln's appearance: "Dedication Remarks by the President of the United States," making it appear as if he were the featured speaker. Mr. Everett probably was not pleased with this oversight and at the bottom of the page he completely obliterated the name Ward H. Lamon who had the programs printed in Washington. There were two bands and two chorus numbers and Everett mentions in his diary "the very long musical voluntary" and then again "more music."

It was hoped that one of the famous New England poets could be persuaded to prepare some verse to be set to music. As late as November 13, the press announced that a dirge selected by Professor Longfellow would be sung. However, he was just then in the process of bringing out his anthology, *Tales of a Wayside Inn*, and could not spare the time to compose an acceptable poem.

Benjamin B. French, associated with the public buildings department of the government, accompanied Ward H. Lamon to Gettysburg on November 12, to assist in making preliminary plans for the dedicatory program. Mr. Wills told Mr. French about the difficulties with respect to a dirge he desired for the exercises. Mr. French, who had written several acceptable poems, offered to work on something appropriate that very night. Inspired by being on the battlefield where so many of the heroic dead were buried, he was able to prepare some very commendable verses. The next morning he handed Mr. Wills the manuscript containing these five stanzas:

> 'Tis holy ground—
> This spot, where, in their graves,
> We place our Country's braves,
> Who fell in Freedom's holy cause
> Fighting for Liberties and Laws—
> Let tears abound.

121. pp. 5–13 / *76.* Nov. 13, 1863 / *173.* p. 232

>   Here let them rest—
> And Summer's heat and Winter's cold,
> Shall glow and freeze above this mould—
> A thousand years shall pass away—
> A nation still shall mourn this clay,
>   Which now is blest.
>
>   Here, where they fell,
> Oft shall the widow's tears be shed,
> Oft shall fond parents mourn their dead,
> The orphans here shall kneel and weep,
> And maidens, where their lovers sleep,
>   Their woes shall tell.
>
>   Great God in Heaven!
> Shall all this sacred blood be shed—
> Shall we thus mourn our glorious dead,
> Oh, shall the end be wrath and woe,
> The knell of Freedom's overflow—
>   A country riven?
>
>   It will not be!
> We trust, Oh God! Thy gracious Power
> To aid us in our darkest hour.
> This be our prayer— "Oh Father! save
> A people's Freedom from its grave—
>   All praise to Thee!

These lines by Mr. French brought him into prominence during the exercises and one observer states that he was invited to introduce Edward Everett, although his presentation words are not known to have been recorded. This fact is certain: his dirge was sung by the Baltimore Glee Club of twelve voices, during the interval between the addresses of the two principal speakers.

121. p. 8 / ibid

CHAPTER 11

Orator of the Day

SEATED side by side on the platform were two distinguished persons, Edward Everett and Abraham Lincoln. They presented one of the most striking contrasts in American public life. Everett was born in the environs of cultural Boston; Lincoln came from the wilderness of a frontier civilization. The former was the son of an educated clergyman, the latter was a child of an unlettered pioneer. Everett was graduated from Harvard; Lincoln was never in a university until he was a man grown and then, as a visitor. When Everett was nineteen, he became pastor of a Unitarian church in Boston and three years later, he preached a remarkable sermon in the House of Representatives at Washington, D. C. When Lincoln was nineteen, he was working on a flatboat en route to New Orleans.

In 1814, Everett was a tutor in Latin at Harvard. Lincoln, in commenting about school conditions in the Indiana country where he grew up, wrote: "If a straggler supposed to understand latin, happened to sojourn in the neighborhood, he was looked upon as a wizard." After serving as a Latin tutor, Everett was appointed to a Harvard professorship in Greek and went to Europe for a four-year course in preparation for the task. Lincoln humbly admitted

1. III, 511, *10.* II, 386–389, *188.* pp. 38–57

to a friend that he had no European acquaintances. In 1846, Edward Everett became the president of Harvard.

The political achievements of Everett and Lincoln, preceeding the election of 1860, offer a vivid contrast indeed. It must be recognized that Everett was fifteen years older than Lincoln, but Lincoln entered politics when he was twenty-three and Everett did not start his political career until he was thirty. Everett was elected to Congress as a representative from Massachusetts in 1824 and continued in this capacity for ten years. At the close of his congressional career, he was elected governor of Massachusetts in 1835 and served in the same office for two succeeding terms. Everett was given a portfolio as minister to England in 1840; in 1850 he became Secretary of State, and in 1853 he was in the United States Senate.

Compared with Everett's long and impressive record, Lincoln's four terms in the Illinois legislature, and one as a representative in Congress, seem insignificant. One can well understand the public mind when it wondered if a mistake had not been made in the nomination of Lincoln for the Presidency, with so many illustrious men opposing him on the other two rival tickets. One of his competitors was Everett, the vice-presidential nominee of the Constitutional-Union Party.

Their respective achievements in oratory were almost as incongruous as were those in the political field. Mr. Everett had an enviable record as a public speaker. His famous oration on Washington had been delivered 122 times over a period of three years and the proceeds netted the Mt. Vernon Memorial Committee $58,000. The grand total received for all of his speeches approached one hundred thousand dollars. On the other hand, Abraham Lincoln had but one speaking engagement for which he was compensated and out of the $200 he received from Cooper Union in New York, he was obliged to pay his traveling expenses.

It is not strange that Mr. Everett was unfavorably impressed with Mr. Lincoln as the President-elect. Both men had been

10. II, 386–399, *1.* III, 511 / *10.* II, 386–389 / *109.* No. 562 / ibid leaders in their respective political parties in the campaign of 1860. This situation does not usually result in increased admiration of one for the other. Mr. Lincoln had made no speeches in the campaign and even after his election, chose the policy of silence, until such time as he could speak with authority. Most of the informal talks he was pressed into making en route to the inaugural were merely commonplace utterances from which no conclusions could be drawn that would add fuel to the flame of unrest already ignited. With respect to these trivial comments of Lincoln, Everett noted in his diary: "These speeches thus far have been of the most ordinary kind, destitute of everything, not merely of felicity and grace, but of common pertinence. He is evidently a person of very inferior cast of character, wholly unequal to the crisis."

The first meeting of Everett and Lincoln may have been on September 25, 1862, when the President handed Everett this letter of introduction: "Whom it may concern: Hon. Edward Everett goes to Europe shortly. His reputation and the present condition of our country are such, that his visit there is sure to attract notice and may be misconstrued. I therefore think fit to say, that he bears no mission from this government, and yet no gentleman is better able to correct misunderstandings in the minds of foreigners, in regard to American affairs.

"While I recommend him to the consideration of those, whom he may meet, I am quite conscious that he could better introduce me than I him, in Europe."

Possibly up to the very day of their meeting at Gettysburg, Everett was lukewarm toward the President. There was a mass meeting arranged by the Loyal Men of Illinois at Springfield for September 3, 1863, for which Lincoln wrote his famous Conkling letter. Upon publishing it in the Illinois *Journal*, the editor commented that it is "probably the subject of more intense interest than any other similar document addressed to the country." Everett also prepared a letter for the identical assembly, and with

74. pp. 457, 458 / 1. V, 437–438

Lincoln's correspondence, it was published in the same issue of the *Journal* and probably read by both men. Everett wrote to the convention: "I have doubted the policies of some measures of the administration, and strongly disapprove of others, but regard the persons in power for the time being, as the constitutional agents of the people for carrying on the government."

It is not likely that in the intervening four months between this writing and the Gettysburg occasion, Mr. Everett changed his opinion of the President and his administration. It is true that he forwarded a copy of his Gettysburg address to Mr. Lincoln, but there is no indication that when they met in the home of Mr. Wills at the evening meal on November 18, there was any cordiality. Although at the close of the repast, Mr. Everett's opinion of the President apparently had been raised considerably, as has been noted in his later remarks.

A Massachusetts newspaper made this comment about the departure of the orator for the dedication: "Hon. Edward Everett left Boston Sunday evening on his way to Gettysburg." Another dispatch announced his arrival on a special train furnished by Mr. Du Barry of the Northern Central Railroad on the evening of November 16. From Everett's own diary some details of the plans for his entertainment may be ascertained. He had been invited to stay with Mr. Wills where the President and thirty-six other guests were to find lodging. Everett states: "At first it was proposed to put the Governor (Curtin) into my bed with me. He kindly went out and found a lodging else where . . . I did not get to bed until ½ past 11 & the fear of having the Executive of Pennsylvania tumble in upon me kept me awake until one." Everett was nearly seventy years old and somewhat particular about his surroundings, as we shall observe.

Having arrived on the evening of the sixteenth, he could have "at least one day on the battlefield," which he had suggested in his letter would be needed for orientation. It was stated by Clark E. Carr that Everett "had come to Gettysburg soon after accepting

97. Sept. 4, 1863 / *30.* pp. 394, 395 / 27. Nov. 17, 20, 1863, *121.* p. 2

the invitation September 23, and for several days had gone over and studied the battlefield with maps and drawings that had been prepared, before him." There is no confirmation of this September sojourn.

When Everett arrived, his address was already finished and put into print. Professor Michael Jacobs of the local college had been chosen as Mr. Everett's guide over the battlefield. They found plenty of atmosphere out of which to recreate the days of the July contest. According to one visitor at the dedication; "There were trees marked, limbs and branches torn, breast works and rifle pits before and around us, the houses scarred and torn in various ways—some peppered, some with holes large enough to admit a barrel, some almost destroyed, certainly ruined." One near by Pennsylvania author who has given much attention to the local history states that "Even on the following day, Everett and his guide were still traveling the battlefield at the very hour the exercises were to begin."

From the orator's diary it is not clear just when he started for the place where the exercises were to be held. He states: "I went in a carriage with the President of the College, Doctor Stockton the chaplain, and Mrs. Wills." In the prospectus for the line of march, the spot assigned to Everett and Stockton was some distance behind Mr. Lincoln and just in advance of the group of commissioners from the states. One of these men was positive that Everett was not in the parade and had no idea how he reached the cemetery. The notation by Everett that "at length the President arrived," indicates he was there before Mr. Lincoln. One citizen of Gettysburg remembered having seen Mr. Everett and one or two others being driven toward the cemetery, and another person observed both Mr. Everett and Mr. Stockton in a carriage headed toward the place where the exercises were to be held. An explanation for this irregular procedure may be found in a letter which Everett wrote to a friend with reference to an earlier speaking engagement: "I hope that no one of the trustees will be at the

9. pp. 35, 36, 38. p. 40 / *191*. Nov. 19, 1863, *136*. I, 28

trouble to attend me, I do not like to talk while the carriage is in motion, it is more agreeable to me just before speaking, to be alone."

This desire for some privacy just before speaking, requiring Everett's own supervision, may have been an added consideration for an extra day at Gettysburg. He states in his diary that there was "a tent pitched at my request in the rear of the platform. I requested and was promised, that it should be in two divisions, one for my private use. . . ." He further comments that the tent was not divided and "that all privacy was out of question. . . ." When he arrived at his improvised suite he states; "Into this tent I was ushered with 8 or 10 men and women. They by degrees comprehended the nature of the position, left me alone, master of it."

The facts about the time the orator of the day arrived on the grounds, ready for his part in the program, are just the reverse of the statements made by Secretary Nicolay and Commissioner Carr. The latter claimed: "I distinctly remember that we waited for him a half hour before the exercises commenced." This observation has been accepted as authentic by nearly every subsequent author who has written on the ceremonies. This untenable accusation has done Mr. Everett a great injustice as it implies a lack of respect in keeping a vast audience as well as the President of the United States waiting—and places the distinguished speaker entirely out of character. He was the one who did the waiting.

Mr. Selleck, the commissioner from Wisconsin observed: "At the east end of the stand was a tent, and from it a short time after all were seated on the stand, came forth Edward Everett, the orator of the day." Mr. Everett noted in his diary: "A committee of four governors (Seymour, among them) conducted me to the platform where I was seated on the President's right hand." One reporter who apparently held a watch on the progress of events, noted that Mr. Lincoln came to the platform at 11:20, directly

121. p. 12, *179.* No. 142 / *121.* p. 12 / *41.* Feb. 1894, p. 602, *38.* p. 40

from the parade. Before other units had arrived and all were in their seats, it was 11:40.

At noon on this significant day, the elder statesman arose, turning to the left, and making a very low bow, said: "Mr. President." The salutation was acknowledged by the recognition: "Mr. Everett." The speaker then turned to the expectant crowd and began one of the great orations of the war period.

His informal salutation and timely historical introduction were followed by a well-arranged argument. The influences of his training as a clergyman finds expression here, as the subject matter falls into three general divisions: 1. The Battle, with each day's movements clearly and authentically set forth. 2. The cause and the character of the war. 3. The objectives and guarantees of victory. The conclusion invokes a benediction on the honored graves and declares that "in the glorious annals of our common country there will be no page brighter than that which relates to THE BATTLE OF GETTYSBURG."

The President paid strict attention to the address and thought it to be "eminently satisfactory." The passages which "transcended" his "expectations" were those renouncing "the theory of the general government being only an agency, whose principals are the States," and the "tribute to our noble women." When Mr. Everett concluded, the President arose, grasped his hand and said: "I am more than grateful, I am grateful to you."

The length of time it took Mr. Everett to make this address has also been a matter of exaggeration. Again, Clark E. Carr is in error by stating that "An address so exhaustive was necessarily long occupying nearly three hours." The usual reference to the time element is "about two hours" but to be exact, one man who timed the speech called it "one hour and fifty-seven minutes." A person who heard it, stated: "He spoke slowly and appeared to deliberate on each sentence. The grace and beauty of his delivery and of his language impressed me more than did his thought."

127. Feb. 4, 1909, *38.* p. 40 /—/ *127.* Feb. 4, 1909, *142.* VIII, 194 / *1.* VII, 24, *121.* p. 13

Another observer, while pleased with his presentation, felt that his voice was not properly pitched for outdoor audiences, and regretted that comparatively few of the large assembly could follow his argument. A reporter on the platform wrote this impression as Mr. Everett spoke: "Every word is memorized; there is no hesitation; the stream of eloquence flows steadily on; and there is the gesture, once observed never to be forgotten, when the orator rises to some climax, and the arms outspread and the fingers quivering and fluttering as one said, like the pinions of an eagle, there seems to rain down upon the audience the emotions with which they vibrate."

However, there was some adverse criticism of the address, prompted as usual, by personal, political or provincial bias. Three New York papers, apparently convinced that nothing of value could come out of Boston, found little to praise in the address. The New York *Times* took occasion to compare the speech of Henry Ward Beecher of Brooklyn, who spoke that same day at the academy, with Edward Everett's oration "to the disadvantage of the latter." The *Herald* avowed Everett's presentation was "milk and water; utterly inadequate, although his sentences were as smooth as satin and his metaphors as white as snow." The *World* concluded that Mr. Everett: "has fallen below his own reputation in the greatest opportunity ever presented to him, for rearing a monument more enduring than brass."

The most severe denunciation of the oration came from *The Daily Age* of Philadelphia: "Seldom has a man talked so long and said so little. He told us nothing about the dead heroes, nothing of their former deeds, nothing of their glories before they fell like conquerors before their greater conqueror, Death. He gave us plenty of words, but no heart. His flowers of rhetoric were as beautiful and as scentless and as lifeless as wax flowers. His style was as clear and cold as Croton ice. He talked like a historian, or an encyclopaedist, or an essayist, but not like an orator, but a great disappointment."

136. II, p. 2, *191.* Nov. 20, 1863, *52.* Nov. 19, 1863 / *138.* Feb. 12, 1909, *137.* Nov. 20, 1863, *140.* Nov. 26, 1863 / *136.* I, 28

Orator of the Day

Neither was *Harper's Weekly* complimentary in this comment: "The oration by Mr. Everett was smooth and cold. Delivered, doubtless, with his accustomed graces it yet wanted one strong thought, one vivid picture, one thrilling appeal."

Nevertheless, the Washington *Chronicle* esteemed it so highly that it was printed in full and the next day, published in pamphlet form. This excerpt from a full column editorial also appeared: "It would be superfluous to say that the orator rose to the patriotic and solemn granduer of the occasion. Yet higher praise than this could not be given to human intellect or human eloquence, for the occasion has no parallel in modern times."

The Boston *Journal* was especially pleased with the section relating to the war, observing that "the detailed narrative of the campaign ending in the battle of Gettysburg, reads like the most brilliant pages of Macaulay or Prescott. As Mr. Everett has taken great pains in collecting the data for the narrative, having access to official authorities, it is probably the best history of the campaign which this generation shall have the privilege of reading." This highly complimentary tribute to its historical value, supplemented by other equally important factors, almost demand that the address be laid before the reader. However, the exhibiting of it at this particular place in the thesis, primarily concerned with Lincoln's short speech, would seriously interrupt the development of the argument.

The President's receipt of the proof sheets of Mr. Everett's address is usually associated with two reported appearances at Gardner's Gallery, the first on November 8, noted in Hay's diary, the other on November 15, recalled by Noah Brooks. Stories associated with both visits identify a rectangular piece of paper on a table at the studio as a printed copy of the oration. Everett's diary indicates that the manuscript was sent to the Boston *Daily Traveler* on November 14 "to be set in a proof sheet." This was too late for type setting, printing, proof reading, correcting and reading, to be completed in time to reach Mr. Lincoln the following day, to say nothing about the alleged receipt a week

84. Dec. 5, 1863 / *191*. Nov. 20, 1863 / 27. Nov. 20, 1863

before. Yet, it must have been ready by the evening of the fifteenth when Everett left for Gettysburg, as he had a copy with him on the platform when he gave the address.

The orator explained that the preliminary printing was "to prevent it being mutilated and travestied by the reporters." This precaution did not prevent the author himself from making several changes upon its delivery. He noted in his diary: "I omitted a good deal of what I had written . . . parts of the address were poorly memorized, several long paragraphs condensed, several thoughts occurred at the moment which happens generally." From this critical analysis of his own speech, we may conclude that both the news release and the "Authorized Version" were, at best, what he intended to say. Reporter Gilbert claimed to have taken down the full text but there appears to be no verbatim record in print of what he said. There is evidence that on his manuscript copy he deleted some portions of the address which he planned to omit upon delivery.

The transcript used in the Appendix of this book is the one noted by Mr. Everett in his letter to the President and designated as the "Authorized Version." It differs slightly from the copy prepared for the press, but is identical with the one printed in the proceedings, published for the benefit of the Cemetery Monument Fund.

64. p. 117, *31.* p. 285, *121.* p. 2 / *121.* p. 13, *20.* pp. 78, 190 / *173.* pp. 198–231

CHAPTER 12

Appropriate Remarks

ON THE printed "Programme of Arrangements," after noting the "*oration*" and "*music*," this number appeared: "Dedication Remarks by the President of the United States." No one, not even Mr. Lincoln himself, could have anticipated that in responding to this casual announcement, one of the world's most eloquent utterances would be delivered. Newell Dwight Hillis draws this striking contrast: "Everett's oration was a bushel of diamonds carefully polished, Lincoln's, a handful of seed corn that has sown the world with the harvest of liberty."

The meticulous copy of the speech made by Charles Hale of Boston, has been accepted as the most accurate "word-for-word" recording of the President's remarks. This version is superior also to other abstracts, because careful punctuation indicates the flow of Mr. Lincoln's diction. Another improvement is paragraph indentation, to note brief pauses. An entirely different concept of the address is received while reading Hale's version, when compared with those reproductions where all the sentences are run together irrespective of context. The Hale copy follows:

> Fourscore and seven years ago, our fathers brought forth upon this continent a new nation, conceived in liberty and dedicated to the proposition that all men are created equal.

136. V, 20 / 7. LXXII

Now we are engaged in a great civil war, testing whether that nation—or any nation, so conceived and so dedicated—can long endure.

We are met on a great battle-field of that war. We are met to dedicate a portion of it as the final resting-place of those who have given their lives that that nation might live.

It is altogether fitting and proper that we should do this.

But, in a larger sense, we cannot dedicate, we cannot consecrate, we cannot hallow, this ground. The brave men, living and dead, who struggled here, have consecrated it, far above our power to add or to detract.

The world will very little note nor long remember what we say here; but it can never forget what they did here.

It is for us, the living, rather, *to be dedicated*, here, to the unfinished work that they have thus far so nobly carried on. It is rather for us to be here dedicated to the great task remaining before us; that from these honored dead we take increased devotion to that cause for which they here gave the last full measure of devotion; that we here highly resolve that these dead shall not have died in vain; that the nation shall, under God, have a new birth of freedom, and that government of the people, by the people, for the people, shall not perish from the earth.

Fourscore and seven years ago,

The introductory word, "Fourscore," sets the tone for the terminology of the whole address. The nineteeth psalm with its "three score years and ten; and if by reason of strength there be four score years," was very familiar to the President, as were other biblical quotations using this antiquated form in relating to the passing time. As early as 1840 he referred to the struggle for freedom, "more than three score years ago."

our fathers

The funeral oration of Pericles commences: "I will begin then with our ancestors. Our fathers inherited . . ." There is much in common in the orations of Pericles and Lincoln, as both were spoken over the remains of soldiers engaged in fraternal strife.

7. p. LXXII / 92. Psalm, 90, *110.* Microfilm

The heroic efforts of the founding fathers so vividly portrayed in Weems' *Washington*, deeply impressed Lincoln.

brought forth

Before speaking a dozen words, he again reverts to biblical diction, using the 'brought forth' he had so often heard his mother employ in telling the Bethlehem story: "And she brought forth her first born son." Here he introduced the underlying nativity theme, which he continued to stress up to the conclusion of his discourse.

upon this continent

Words from the Scriptures predominate and there are but three exceptions: "continent" is one, "proposition" and "civil," the other two.

a new nation,

Referring to the origin of Greece, Pericles spoke of it as having been "inherited." America, as Lincoln was well aware, was no heirloom but had come into being through courageous and sacrificial efforts.

conceived in liberty

The paraphrasing of the Bethlehem story continues in the reference to the nation as having been "conceived" in liberty. Lincoln, at Trenton, New Jersey, in 1861, recalled that as a boy he read Weems' *Washington* and stated: "I remember all the accounts there given of the battlefield and struggles for the liberties of the country."

and dedicated

In the introduction to his *Rhetoric of Aristotle*, published in 1931, Lane Cooper makes this comment on the opening words of Lincoln's address: "The metaphor of the dedication of a child

136. II, 90 / *92.* Luke II, 7 / *200* / *136.* II, 90 / *1.* IV, 235

runs through the speech beginning with the violent figure of sires 'conceiving,' 'bringing forth' and 'dedicating' the newly born."

to the proposition

The word, proposition, was often used by Lincoln, long before he studied the *Six Books of Euclid*. He said it was the ambition of the founding fathers to present: "a practical demonstration of the truth of a proposition . . . the capacity of a people to govern themselves." Charles Sumner thought the address was perfect except for that one word, but he was unsuccessful in the quest for one more acceptable.

that all men are created equal.

Upon pronouncing a eulogy on Henry Clay, Lincoln avowed: "I would also, if I could, array his name, opinions, and influence . . . against an increasing number of men, who . . . are beginning to assail and ridicule the white-man's charter of freedom—the declaration that 'all men are created equal.' "

The equality pronouncement concludes the first division of the address. The Chicago *Tribune* stated that it "summarizes in twenty-nine words, the essence of the revolutionary period, perhaps better than it has ever been written before or since."

Now we are engaged in a great civil war,

Lincoln moved the time element from "Fourscore and seven years ago," to "Now." A "civil war" replaces the "revolution." A few days before, in his Thanksgiving Proclamation, he observed: "in the midst of a civil war of unequaled magnitude and severity . . . the laws have been respected and obeyed, and harmony has prevailed everywhere except in the theatre of military conflict; while that theatre has been greatly contracted by the advancing armies and navies of the Union."

136. III, 19 / *1.* I, 113 / *1.* II, 130 / *49.* Feb. 6, 1930 / *1.* VI, 496

testing whether that nation—or any nation,

In February, 1863, the President wrote: "It seems to have devolved upon them (the American people) to test whether a government, established on the principles of human freedom, can be maintained against an effort to build one upon the exclusive foundation of human bondage."

so conceived and so dedicated—

On July 4, 1861, in his message to Congress, the President wrote: "Our popular government has often been called an experiment. Two points in it, our people have already settled—the successful *establishing*, and the successful *administrating* of it. One still remains—its successful *maintenance* against a formidable internal attempt to overthrow it."

can long endure.

The closing episode of the biblical nativity story presents the flight of the Holy Family into Egypt, "for Herod is about to search for the child to destroy him." The war was being fought primarily for the survival of the young republic, under the slogan, "The nation must be preserved."

We are met on a great battlefield of that war.

Everett in his address stated: "The whole rebel army estimated at 90,000 infantry upwards of 10,000 cavalry and 4,000 or 5,000 artillery making a total of 109,000 of all arms was concentrated in Pennsylvania." General Halleck reported the size of the armies to have been equal.

We are met to dedicate a portion of it

"We are met," is repeated by Lincoln although later he changed it to "we have come." As early as 1842, in a Washington's birthday speech, he used the idiom: "We are met" to celebrate

1. VI, 89 / 1. IV, 439, 426 / 92. Matt. II, 13 / 171. p. 41

this day. Major Nickerson commented that while Lincoln was speaking he was facing the spot where: "We had our death grapple with Pickett's men, and he stood immediately over the place where I had lain and seen my comrades torn in fragments by enemy cannon ball."

as the final resting-place

The evening before he left for Gettysburg, William Saunders, who drew the plans for the cemetery, was with the President and explained the map of the cemetery area with its semi-circular courses of interments. Lincoln said it was "an admirable and befitting arrangement."

of those who have given their lives

The orator of the day had observed: "Few of the great conflicts of modern times have caused victors and vanquished so great a sacrifice. . . . On the Union side there fell below the rank of general, 2,834 killed, 13,709 wounded." A great number of the latter died in the nearby hospitals.

that that nation might live.

The national emblem, "elegantly executed," had been presented to the President by some Philadelphia women. In the President's acknowledgment, written on August 10, 1863, he mentioned: "the heroic men, who had suffered and bled in our flag's defense." He concluded his letter with this note of appreciation: "We never should and I am sure, never shall be niggard of gratitude and benefaction to the soldiers who have endured toil, privations and wounds, that this nation may live."

It is altogether fitting and proper that we should do this.

In his eulogy on Henry Clay, Lincoln commented that it was "customary and proper" to present a brief sketch of the departed. In his 1863 Thanksgiving Proclamation, referring to the gracious

1. I, 279 / 151. p. 393 / 136. I, 19, 171. p. 59 / 1. VI, 376

Appropriate Remarks 109

gifts received, he wrote: "It has seemed to me fit and proper, that they should be solemnly, reverently and gratefully acknowledged."

But, in a larger sense, we cannot dedicate, we cannot consecrate, we cannot hallow this ground.

The futility of doing anything in the way of commemorative service that would approach the significance of what had already been done by those participating in the battle, was evident. However, Lincoln did give further emphasis to the underlying current of the nativity theme which he was weaving into the development of his argument.

The brave men, living and dead, who struggled here,

Recalling one of Weems' stories of the Revolution while en route to his first inaugural, the President-elect said: "I recollect thinking then, boy even though I was, that there must have been something more than common that those men struggled for." A group of soldiers whose time of enlistment had expired, passed through Washington and received this word of appreciation from the President: "Thank you for the part you have taken in this struggle for the life of the nation."

have consecrated it, far above our power to add or to detract.

Governor Andrew of Massachusetts expressed the above sentiment of Lincoln's in these words: "The soldiers who fell in the battles of Gettysburg . . . baptising with their blood the ground which their valor rendered immortal, are now commemorated by a National Cemetery where they repose in becoming interment."

The world will very little note nor long remember what we say here; but it can never forget what they did here.

Possibly a large number of the visitors at the dedication agreed with the above comment. The New York *Times* stated that while

1. II, 124, *1.* VI, 497 / 109. No. 934 / *1.* IV, 237, *1.* VII, 528 / 7. pp. 36, 37

Mr. Everett was delivering his splendid address; "there were about as many people wandering over the battlefield as were assembled around the platform." The *Times* concluded: "They seemed to have agreed with President Lincoln, that, it was not what was *said* here, but what was *done* here, that deserved their attention."

At this point in the address, Lincoln's argument takes on an unexpected shift of emphasis in its context by turning attention from the dead, to the living; from eulogizing, to exhorting. The people could not have anticipated that they likewise—as well as the ground on which they stood—were to be dedicated.

It is for us, the living, rather, to be dedicated, here,

The audience must have been strangely awakened by the President's vibrant voice as he uttered this dynamic challenge following a somewhat somber and compassionate presentation. However, he still retained the dedication terminology, keeping the atmosphere of the occasion ever in mind. General Howard, later on, speaking at Gettysburg, said: "He, Abraham Lincoln, never forgot his own dedication until the work was finished. He did display ever increased devotion if it were possible."

to the unfinished work that they have thus far so nobly carried on.

Lincoln had but two supreme motivating slogans in his career. Prior to becoming president, one was: "No extension of slavery." After his inauguration: "The Union must be preserved." His uppermost objective is concisely stated in his letter to Horace Greeley in 1862: "My paramount object in this struggle *is* to save the Union."

It is rather for us to be here dedicated to the great task remaining before us;

Replying to Governor Curtin at Harrisburg on February 22, 1861, Lincoln said: "Reference has been made . . . to the great

138. Nov. 19, 1863 / *109.* No. 924 / *173.* p. 265 / *1.* V, 388

task that lies before me in entering upon the administration of the general government." Now again Curtin hears about "the great task" to which all the people must be dedicated. In his first message to Congress the President made this appeal: "With a reliance on Providence, all the more firm and earnest, let us proceed in the great task which events have devolved upon us."

that from these honored dead we take increased devotion to that cause for which they here gave the last full measure of devotion;

Here the inspirational note of encouragement, spoken to spur on to still greater efforts those loyal to the Union, reaches again into biblical terminology for an expression adequate to acknowledge the supreme sacrifices offered on those grounds. They had given "good measure, pressed down, and shaken together, and running over" a full measure of devotion.

that we here highly resolve that those dead shall not have died in vain;

While there may be some religious implication in the sentiment of having not "died in vain," there is a scene portrayed in Weems' Washington that Lincoln could not have forgotten. Washington is pictured as observing the graves of some soldiers of the Revolution and commenting: "There the battling armies met in thunder. The stormy strife was short. But yonder mournful hillocks point the place, where many of our fallen heroes sleep; perhaps some good angel has whispered, that their fall was not in vain."

that the nation shall, under God, have

The two words, 'under God,' which had not been used in the preliminary writings of the address, apparently came to Lincoln on the spur of the moment. Their inclusion between two parts of a verb indicates a failure to give sufficient attention to the grammatical construction of the thought expressed. In subsequent copies of

1. IV, 243, V, 53 / 92. Luke, VI, 38 / 193. p. 126

the address, the error was corrected. Possibly Everett's use of the term, "under Providence," about half-way through his speech, may have called to Lincoln's attention the recognition of Deity, although his whole address was a requiem.

However, the expression 'under God' had been a familiar one with Lincoln since childhood, when in Weems he often came across this favorite idiom. Weems, emphasizing the people's reliance on Washington, said; "They had so long and fondly looked up to as, Under God, their surest and safest friend." Again: "The people everywhere welcomed him as the representative of a beloved nation, to whom, Under God, they owed their liberty." And on the death of Washington, Weems used this tribute: "To whom you and your children owe, Under God, many of the best blessings of life." Not only in the early days but even after the Gettysburg occasion, Lincoln continued to use the expression. In a speech at the Great Central Sanitary Fair at Philadelphia he said: "We accepted this war for an object, a worthy object, and the war will end when that object is attained. Under God, I hope it never will until that time." There was, however, another objective which Lincoln had in mind in the use of these two interpolated words. They were inserted just prior to the pronouncement of the grand climax of the address. They furnished the necessary pause which would call attention to the significant declaration which he had been approaching.

a new birth of freedom,

The paraphrasing of the Bethlehem story in recounting the genesis of the country, and the numerous nativity terms used throughout the address, would almost demand that the chief emphasis in the President's declaration should be couched in relevant terms. The nation that was "conceived in liberty" that the "fathers brought forth" and that was "dedicated to the proposition that all men are created equal," now, under God, shall have "A NEW BIRTH OF FREEDOM." Lincoln was conscious that a

136. I, 25 / 193. pp. 168, 162, 140, 1. VII, 395

Appropriate Remarks 113

nation "conceived in liberty" by its very nature, periodically, must be rejuvenated, rededicated, and even reborn, if it were to survive.

There was never any question among those who heard the address as to when the President reached his grand climax. Colonel John Forney prepared for his paper an account of the high points in the speech and concluded with the expression "that this nation shall have a new birth of freedom." General Howard, who gave the oration at the Soldiers' Monument two years later, stated: "The nation has already experienced the 'new birth of freedom' of which he spoke." Those not present who saw it in print, sensed the placing of the emphasis. Horace Greeley, in his New York *Tribune*, used the "Freedom resolution" as the outstanding pronouncement. Even the opposition press put its finger on the crux of the speech by denouncing the declaration about the "new birth of freedom."

Possibly the most striking illustration of Lincoln's grand pronouncement, when he virtually confirms the theses he had been developing, is found in the closing words of his message to Congress which was spoken less than three weeks after the Gettysburg remarks. The President, in bringing his message to a close, stressed the point that it was the armed forces "to whom, more than others, the world must stand indebted for the home of freedom disenthralled, regenerated, enlarged, and perpetuated."

The freedom motif, so fundamental in Lincoln's political philosophy and so prevalent in the sources leading up to the address, has been set forth with some detail in chapter 2, which precludes in this section, any extensive summary. The rather exhaustive discussion about the remainder of the speech is necessary in order to give attention to the most controversial part of the oration. The phrase which has been worked over to throw stress on three prepositions, has become the most familiar and more often quoted statement in the entire address.

109. No. 924 / *71.* Nov. 28, 1863, *173.* p. 265, *139.* Feb. 12, 1930, *48.* Dec. 2, 1863 / *1.* VII, 53 / *109.* No. 781

and that government of the people,

Lincoln, as a youth, must have pondered long over the following pronouncement in Weems' book: "A republican form of government, that is a government of the people, can never long subsist when the minds of the people are not enlightened." As a young man he made the observation: "Most governments have been based practically, on the denial of equal rights of men . . . ours began by affirming those rights." Speaking at Cincinnati when fifty years of age, he used this expression: "We know that in a Government like this, a Government of the people." Presumably, among the many definitions for Democracy, he came across its Greek origin, Demos Kratos, literally translated "The government of the people." The President is said to have advised his friend Governor Richard Oglesby of Illinois: "Dick, remember to keep close to the people; they are always right; they will never mislead anyone." In his First Inaugural Address he stated: "The Chief Magistrate derives all his authority from the people, . . . why should there not be a patient confidence in the ultimate justice . . . of this great tribunal, the American people."

The primary style in public announcement in the press was not in display advertising but in the use of repetition. A whole column might be utilized to repeat over and over again one phrase only. Emphasis was achieved by reiteration. Do we need any further proof as to where Lincoln placed the emphasis, in a phrase of ten words, when six of them are expressed in the term "the people?" Lincoln's most significant statement which may be associated with his concluding phrase is found in the message to the special session of Congress in 1861, so appropriately called to convene on the birthday of the nation. The affair at Fort Sumter presented the question; "Whether a constitutional republic, or a democracy—a government of the people, by the same people,—can, or cannot, maintain its territorial integrity, against its own domestic foes." Between the dashes we have the President's definition of Democ-

193. p. 203, *1.* II, 22, *1.* III, 441, *49.* Mar. 1, 1884, *1.* IV, 270

racy. Here, with no chance left for argument the emphasis falls on the word "people."

by the people, for the people,

In the brief definition of Democracy just mentioned, if the word "same" is removed, and the clause "for the people" added, we have the quotation as it appears above. Instead of leaving the emphasis on the word "people," where it belongs, through some strange quirk, the stress has been shifted to the prepositions, not only the two noted above, but reaching back to the first one, "of."

One of the earliest attempts to give the concluding clause some emphasis, is found in Isaac N. Arnold's *Abraham Lincoln*, in which he copies the address and then places in italics: "of the people, by the people, and for all people." The interpolation of "all" would seem to throw the emphasis on "people." Arnold, again in 1885, uses the phrase "of the people, for the people, by the people" set in italics with a change in order of the prepositions and dropping the word "all." Nicolay placed the emphasis on "people."

An early attempt to stress the "by," "for," and "of" series, with "to" added, is found in a sort of a parody published by *Harper's Weekly* in 1866: "Gettysburg was fought *by* the nation, *for* the nation, *to* save the nation. It should have been the work *of* the nation." This is clearly a political inference, and through the years politicians generally have captured this prepositional interpretation, until the vigorous enunciation of the three "two letter" words have almost drowned out the major thesis of the address. Directing the remarks as a political thrust at Gettysburg would have been far from Lincoln's intention. There would be little point in spending much time in attempting to find an original combination of these prepositions, unless all three were given an emphasis by the President. The lack of any punctuation mark after "Government" and the removal of the conjunction "and" before the third preposition, argues against such an interpretation.

1. IV, 426 / ibid / *12.* p. 424, *13.* p. 165, *12.* p. 424, *41.* Feb. 1894, p. 608 / *48.* July, 1866

Much time has been spent in attempting to find an early combination of these three prepositions which may have accounted for Lincoln's use of them. The search still continues and just a few of the contributors and the dates on which their statements appeared, are presented chronologically: Cleon, 430 B.C.; Thomas Cooper, 1794; Patrick Henry, 1818; Chief Justice Marshall, 1819; President Monroe, 1820; Schinz (Swiss), 1830; Daniel Webster, 1830; Nathaniel Pilcher, 1834; Theodore Parker, 1850–1857; Mathew F. Maury, 1851; Henry Wilson, 1860. The most reasonable explanation for the use of the prepositions, without reference to emphasis, is by Samuel A. Green, onetime librarian of the Massachusetts Historical Society: "The resemblance between these several citations is only a coincidence. It is a case where a somewhat similar idea existed in the brains of different individuals . . . but it was left for Mr. Lincoln to mould it into its final shape, and to give utterance to an expression that is now well-nigh classical."

There seems to be no contemporary evidence that the President emphasized the prepositions. There were many prominent members of the press in attendance who would have sensed immediately any such unusual play on words, and featured it in their reports. No such dispatches have been discovered. Even the rather casual accounts of the address offer strong support that no special stress was given to the prepositions. Lincoln's home paper, The Illinois *Journal*, printed this version of the closing lines: "That the government of the people, founded by the people, shall not perish." In the Philadelphia *Inquirer* it appeared: "That the government of the people, for the people and for all the people." The Hastings (Minn.) *Conservator* has it: "That the government the people founded by the people shall not perish." The *Boston City Document No. 106:* Report of the Joint Special Committee uses this form: "That the government from the people for the people and by the people shall not perish."

109. No. 781, 136 II, 85, *121.* p. 92 / *97.* Nov. 21, 1863, *154.* Nov. 20, 1863, 87. Dec. 1, 1863, *25.* p. 21

Joseph L. Gilbert, the reporter who took down at least a part of the address at Gettysburg, was under the impression that Mr. Lincoln accentuated the word "people," but could not be positive about it. After a program in the Philadelphia Athletic Club in 1946, in a conversation about the Gettysburg speech, an elderly gentleman said that his father, who had heard the address, always became very much irritated when speakers put tremendous stress on the prepositions, because Lincoln, he claimed, emphasized the word, "people."

Nearly every boy and girl in the schools, until these later years, has given great stress to the prepositions, and the stronger they could be intoned, the more satisfactory the effort. The best comment on the manner of presentation by boy or man is found in the query, "Can anyone imagine the Gettysburg Address being declaimed?" Santayana, one of the most prominent world figures of the present century, commented: "I think my American cousins give a wrong interpretation to Lincoln's Gettysburg Address when they emphasize the prepositions. My feeling is that Lincoln placed the emphasis on the word 'people.'"

shall not perish from the earth.

It may seem strange to turn to Lincoln's boyhood for the expression of a sentiment that contemplates eternity. After telling the legislators at Trenton in February, 1861, about his perusal of Weems' book when a small lad, he made this thought provoking statement: "I recollect thinking then, boy even though I was, that there must have been something more than common that those men struggled for, that something more than National Independence; that something that held out a great promise to all the people of the world to all time to come."

Contemplating the magnitude of the prospects of the civil war which had just begun, the President said in his first message to Congress: "The struggle of today is not altogether for today—it is for a vast future also." In reply to a committee from the General

136. III, 4 / 49. Apr. 27, 1948 / 1. IV, 236

Synod of the Evangelical Lutheran Church, Lincoln said that the crisis involved "not only the civil and religious liberties of our own dear land, but . . . of mankind in many countries and through many ages." It is in the letter to James C. Conkling, written a few weeks before he prepared the address for the dedication, that we find Lincoln's most dramatic statement about the perpetuity of the nation: "Thanks to all. For the great republic—for the principle it lives by, and keeps alive—for man's vast future,—thanks to all."

    1. V, 53, 212, 1. VI, 410

CHAPTER 13

Presentation Notes

NEARLY every phase of the Lincoln story, from his parentage and birth to his assassination and the trial of the conspirators, even now, is in controversy. No single episode has presented so many divergent opinions as the incidents associated with the writing, presentation, and evaluation of the remarks at Gettysburg. The many contradictions relating to its composition have already been noted. Even more disconcerting are the testimonies referring to its manner of delivery, because many of the conflicting accounts are by eye-witnesses or those within earshot of the proceedings.

Some of the inconsistencies were caused by the similarity of three ceremonies arranged at Gettysburg within a period of six years. All were about equally attended, and attracted about the same group of Adams County citizens. The laying of the cornerstone of the Soldiers' Monument on July 4, 1865, less than two years after the dedication, again presented Governor Curtin serving as host. Also, the home of David Wills offered hospitality to the special guests who in this instance, were General Meade and General Howard. There were distinguished visitors, marshals, military personnel, cemetery commissioners, bands of music, a Baltimore chorus, local singers, and officiating clergymen. There was a parade which proceeded out Baltimore street to

109. No. 162

the platform "erected in the center of the cemetery where the memorial is to be located." When the monument was dedicated on July 1, 1869, General Meade and Governor Morton of Indiana were the speakers.

One group of observers in 1863, was sure that: "Governor Curtin presented President Lincoln" as was entered by Professor Halloway in his diary. Still others recalled that it was Ward H. Lamon who said: "The President will now make a few remarks." The consensus favors Lamon.

Another group, mostly members of the press, avers that when the President started to speak, a newspaper photographer stole the show, or as a feature writer in later years put it, "Killed Lincoln's Gettysburg Address." John Russell Young, a twenty-one-year old reporter from Philadelphia, was largely responsible for the early circulation of the story, and he admitted that he was "more interested in his (the photographer's) procedure than in the address" of the President of the United States. However, on another occasion Mr. Young stated: "So when the President arose . . . I took up my pencil and began to take him in short hand."

Lincoln, throughout his early years, in fact, during most of his life, was an open-air speaker, to which the quality of his voice was well adapted. Through self-teaching in public speaking he had cultivated a high pitched tone. It may have sounded unpleasantly shrill when he started to speak, but it quickly found its proper range. One who heard the Gettysburg speech commented: "Loud, and far reaching, was his voice. He had it under perfect control and observing every proper inflection, he maintained its strength until he closed." Another, who heard him, recalled that the President's voice: "was somewhat raspy" but was "penetrating" and probably reached the "farthest ear" in the audience. P. H. Bikle stated: "His voice was loud and clear and many more of that immense crowd heard him, than heard Everett." According to

79. July 4, 1963, 76. Nov. 26, 1963 / 20. p. 181, 58. p. 227 / 136. III, 5, 199. p. 69, 134. Dec. 1938, pp. 22, 30

Benjamin French: "Even the language he used was as peculiar to him as was any other peculiarity of his nature—terse, pointed, plain; never wandering among the mazes of rhetoric after adornment, but simple as the man himself; and going as straight to the mark at which he aimed as an arrow from the bow of Tell."

Gestures were seldom used by Lincoln, but he relied on inflections in his enunciations and appropriate facial expressions to give weight to his thought. Chauncey Depew in later years remarked: "In speaking, Lincoln had a peculiar cadence in his voice, caused by laying emphasis upon the key word of the sentence." Lincoln probably had picked up one of the early theorems in public speaking: "A sentence has as many meanings as it has words," and placed the stress accordingly. One admirer said that to fully understand Lincoln, he should be seen when speaking. Austin Bierbower closely observing him, concluded "his delivery added much to the impressiveness of his speech, we all noticed his earnestness and deep sincerity." Andrew C. Wheeler, a member of the press wrote: "I stood close by and heard the speech delivered. It came upon us after the ponderous and elaborate rhetoric of Edward Everett like a blaze of real fire after a matchless picture of fire."

One controversy, of three parts, which may never be settled to the satisfaction of all, centers about the query as to how Lincoln delivered his address: Did he read from a manuscript held in his hand, casually refer to it as he spoke, or speak without notes? Almost unanimous testimony confirms that when Edward Everett approached the conclusion of his address, Mr. Lincoln, who had been giving strict attention to it, reached into one of his coat pockets and drew forth the manuscript of his speech. He adjusted his steel-rimmed spectacles to a point near the end of his nose, briefly glanced over the speech and returned it to his pocket.

It was the opinion of an eyewitness, that after being introduced, the President, with the "utmost deliberation," proceeded to read

136. II, 2, *136.* I, 79, *136.* I, 77, *55.* 1868, Report 98 / *109.* 340, *136.* II, 59, *45.* Feb. 12, 1908 / *136.* II, 56

his address. Dr. Henry Jacobs recalled that while he was speaking, "he drew his notes from his pocket and read them." A college student observed: "He barely took his eyes off the manuscript," as he read. When he arose to speak, according to James B. Batterson, the President placed his papers "on the top of his hat," and read the address. Noah Brooks claimed that he read from a manuscript and made a few changes. The Associated Press reporter who took down his address in shorthand, mentions the "manuscript from which he read." Ward H. Lamon, in one of his reminiscences, affirms that Mr. Lincoln "read his speech," but in a later printing of his memoirs, the statement was changed to, "delivered his speech." The reporter of the Cincinnati *Commercial* observed: "The President rises slowly, and, when commotion subsides, in a sharp unmusical voice reads the brief and pithy remarks." Another scribe mentioned that he produced "from the pocket of his Prince Albert coat several sheets of paper from which he read slowly and feelingly." According to the New York *Times*, the address was "delivered (or rather read from a sheet of paper which the speaker held in his hand) in a very deliberate manner, with strong emphasis and a business like air." William H. Lambert of Philadelphia, the dean of Lincoln collectors, in an excellent article appearing in the Pennsylvania *Magazine of History and Biography* in 1909, concluded: "All authorities agree that the address was read from manuscript." But not quite "all."

Several people present did not think Lincoln followed his script closely. Dr. T. C. Bielheimen said: "The copy was occasionally raised during the address." While Dr. P. H. Bikle claimed: "With a hand on each side of the manuscript. . . . throughout the speech. . . . he looked at it seldom." One observer recalled: "he held in his left hand two or three pages of manuscript, at which he glanced but once during the address."

There were many present who were very sure that he made no reference whatever to the written pages while speaking. A. H.

136. I, 80, *136.* III, 7, *30.* p. 394, *52.* Nov. 23, 1863 / *76.* Nov. 26, 1913, *153.* Nov. 18, 1933, *73.* Feb. 6, 1932

Nickerson, who stood just in front of him, wrote that he had a slip of paper in his hand but "He did not, however, look at it or refer to it in any way." One visitor at Gettysburg, John J. MacFarlane, noted: "He rested his hands on the rough wooden bar of the platform and began his speech." John A. Sprengle was sure: "He folded his large hands and began speaking in a conversational tone of voice." Amos Sullivan commented: "He looked over the paper, returned it to his pocket and commenced his speech." John Hay wrote in his diary: "The President in his firm free way, with more grace than was his wont, said his half dozen lines of consecration." John Nicolay affirmed: "The President did not read from a manuscript."

One argument put forth by those who are in accord with this last group, points to the fact that stenographic reports of what he said reveal that Lincoln left out some words appearing in his written draft, and included other expressions not appearing in the earlier writings. This inconsistency, they feel, would not have appeared, had he read the address or closely referred to the copy. With one or two exceptions it is acknowledged that the President held a manuscript in his hand. The fact should not be discounted that he never had difficulty committing subject matter to memory. Would not Lincoln have been embarrassed to have *read* his few lines, after Everett had spoken—without notes—for two hours?

The difference of opinion about both the writing and the delivery of the address, neither exceed in number, nor surpass in variety, the traditions extant on the reaction to the address by those who heard it.

Dr. Baugher, president of Pennsylvania College, who sat next to Edward Everett on the right, and in a position to hear what was said, recalled that immediately at the close of the address, he heard Mr. Everett say to the President: "I spent much time and painstaking effort on my speech of an hour or more, but yours of a few minutes will live and mine will be forgotten."

169. July, 1893, *136.* III, 113, *109.* No. 240 / *109.* No. 343, *136.* I, 74–76, *88.* I, 122, *41.* Feb. 1894 /—/ 76. Nov. 26, 1913

Wayne MacVeagh, who also sat on the platform, remarked: "I waited until the distinguished guests who wished to do so had spoken to him (The President) and then I said to him with great earnestness: 'You have made an immortal address.' To which he quietly replied: 'Oh, you must not say that. You must not be extravagant about it.'" MacVeagh also congratulated the orator of the day on his splendid address. Mr. Everett thanked him and then continued: "You are very kind but Mr. Lincoln perhaps said more to the purpose, in his brief speech than I in my long one."

John Morrow, a superintendent of schools in Alleghany County, Pennsylvania, who stood at the edge of the platform within hearing range of Mr. Everett and Mr. Lincoln, put their conversation at the conclusion of the President's speech in dialogue form:

MR. EVERETT: Mr. Lincoln, allow me to congratulate you on those noble sentiments.
MR. LINCOLN: I am sorry I could say so little I had only twenty lines.
MR. EVERETT: Yes, Mr. Lincoln but there was more in your twenty lines than in my twenty pages.
MR. LINCOLN: We shall not try to talk about my address, I failed: I failed: and that is about all that can be said about it.

Arthur B. Farquhar, who was also on the platform, stated that he heard Mr. Everett say to Mr. Lincoln: "Mr. President you have made a great speech, my address will only be remembered because it was made on the same day." One of the earliest complimentary statements by Mr. Everett to appear in print, is found in Isaac N. Arnold's Lincoln volume, published in 1866. Although not present on the occasion Arnold states he secured his information from Governor Dennison who sat on the platform not far from the President. Mr. Everett is reported as saying: "Oh, Mr. President how gladly would I give all my hundred pages to be the author of your twenty lines."

The day after the celebration, the President received from Edward Everett a letter which said in part: "I should be glad, if I

41. Nov. 1909 / 58. p. 230 / 136. III, 7, 13. p. 334

could flatter myself that I came as near the central idea of the occasion, in two hours as you did in two minutes. My son, who left me at Baltimore and my daughter concur in this sentiment."

Ward H. Lamon who had gained the ill will of Lincoln students by securing Chauncey F. Black to ghost write Lamon's *Lincoln*, published in 1872, submitted a letter to the Chicago *Tribune* in 1889, in which there appeared these uncomplimentary statements concerning favorable notices about Lincoln's speech: "unworthy gush . . . purely apocryphal . . . rhetorical bombast . . . baseless adulation . . . falsification of history." He then proceeded to give his account of what was said on the platform at the close of Lincoln's address: "Only a moment after its conclusion, Mr. Seward turned to Mr. Everett and asked him what he thought of the President's speech. Mr. Everett replied: 'It was not what I expected of him: I am disappointed.' In his turn, Mr. Everett asked: 'What do you think of it Mr. Seward?' The response was: 'He has made a failure, and I am sorry for it; his speech is not equal to him.' Mr. Seward then turned to me and asked: 'Mr. Marshal, what do you think of it?' 'I am sorry to say it does not impress me as one of his great speeches.'"

Mr. Everett's cultural background would not have allowed him to speak disparagingly about the address of an associate on the same program, especially if he were the President, and the recipient of his comment was the Secretary of State. Mr. Everett, in common with everyone else, did not expect Mr. Lincoln to speak as he did. Twenty-six years having passed, Mr. Lamon's memories must have played a trick on him when he quoted Mr. Everett as saying: "I was disappointed." Mr. Everett was not a man to contradict himself within twenty-four hours and the sincerity of his complimentary tribute in the letter the following day, cannot be successfully challenged.

Lamon also stated the President said to him: "That speech wont scour! It is a flat failure and the people are disappointed." Lamon commented: "As a matter of fact Mr. Lincoln's great

1. VII, 24, 25 / *109.* No. 739, *136.* III, 62 / *136.* III, 48

Gettysburg Speech fell on the vast audience like a wet blanket." In Lamon's *Recollections*, this wet blanket assertion was placed in quotations but credited to Lincoln rather than Lamon. There can be little doubt that from Lincoln's viewpoint, any brief comments he might have made would have been completely overshadowed by the preceding great oration. The anticipation of this situation may have been responsible for his telling Seward in Washington, as reported by the New York *Times* "that he was nervous about his speech." Again, he is said to have commented to Seward on the platform before speaking: "It is a failure they wont like it."

The "wont scour" expression sounds much like Lincoln and there seemed to be a lingering doubt in his mind about the success of the speech, expressed in his reply to Everett's letter of the following day when he wrote: "I am pleased to know that, in your judgement, the little I did say was not entirely a failure." Whether the "wet blanket" statement was coined by Lamon or Lincoln, it found a responsive chord with two subsequent writers who, with Lamon, greatly influenced public sentiment about the reaction to Lincoln's speech.

One of these authors, Clark E. Carr, copied, verbatim, much of the Lamon story that appeared in the *Tribune*, and also in a later publication, the *Recollections of Lincoln*, published by Lamon's daughter. He commented that he agreed with Lamon's conclusions. Mr. Carr states that when the President was introduced: "It was the first opportunity the people had to really see him. There was the usual craning of necks, the usual exclamations of 'down in front,' " but Mr. Carr makes no mention of any applause. At the conclusion of the address, he comments that "the applause was not especially marked."

Another writer who featured the little or "no applause" reaction to the President's speech, was Mrs. Andrews, author of the *Perfect Tribute*. She seems to have been the first one to publish the absence of any hand clapping or acclamation whatever. When

138. Feb. 12, 1909, *136*. III, 62 / *1*. VII, 24 / *38*. pp. 56, 57, 60

Mr. Everett finished his oration, she states: "They clapped and cheered him again, again and again." When Lincoln concluded, about seven minutes later, she observes: "There was no sound from the silent, vast assembly . . . not a hand was lifted in applause, there was no sound of approval, or recognition from the audience." In later years, this allegation of Mrs. Andrews, as well as the Lamon and Carr uncomplimentary sketches, was reflected in the testimonies of those trying to recall incidents occurring at the dedication. Reputable contributors to magazines, wrote: "Not a sound broke the solemn stillness," "When he finished a dead silence greeted him." "No one applauded him," "The address seemed like a benediction, an applause would have been out of place."

The Washington *Daily Chronicle* reported the next day that when the President was introduced, he was "vociferously cheered by the vast audience." Joseph L. Gilbert, reporter for the Associated Press, put in brackets the word "(applause)" at the end of four sentences, at a break in another, and at the end: "(Long continued applause)." Mr. Lincoln's home paper, the Illinois *Journal*, on November 23, printed an independent version of the address which contained at intervals, these three comments set in brackets: "(applause), (great applause), (immense applause)." Also this additional notation: "The conclusion of the President's remarks was followed by immense applause and three cheers were given for him and the governors of the states."

Governor Curtin, who was but two seats away on Lincoln's left, stated: "He pronounced that speech in a voice that all the multitude heard. The crowd was hushed into silence because the President stood before them. But at intervals there were roars of applause. My God! It was so Impressive! It was the common remark of everybody. Such a speech, as they said it was! Everett and all went up and congratulated the President, shaking him by the hand." Shortly after Benjamin French returned to Washing-

8. pp. 11–17, *109*. No. 782, *98*. Apr. 24, 1913 / *191*. Nov. 20, 1963, *97*. Nov. 23, 1963

ton, he made this statement: "Anyone who saw and heard, as I did, the hurricane of applause that met his every movement at Gettysburg would know that he lived in every heart. It was no cold, faint shadow of a kind reception; it was a tumultous out pouring of exultation from true and loving hearts. . . . It was the spontaneous outburst of the heartfelt confidence of the people in their President."

Were the people disappointed in its brevity? When the President was invited to make a few appropriate remarks, the cemetery commissioners may not have known that brevity was his specialty. Lincoln once referred to a person given to wordiness, as being able to compress the most words into the smallest ideas of any man he had ever met. With Mr. Lincoln it was just the reverse. He could compress the most profound and comprehensive ideas into the most condensed wordage of any contemporary statesman. On another occasion, one man hearing him, in a reflective mood, commented: "So 'many things' in 'so few words,' I never heard before."

Although Lincoln lived in a day of lengthy discourses—his own no exception—his inclination was to brevity. One of his legal associates in Illinois, noted: "He always said things short, things shorter than anyone else." So when Noah Brooks asked him about the speech he had prepared for the dedication, the answer was "very short" or as he "emphatically expressed 'short, short, short.' " After Brooks had glanced over the copy of Mr. Everett's extended discourse which Mr. Lincoln had received, the President smiled and quoted a line he thought he had read in Webster's writings: "Solid men of Boston, make no long orations!" However, it originated with Charles Morris and is associated with a preliminary line: "Solid men of Boston, banish long potations." While the various versions of the address differ slightly in length, the Hale word-for-word copy, which have been presented in the preceding chapter, contains 265 words, of which 189 are of one syllable, and 76 of two syllables or more. It is not known that

20. p. 167, 170 / *136*. III, 4

anyone held a stop watch on Lincoln while he made his speech, although this statement by James Grant Wilson might imply it: "The immense audience that was within the sound of his strong tenor far reaching voice, listened almost breathlessly during its delivery which occupied precisely 135 seconds." Possibly Mr. Everett's estimate of the time of the two addresses: "two hours" for his own and "two minutes" for Mr. Lincoln's is close enough, but presumably the President's speech was nearer three minutes, including applause.

The reporter, John Russell Young, apparently speaking for the press, stated: "We all supposed that Mr. Lincoln would make rather a long speech—a half hour at least." Why there should have been any such notion is difficult to conceive. All the publicity that had been given to the dedication mentioned the *few remarks* to be made by the President. John Nicolay gives a logical and satisfactory explanation of what the people may have anticipated in the speech: "It was entirely natural for everyone to expect that this would consist of a few perfunctory words, the mere formality of official dedication . . . and took it for granted that Mr. Lincoln was there as a mere figure-head, the culminating decoration, so to speak of the elaborately planned pageant of the day."

It would not be difficult to build up an argument to affirm that the people must have been greatly pleased at the brevity of the speech. The women had been urged to occupy the ground set apart for them by 10:00 a.m., and when Mr. Lincoln began to speak, it was after 2:00 p.m., resulting in four solid hours of standing for them. Furthermore, most of those present had been without food since breakfast, and for some it was a very early meal at that. Mr. Lincoln, having seen the long Everett discourse in print, must have anticipated the weariness of the people at the hour when it came time for him to speak. He wrote to Mr. Everett the next day: "You could not have been excused to make a short address nor I a long one."

95. VI, No. 1, *41.* Jan. 1895, *19.* p. 432, *98.* Apr. 24, 1913 / *126.* III, 21, *41.* Feb. 1894 / *1.* VII, 24

CHAPTER 14

Dedication Aftermath

CONSIDERING the time designated for the program, the completion of Mr. Everett's address almost brought the exercises to a conclusion. Five minutes were consumed by the dirge which followed, three minutes, by the President, another five minutes, for the chorus and then came the benediction. The dirge was sung by a volunteer chorus of Gettysburg men and women and was prepared especially for the occasion. The words were by James G. Percival, the music by Alfred Delany. It was dedicated to Governor Curtin. Only the first of the four verses is presented here:

> O! it is great for our country to die
>   whose ranks are contending:
> Bright is the wreath of our fame; glory
>   awaits us for aye:
> Glory that never is dim, shining on
>   with a light never ending—
> Glory, that never shall fade, never, O!
>   never away!

There is some confusion about the wording of the benediction by Reverend Henry L. Baugher, D.D. The Adams *Sentinel* of December 1, printed it in full and it agreed with the recorded copy made by Mr. Hale of Boston. However, one week later, the *Sentinel* presented what it called, a "correct" copy of the bene-

171. pp. 85–87

diction, which differs considerably from the former printing. It was this second version that Mr. Wills used in his published report of the ceremonies. The one transcribed by Mr. Hale which is reproduced here, is more likely to contain the exact words used, while the second copy appears to be a revision.

"O Thou King of Kings and Lord of Lords, God of the Nations of the Earth, who permitteth them to do only whatsoever Thou willest, we beseech Thy blessing on these holy services. Bless this spot, Bless these holy graves. Bless the President of the United States and the Cabinet. Bless all governments of the earth. Bless the representatives of the States, and bless those whose hands embroiled the nation in war—that their hearts may be influenced by Thy grace to return. Bless the efforts to subdue the Rebellion, that it may be overthrown, and now may the grace of our Lord Jesus Christ, the love of God, Our Heavenly Father and the fellowship of the Holy Ghost be with you all, Amen."

With the pronouncing of the benediction, Marshal Lamon declared the close of the exercises of the day. Whereupon, a battery of artillery stationed on one of the highest points of the ridge, fired a salute. When the President came down from the platform, he stopped to shake hands with the wounded veterans who had fought so gallantly on that very field. Possibly he recalled a visit to the executive mansion earlier that same year, of some convalescent veterans known as "The One-Legged Brigade." He said, in reply to their chaplain: "The men upon their crutches were orators; their very appearance spoke louder than tongues." Lincoln would have agreed that the real orators of the day at Gettysburg were before him. The military led by the Marine Band escorted the President and his associates back to town.

The aftermath of the exercises provides an interesting reaction of the commissioners to the speech of the President. It will be recalled that Mr. David Wills had written a letter to Mr. Lincoln confirming the wish of the commission that he might appear on the program. The letter has been given wide attention, even to the

2. Dec. 1, 1863, 2. Dec. 8, 1863, 27. Nov. 23, 1863 / 27. Nov. 23, 1863 / 1. VI, 226

casting of its contents in bronze on a tablet of the Lincoln Speech Memorial at Gettysburg.

Some critics feel they have discovered in the letter, the essence of Mr. Lincoln's address. Robert Bruce, in a contribution to the New York *Times* on February 15, 1939, made this comment: "The celebrated address was an earnest, thoughtful effort to carry out Judge Wills' suggestion. The same feelings permeate both, and their languages strikingly similar." Joseph L. Eisendrath, Jr. of Chicago, released to the press on November 20, 1948, a comparative study of the Wills letter and the address, in which he felt he had discovered striking similarity, and that the President made "a noteworthy attempt to follow out Wills' suggestions." The 1962 fall issue of the *Lincoln Herald*, presents a monograph by Clifford P. Owsley, entitled: "Genesis of the World's Greatest Speech." It is a more exhaustive presentation, attempting to point out certain passages in Wills' letter that found expression in the composition of Lincoln's address. One indisputable similarity is that the Wills letter and the Lincoln address are about the same in length.

The most significant instruction which Mr. Wills included in his letter to the President, specified that the commissioners wanted him to present a few appropriate remarks. No one can question Lincoln's attempt to literally carry out this request. His words could not have been more appropriate and his remarks were few. Yet the statements published by Mr. Carr in his Gettysburg book, allege that the commissioners, as well as many of the people, were greatly disappointed in the President's contribution.

After the program, according to Carr: "Many persons said to me that they would have supposed that on such a great occasion the President would have made a speech." Mr. Carr also claims that the writer of the invitation letter and chairman of the commission, David Wills, remarked in the same critical tone: "Instead of Mr. Lincoln delivering an address he only made a

111. Wills to Lincoln Nov. 2, 1863 / *138.* Feb. 15, 1939, *136.* II, 59, *108.* Fall, 1862 / *38.* p. 59

few dedicatory remarks." If Mr. Wills thought them to be appropriate as well as brief, he heard just what he ordered. It is strange that Mr. Carr, who claimed the honor of proposing that Mr. Lincoln be invited to speak, and Mr. Wills, with his alleged thought-laden invitation, should count Mr. Lincoln's effort a failure.

In the 1900 newspaper contribution, Mr. Carr said the address had "all the elements of a finished oration. There is the exordium, introduction, or premise, laid down with the most perfect exactitude. There is the argument so strong as to be irresistible. There is the illustration that arrests the attention and makes clear the arguments and there is the peroration so striking so lofty and sublime." Yet, in his 1906 publication, he stated: "We on the platform heard every word and what did we hear? A dozen common place sentences, scarcely one of which contained anything new, anything that when stated was not self evident."

The program having been completed a few minutes after two o'clock, the rest of the afternoon was occupied by many in walking over the battlefield. Some visitors were trying to find where relatives or friends had fallen or were buried. A large number of the soldiers had not as yet been removed from their original burial places in the cemetery area. The Adams *Sentinel* gives a good description of the surroundings at the time of the ceremonies: "The ground is yet strewn with the remains and relics of the fearful struggle, ragged and muddy knapsacks, canteens, cups, haversacks, thread bare stockings trodden in the mud, old shoes, pistols, holsters, bayonet sheafs, and here and there fragments of blue and gray jackets—mournful and appealing mementoes of the civil strife, . . . Hundreds gathered up to bear with them, the spirit of Gettysburg to every quarter of the state, relics more eloquent than orations." Later, the *Sentinel* stated that a total of 28,000 muskets had been picked up on the battlefield since the engagement.

38. p. 59, 96. No. 23, p. 10 / 49. Feb. 12, 1900, 38. pp. 59, 60 / 136. III, 60, 61, 2. Feb. 9, 1864

While there were souvenirs to be recovered, there were still others which should have been buried. The day after the ceremonies, Russell M. Briggs of Philadelphia, was in Gettysburg for the purpose of removing the body of his son. On his way to the place of the son's death, Mr. Briggs observed a lad, twelve or fourteen years of age on the sidewalk playing with a shell. Briggs discovered the shell to be loaded. Attempting to remove the charge, it exploded and severed both of his hands. Another account of the story states that Mr. Briggs himself had found the shell on the battlefield, and was attempting to unload it in front of the house of Solomon Powers, when young Allen Frazer, who lived with Mr. Powers, was killed by the explosion.

The time passed rapidly on the afternoon of the ceremonies and it was nearly three o'clock before a dinner was served "at the home of Mr. Wills for a very large company," according to Mr. Everett. The dinner was followed by an informal reception. The President, taking his position in the hall opening on York Street, greeted guests as they entered. Governor Curtin shook hands with them as they passed into the public square.

While the hour-long reception was in progress, the Fifth New York regiment of heavy artillery with Colonel Murray in command, marched in review before Governor Seymour at the residence where he was staying. After a "Glorious banner from the merchants of New York City," had been presented he said: "Sergeant, I place these colors in your hands, in the firm confidence that they will be borne through every field of triumph, of toil, and of danger, in a way that you will do honor to yourselves; to the great state which you represent and the still greater country to which you belong." The Albany *Evening Journal* reported that he closed his address, asking the men of New York to give "three cheers for the Union of our country and three cheers for the flag of our land." The Gettysburg *Compiler* reported: "His remarks were those of a statesman, not of a groveling political partisan.

27. Nov. 25, 1863, 2. Nov. 24, 1863 / *121.* p. 13, *136.* I, 43

His allusions to the occasion which had brought him here—the sacred work of dedication to the soldier dead a portion of the battlefield on which they had fallen—were not only appropriate but feelingly beautiful."

One of the most interesting persons whom Lincoln met at the close of the reception, was the local Gettysburg hero, John L. Burns. Upon learning the story of the old man's bravery, the President expressed a desire to meet him. Mr. Wills and Secretary Seward were commissioned to arrange his introduction to the President. The best story of his valor is found in an interview by a reporter of the Washington *Chronicle* the day before the ceremonies. "Your correspondent deemed himself exceedingly fortunate to fall in with brave old John L. Burns—an old hero of the war of 1812, and the only citizen of Gettysburg who took part in the battle. Mr. Burns to his honor be it recorded, shouldered a rifle and nobly did his duty, in the Wisconsin Iron Brigade on Wednesday and fell wounded in three places, and lay four and twenty hours on the field among the rebels in sight of his own home, before he could be carried there and obtain relief. While lying in his bed a rebel minnie ball cut a clean hole through his window, took off the back of a chair and passed through the opposite wall above his head, and not a foot from it, and your correspondent now is writing beside these marks of battle."

Burns had been the town's cobbler, had served as a constable, and, as one citizen put it he was "treated with scant courtesy by the town's people," due to a fondness for intoxicants. Although seventy years of age, his behavior on July 1, when the town was attacked, brought him much deserved distinction. It was the dedication exercises and his recognition by the President that gave him wide publicity. In its issue of December 15, the Adams *Sentinel* reported that Mr. (Daniel) Clark of New Hampshire, in the Senate of the United States, introduced a bill to grant a pension to John L. Burns, and on February 23, the *Sentinel* announced it had passed both houses of congress. The bill

76. Nov. 23, 1863 / *191.* Nov. 21, 1863

provided for "a pension of $8.00 per month for valor on the battle field". It was retroactive to July 1, 1863.

After Mr. Lincoln had met Mr. Burns, and the reception at Mr. Wills' was concluded, Burns, with President Lincoln on his right and Secretary Seward on his left, was conducted to the Presbyterian church, where the ceremonies of the afternoon were to begin at five o'clock. The pew which they occupied has become one of Gettysburg's most interesting memorials. The citizens of the town were somewhat disturbed by the John Burns stories, which seemed to imply he was the only Gettysburg citizen who had participated in the battle. It is said that when the Governor called for troops, the college at Gettysburg sent the first company to report at Harrisburg. Nearly 200 soldiers were furnished to the Army from the small community.

This is the place where the story of Virginia Wade should be mentioned. In the same copy of the Adams *Sentinel* which told of John Burns' injury, this short notice appears: "Killed—Miss Virginia Wade by our own sharp shooters." It was the dedication which also brought the story of Miss Wade into prominence. On December 1, The *Sentinel* copied an article from the Harrisburg *Telegraph* which is presented in part: "Jennie Wade was busily engaged in baking bread for the national troops. She occupied a house in range of both armies and the rebels had sternly warned her to leave the premises, but this she refused to do. While she was busily engaged in her patriotic work, a minnie ball pierced her pure heart and she fell a holy sacrifice in her country's call . . ."

Apparently John Burns was somewhat jealous of eulogistic comments in the press about Miss Wade. On January 20, 1899, he answered a letter of inquiry in this manner: "The story about her loyalty, being killed while serving Union soldiers etc. is all a fiction. . . . The only fact in the whole story is that she was killed during the battle in her home by a stray bullet. *I could call*

2. Dec. 15, 1863, 2. Feb. 23, 1864 / 2. Nov. 21, 1863, 76. June 22, 1863 / 2. July 7, 1863, Dec. 1, 1863

her a *she-rebel*." Nevertheless, she was engaged to a Union soldier. Her tombstone in Evergreen Cemetery bears this inscription: "Killed July 3, 1863, while making bread for the Union soldiers." The memorial shaft was: "Erected by the Relief Corps of Iowa, A.D. 1901."

The guest speaker at the Presbyterian Church was the newly elected Lieutenant Governor of Ohio, Honorable Charles Anderson, brother of Robert Anderson of Fort Sumter fame. The *Sentinel* reported that the building was "filled to repletion and for everyone inside there were ten on the outside, who wanted to get in." A newspaper condensed Colonel Anderson's speech into this brief paragraph: "The address was a bold and able exposition of the causes which led to the present war, the issues involved in the contest, and the importance of its termination. It was the first human contest between freedom and despotism which was to end in the triumph of one or the other." The address which Mr. Anderson delivered at Xenia, Ohio, on May 2, 1863, covered much of the same ground.

The President allowed just enough time after leaving the church, to go back to the Wills house, and then directly to the depot. A reporter from the New York *Times* stated that the first train allowed to depart during the day was the "special" which left at 6:30 p.m., "bearing the President and his party." After the last train had gone, late in the evening, a reporter for the Boston *Journal* wrote: "All is now quiet in the streets of Gettysburg, the imposing ceremonies of the day having been completed in admirable order and without being marred in any respect."

It had been a strenuous day for the President. Wherever he appeared, he was surrounded by people who wanted to shake his hand. After the train pulled out, he is said to have retired to the room especially reserved for him. Here he "lay in a relaxed position with a wet towel across his head." Although he was not well, he chatted with Wayne MacVeagh at some time during the

79. July 1, 1963 / *136*. III, 60, 2. Nov. 24, 1863 / *138*. Nov. 21, 1863, 27. Nov. 20, 1863

return trip. They had talked about political affairs in Missouri on the way to Gettysburg, and later resumed their conversation. Many politicians looked upon Lincoln's chances to be renominated as the party standard bearer in 1864, as most unlikely. When it was learned that the President was to speak at the dedication of the cemetery, one of his critics commented derisively: "Let the dead bury the dead." The train finally pulled into Washington at one o'clock the next morning.

Friday, November 20, brought to Mr. Lincoln one of his most cherished personal letters, Edward Everett's complimentary words about his few remarks, and this line of inquiry about Tad: "I hope your anxiety for your child was relieved upon your arrival." That very day, the laudatory and gracious communication was answered, his own appreciation of Mr. Everett's oration expressed, and Tad's improvement noted.

James Speed, whom Lincoln appointed attorney general the following year, recalled an interview with the President in which the Everett letter was mentioned. Mr. Lincoln promptly handed the letter to Speed and acknowledged that "he had never received a compliment that he prized more highly."

20. p. 195, *88.* I, 121, *191.* Nov. 20, 1863 / *1.* VII, 24, 25 / *16.* II, 209

CHAPTER 15

Press Reaction

A GROUP of Washington reporters in Lincoln's day called themselves the Press Bohemians. At least one of them was on the Gettysburg train, and stated that the President was asked for an advance copy of his speech, whereupon the impression was left that he had no speech to make, but that his part on the program was to introduce Mr. Everett, "who would do the speech making." However, when further pressed for a copy, as the story goes: "The President asked for a pencil and a piece of paper and wrote out the address for them."

Another account of Lincoln's aid to reporters comes from Joseph I. Gilbert, one of the best known Associated Press shorthand artists of that day. He had taken down what Lincoln said, at both Philadelphia and Harrisburg when en route to the inaugural. Mr. Gilbert thought the President was the most easily reported person among all the public speakers of his time, and commented: "His lucid thinking and distinct articulation—qualities in a speaker which most delight a reporter—and his natural unaffected style of delivery, made him the orator par excellence for a short hand novice like myself."

After Lincoln became President, Gilbert reported virtually all of his speeches for the Associated Press. He was at Gettysburg,

136. II, 36 / *153.* Nov. 12, 1940

prepared to take down Mr. Lincoln's address, and stood directly in front of him. Years later he commented: "Fascinated by his intense earnestness and depth of feeling, I unconsciously stopped taking notes and looked up at him as he glanced at his manuscript with a far away look in his eyes. . . . Before the dedication ceremonies closed, the President's manuscript was copied with his permission." The Gilbert or Associated Press copy follows:

> Four score and seven years ago our fathers brought forth upon this continent a new nation, conceived in liberty, and dedicated to the proposition that all men are created equal. (Applause) Now we are engaged in a great civil war, testing whether that nation, or any nation so conceived, and so dedicated, can long endure. We are met on a great battle-field of that war. We are met to dedicate a portion of it as the final resting place of those who here gave their lives that that nation might live.
>
> It is altogether fitting and proper that we should do this. But in a larger sense we cannot dedicate, we cannot consecrate, we cannot hallow this ground. The brave men, living and dead, who struggled here have consecrated it far above our power to add or detract. (Applause) The world will little note nor long remember what we say here, but it can never forget what they did here. (Applause) It is for us, the living, rather to be dedicated here to the unfinished work that they have thus far so nobly carried on. (Applause) It is rather for us to be here dedicated to the great task remaining before us, that from these honored dead we take increased devotion to that cause for which they here gave the last full measure of devotion; that we here highly resolve that the dead shall not have died in vain (Applause); that the nation shall, under God, have a new birth of freedom; and that Government of the people, by the people, and for the people, shall not perish from the earth. (Long-continued applause)

Among Gibson's many reminiscences, he recalled: "No one of the many orators whom, in after years, I heard repeat the address, ever made it sparkle with light and meaning as its great author did. . . . These reminiscences were related to an association of shorthand reporters in 1917, fifty-four years after the dedication took place.

20. p. 188–192 / *1.* VII, 18, 19 / ibid / *20.* p. 188

Still another reporter who recorded Lincoln's speech, was Charles Hale, a younger brother of Edward Everett Hale. He was born in Boston in 1831, was graduated from Harvard in 1850, published a literary journal, *To-Day*, and became junior editor of the Boston *Daily Advertiser*. Later he was elected a state senator and was then appointed assistant secretary of state, under Hamilton Fish. He visited Gettysburg as a member of the Massachusetts commission, and this excerpt, from a report which he prepared, is of interest:

> "The oration was delivered by Hon. Edward Everett, a distinguished citizen of Massachusetts, and was heard with close attention; and the brief speech of President Lincoln, which followed, likewise made a profound impression. . . . the latter, which has not generally been printed rightly, having been marred from errors in telegraphing, is appended, in the correct form, as the words actually spoken by the President, with great deliberation, were taken down by one of the undersigned."
>
> All of which is respectfully submitted
> Henry Edwards
> Geo. Wm. Bond
> Charles Hale
> Commissioners.

As an exact statement of what Lincoln said, the Hale copy, already presented in chapter 12, is given first choice. It was not changed in any manner from the word-for-word recording of the presentation. The Gilbert version, slightly different, is preferred by some students, because it was corrected against the manuscript Lincoln held in his hand. It is the Associated Press copy that indicates places where applause was received—six in all. In Mr. Hale's sentence: "The world will very little note. . ." Mr. Gilbert left out the word "very." Mr. Hale referred to "these dead," where Mr. Gilbert used, "the dead." In the closing sentence, Mr. Hale omits the word "and," from the Gilbert copy appearing in the phrase; "and for the people." If we may overlook

10. III, 32, 7. p. XXXV

these trivial differences, we may accept either one of them as recording what Lincoln said at Gettysburg.

While there are many widely divergent stories of how, when, and where the speech was written, there is no need for speculation as to what was said. Yet, an "Associated Press Writer," under the caption: "Text of speech at Gettysburg, still uncertain," makes this statement: "And today (November 11, 1950), no one is positive exactly what he said there." It is doubtful that there could be found two separate transcriptions of an address made in 1863, more in harmony (as far as wordage is considered) than the independent recordings made by Charles Hale and Joseph Gilbert. We do know what Lincoln said. Both shorthand and telegraphy were still in their infancy, with few experts in either field, which was largely responsible for so many versions of the address as reported throughout the country. There is no special interest in noting these variations which, for the most part, were typographical in origin.

The newspapers in the larger American cities had been provided with copies of Mr. Everett's address prior to the dedication. In many instances, it was published in full, occupying an entire page or more, thereby invariably inviting editorial comment. Henry Ward Beecher had just returned from a lecture tour in Europe and spoke in Brooklyn on the very day Everett was at Gettysburg. Some papers compared the two addresses. The few lines of Lincoln's speech, received late in the evening by telegraph, and because of their brevity, were hastily set in type and commanded little attention. This apparent neglect, with scant editorial comment, is well understood by publishers.

The reporters for the Washington *Chronicle* returned from Gettysburg on the Lincoln train, and immediately prepared copies for their paper which had printed the Everett address in its first edition. Some comment has been made about Lincoln's speech not appearing in this issue, but it was published in the "Second Edition" at 5 a.m. The paper for November 20, stated: "Edward

136. III, 60 / *136.* IV, 15 / Appendix, *136.* I, 25, *191.* Nov. 20, 1863

Everett's great oration and the proceedings of the dedication of the National Cemetery at Gettysburg will be issued tomorrow in pamphlet form.—For sale at the *Chronicle* office."

The pamphlet bore this title: *The Gettysburg Solemnities: Dedication of the National Cemetery at Gettysburg, Pa. November 19, 1863 with the oration of Edward Everett, Speech of President Lincoln.* This was the first printing of Lincoln's address in a pamphlet. For many years the Baker & Goodwin booklet, dated 1863, and containing both addresses, was thought to be the earliest, and on the strength of that claim, at one time brought as much as $200.00 per copy. *City Document No. 106* published by J. E. Farwell and Company, Boston, was also dated 1863, but the exact day of its appearance is not known. Little Brown & Company, also of Boston, was not able to bring its cloth bound book from the press until January 23, as noted by Mr. Everett in his letter to Lincoln. A little earlier in the month, another Boston printing of the address appeared in *Addresses of his Excellency John A. Andrew.*

Back somewhere in the early nineteen twenties, editors of newspapers were asked to vote on what might be considered the most outstanding editorial column in American newspaper history. First place was given to the Springfield (Massachusetts) *Republican.* One of its editors who had contributed much to its reputation, was Josiah G. Holland, born in Massachusetts in 1819. He became its associate editor under Samuel Bowles in 1849, and soon began writing most of the editorials. As might be expected, when in 1863, Lincoln's brief lines passed over his desk, they did not escape his notice. From his pen came one of the earliest editorial tributes to the address:

"Surprisingly fine as Mr. Everett's oration was in the Gettysburg consecration, the rhetorical honors of the occasion were won by President Lincoln. His little speech is a perfect gem, deep in feeling, compact in thought and expression, and tasteful and elegant in every word and comma. . . . Strong feelings and a

191. Nov. 20, 1863 / *10.* I, 78, *160.* Nov. 20, 1863 / *78.* 110, *25.* III, 7 / *176.* Nov. 20, 1863

large brain were its parents—a little painstaking its accoucheur." When a writer of Mr. Holland's ability gives emphasis to the eloquence of punctuation marks, he must have been deeply impressed. Where would he have found words adequate to express his admiration, if he had seen and heard Mr. Lincoln?

This tribute was no more impressive than one appearing in the Providence *Daily Journal*, of which James Burrill Angell was the editor. He was born in Rhode Island in 1829, was graduated from Brown University, and succeeded Henry B. Anthony as editor of the *Journal* in 1860. He became president of Vermont University in 1866, and in 1871, was called to the presidency of the University of Michigan. He received honorary degrees from Brown, Columbia, Rutgers, Princeton, Yale, and Johns Hopkins Universities. He was United States minister to China and later to Turkey. Mr. Angell wrote, on the day following the delivery of the address: "We know not where to look for a more admirable speech than the brief one which the President made at the close of Mr. Everett's oration. It is often said that the hardest thing in the world is to make a five minute speech. But could the most elaborate and splendid oration be more beautiful, more touching, more inspiring than those few words of the President? They had in my humble judgement the charm and power of the very highest eloquence."

While it is likely that these two editorials were seen by Mr. Lincoln, we are sure he saw the one which was sent to him, written by the editor of The Philadelphia *Evening Bulletin:* "The President's brief speech is most happily expressed. It is warm, earnest, unaffected and touching. Thousands who would not read the long elaborate oration of Mr. Everett will read the President's few words, and not many of them will do it without the moistening of the eye, and the swelling of the heart."

The comments from distinguished members of the press already noted, and those which are to follow, should offer a suf-

176. Nov. 20, 1863 / *10.* I, 78, *160.* Nov. 20, 1863 / *111.* Scoville to Lincoln Nov. 20, 1863, *153.* Nov. 20, 1863

ficient rebuttal to this widely circulated statement by Ward H. Lamon: "I state it as a fact and without fear of contradiction that this famous Gettysburg speech was not received or commented upon with anything like hearty favor by the people, the politicians or the press of the United States until after the death of its author."

> *Army and Navy Journal*, 11–22–63—Decidedly the best feature of the occasion, as well as one of the most felicitious utterances of his career.
>
> Chicago *Tribune*, 11–20–63—The dedicatory remarks of President Lincoln will live among the annals of the war.
>
> Boston *City Document, 106,*—1863—Perhaps nothing in the whole proceedings made so deep an impression on the vast assemblage, or has conveyed to the country in so concise a form the lesson of the hour, as the remarks of the President. Their simplicity and force make them worthy of a prominence among the utterances from high places.
>
> Cincinnati *Gazette*, 11–26–63—The right thing in the right place, and a perfect thing in every respect, was the universal encomium.
>
> Columbus (Ohio) *State Journal*, 11–26–63—The President's calm but earnest utterance of this brief and beautiful address, stirred the deepest foundations of feelings and emotions, in the hearts of the vast throng before him, and when he concluded scarcely a tearless eye could be seen, while sobs of smothered emotion were heard on every hand.
>
> Detroit *Advertiser and Tribune*, 11–23–63—He who wants to take in the very spirit of the day, catch the unstudied pathos that animates a sincere but simple-minded man, will turn from the stately periods of the professed orator to the brief speech of the President.
>
> Hanover (Pa.) *Weekly Spectator*, 11–27–63—The appearance of the President on the stand was the signal for repeated cheers and enthusiasm. Then our great President began to deliver his remarkable speech.
>
> *Harper's New Monthly Magazine*, 7–1866—Mr. Lincoln's brief dedicatory address . . . in the light of subsequent events sounds more like inspiration or prophecy in this connection, than the utterance of mere human lips.

126. III, 62

Harper's Weekly, 12–5–63—The few words of the President were from the heart to the heart. They cannot be read, even, without kindling emotion. . . . It was as simple and felicitous and earnest a word as was ever spoken.

Harper's Weekly, 12–12–63—The most perfect piece of American eloquence, and as noble and pathetic and appropriate as the oration of Pericles over the Peloponnesian dead.

Harper's Weekly, June, 1903—So large and lofty are the thoughts and so exquisitely fitting are the words, that hardy, indeed, would be the rhetorician who should try to edit or retouch them.

Macmillan's Magazine, February, 1865—Looking at the substance it may be doubted whether any king in Europe would have expressed himself more royally than the peasant's son.

New York *World*, 11–20–63—Brief, and calculated to arouse deep feeling.

(Philadelphia) *Forney's War Press*, 12–3–63— Certainly the ruler of the nation stood higher and grander and more prophetic, on that historic height. It was proper that he should utter words such as these.

Presbyterian Banner, 6–30–1909—The two hour address lies in the dust of oblivion, while the two minute address is an immortal English classic.

Review of Two Worlds, 1–15–1866—I do not believe that modern speech has ever produced anything that will excel his eloquent discourse.

Springfield (Ill.) *State Journal*, 11–21–63—The oration of Hon. Edward Everett, the solemn dirge by the choir, and the dedicatory remarks of President Lincoln will live among the annals of the war.

Washington *Daily Morning Chronicle*, 11–20–63—His address which, though short, glittered with gems evincing the gentleness and goodness of heart peculiar to him, and will receive the attention of all the tens of thousands who will read it.

Westminster Review, June, 66—It has but one equal: in that pronounced upon those who fell during the first year of the Peloponnesian War, and in one respect it is superior to that great speech.

This editorial comment in the *Atlanta Constitution* on July 2, 1913, presents a good summary of the earlier tributes: "The sentiments of Lincoln there expressed with such strange prescience and courage have been abundantly justified by the march of time."

All of the comments on the address however, were not favorable. As early as on the occasion of his July 7 speech from the balcony of the executive mansion, the opposition press, looking upon him as a probable candidate for re-election, tried to make political capital of what he said. The Chicago *Times* for July 11, asserted editorially: "Mr. Lincoln never spoke truer words than when he said in his Fourth of July speech, that he was not prepared to make a speech worthy of the occasion, unfortunately he is never prepared to make one worthy of the occasion, and it is a fact becoming a settled conviction that he never will be." The editorial continued: "It is a very bad comment on the capacity of a Chief Magistrate that he cannot get upon his feet and say a few words without blundering through his part as a stripling lawyer would be ashamed to blunder . . . his speeches are too much for equanimity . . . the least he can do is to make no more speeches and write no more letters."

Further criticism came from the East, where the July 7 speech appeared in the Boston *Morning Journal*, with several intervals noting applause. One of these interruptions followed the President's reference to the retreat of the Confederates. This he described by using a typical western idiom, so familiar to those who have observed the actions of a frightened dog. Lincoln commented: "On the 4th the cohorts of those who opposed the declaration that all men are created equal 'turned tail' and run." Although *Webster* defines the identical phrase: "to run away: flee." the Bostonians took exception to this crude figure of speech. Lincoln learned of their resentment and told one of his secretaries, Noah Brooks: "Some very nice Boston folks, I am grieved to hear, were very much outraged by that phrase which they thought improper. So I resolved to make no more impromptu speeches if I could help it."

14. July 2, 1913 / *46.* July 11, 1863 / *27.* July 8, 1863, *109.* No. 1056

It is to be regretted that censure is more apt to receive attention than praise, or as Milton put it: "Evil news rides post, while good news baits" (halts). The two or three politically biased reports of Lincoln's Gettysburg address have been played up out of all proportion to their importance, and they have received more attention by the press than the innumerable complimentary notices. That is true even today.

The Chicago *Times* of November 23, 1863, comments: "Is Mr. Lincoln less refined than a savage! But aside from the ignorant rudeness manifest in the President's exhibition of Daedalism at Gettysburg and which was an insult at least to the memory of part of the dead . . . it was a perversion of history so flagrant that the most extended charity cannot view it otherwise than willful." The *Times* editor also expressed himself in this language: "The cheek of every American must tingle with shame as he reads the silly flat and dishwattery remarks of the man who has to be pointed out as the President of the United States."

The faraway London *Times* published this opinion of the American correspondent: "The ceremony was rendered ludicrous by some of the sallies of that poor President Lincoln. Anything more dull and commonplace it would not be easy to produce."

The nearby *Patriot and Union* of Harrisburg, Pennsylvania, made this comment on the address: "The President succeeded on this occasion because he acted without sense and without constraint in a panorama that was gotten up more for the benefit of his party than for the glory of the nation and honor of the dead . . . we pass over the silly remarks of the President: for the credit of the nation we are willing that the veil of oblivion shall be dropped over them and that they shall no more be repeated or thought of."

There were two papers in Gettysburg, the Adams *Sentinel*, Robert G. Harper, Editor and Publisher, and *The Compiler*, H. J. Stahle, Editor and Publisher. The former supported the administration and the latter was termed a copperhead sheet, whose edi-

18. p. 242 / 48. Nov. 23, 1863 / 136. III, 49, 58 / 85. Nov. 21, 1863

tor had been arrested at the close of the Gettysburg battle for allegedly aiding the enemy in revealing obscure locations of Union soldiers. While Mr. Stahle did not directly condemn Mr. Lincoln at the time of the dedication, he did make this comment on the annual message of the President a few weeks later:

"History is full of examples of ambitious schemers, cut down in the very hour of their pride and the apparent fruition of their selfish calculations. We look to that Power whose hand is apparent in the fast hastening events of the present day, to baffle the projects and confound the cold blooded calculations of the man who, in the President's chair, has thus forgotten in an hour like this, his obligations to the country, and to the cause of constitutional liberty."

The closeness of Gettysburg to the Mason and Dixon's line was noted by Mr. Seward in his address. The state of Maryland formed the southern boundary of Adams County, which contributed to making the environs of Gettysburg, the county seat, nominally Democratic. In the national election of 1864, the county gave McClellan a majority over Lincoln by 2886 to 2362. However, the town of Gettysburg cast 259 votes for Lincoln and 178 for McClellan.

79. July 1, 1963 / 76. Dec. 28, 1863 / 2. Nov. 7, 1864

CHAPTER 16

Preliminary Holographs

THERE ARE five known transcripts of the freedom speech, all in the handwriting of the President, usually identified by the names of those who received them from Mr. Lincoln: John Hay, John G. Nicolay, Edward Everett, George Bancroft, and Alexander Bliss of Baltimore. The appraised total value of these writings is half a million dollars. For their monetary value alone, they are among the most prized of our American manuscripts. Inasmuch as the estate of Abraham Lincoln never realized a penny from their distribution, there is widespread interest in their history and final disposition.

According to Secretary Brooks, several trial sheets were written by the President as the address began to take form. One complete copy and two fragments, usually considered as a single manuscript, are extant. These are termed preliminary holographs, as they were written before the delivery of the speech and are known as the John Hay and the John G. Nicolay copies. After Lincoln's inauguration in 1861, the very first commission which the Chief Executive signed, made John Nicolay his private secretary. Hay was assigned to duties at the executive mansion and became the assistant private secretary. Nicolay was Hay's senior by six years. Both came from Illinois and remained with the President until his

109. No. 1128

death. There were others who served as assistant secretaries for Mr. Lincoln at different intervals.

Nearly every opinion expressed about either the Hay or the Nicolay also, invites controversy: These primary questions still bother the inquirer; where were they written?—and when were they written?—There is no prospect that all the conclusions drawn about either of them, will be unanimously accepted. It is doubtful that many critics are satisfied with their own deductions, once they are put into print. A facsimile of the Nicolay copy did not appear until thirty years after the address was written, and it was forty-five years before the Hay holograph was published.

Miss Bell F. Keyes of Boston, wrote to Robert Lincoln on December 16, 1885, making some inquiries about the Everett copy of the President's speech then in her possession. Robert replied: "I do not know of any other autograph copy or what became of the pencil notes. They were probably used in delivering the address and then destroyed, but as to this I have no knowledge." This letter from Miss Keyes aroused Robert's curiosity about the possibility of the penciled notes still being preserved, and he wrote to John Hay about them which brought this reply on April 12, 1888: "I own a few of your father's mms. which he gave me from time to time. As long as you and I live I take it for granted that you will not suspect me of boning them. But to guard against casualties hereafter, I have asked Nicolay to write you a line saying that I have never had in my possession or custody any of the papers which you intrusted to him. I have handed over to Nicolay to be placed among your papers some of these your father gave me. The rest which are few in number, are very precious to me. I shall try to make an heirloom in my family as long as any one of my blood exists with money enough to buy a breakfast."

Hay made good progress in this direction as at the time of his death, he was in possession, among other Lincoln treasures, of two copies of the Gettysburg Address, the Second Inaugural

---

30. pp. 394, 395, *31.* p. 286, *1.* IV, 271 / *109.* No. 1473 / *55.* Feb. 22, 1950, *88.* II, 245, 246

original manuscript, and Lincoln's, "Memorandum, Concerning His Probable Failure of Re-election." This last paper, dated August 23, 1864, containing his signature and those of all the members of the cabinet, is from the point of view of the autograph collector, an extremely valuable document.

There is an interesting story connected with this last writing. On the day before Christmas in 1908, three years after her husband passed away, Mrs. John Hay wrote to the daughter of the deceased John Nicolay: "As I think you have been cheated out of your share of the Lincoln manuscripts, I want you to accept this one (The August 23, 1864 Memorandum) from me with best wishes of the Holiday season." However, Mrs. Hay requested: "If when you will want it no more you would like to bequeath it to my children, you may do so—but it is your very own till then."

HAY'S CORRECTED WRITING (See endsheet A.)

The first direct reference to John Hay's copy of the address is found in his letter to Richard Watson Gilder, written on January 26, 1891. "Lincoln's Gettysburg speech cannot be considered in any sense an extemporaneous effort. It was not only carefully considered but was reduced to writing before delivered and very little changed in the subsequent issue." Hay knew of but two copies, his own and the "subsequent issue,"—the Bliss-Baltimore copy—published in facsimile, by Nicolay and Hay in their 1890 *History*. Hay's observations about his copy's being "very little changed" in its final form, as it appeared in the Baltimore version, is not only correct, but significant as well.

William Eleroy Curtis, in his *Abraham Lincoln* published in 1902, makes this affirmation emenating from a personal interview: "Col. Hay says he (Lincoln) wrote out a brief speech at the White House before leaving Washington and as usual on such occasions committed it to memory, but the inspiration of the scene led to changes." Hay had no knowledge at this time of the copy in

---

109. Nos. 1437, 1438, *1.* VII, 514 / *109.* No. 1438 / *88.* II, 214, *142.* VIII, 200, 201

possession of John Nicolay, so the changes were noted when he compared his own with the Baltimore copy.

The original manuscript presented to Mr. Hay is the only one of the five writings which contains several corrections to improve the diction. It was written on foolscap, and has every appearance of being a working copy. There is one word, "gave," thoughtlessly written twice in succession, which is deleted. In two places, a caret is used placing the words "poor" and "work" above the line. There are five unimportant monosyllables: "are," "met," "the," "of," "the" crossed out and replaced by "have," "come," "a," "for," "that," respectively. Practically all of these corrections are adopted in later copies and also in the oral presentation as recorded by the press reporters.

The public's first opportunity to view the contents of this version in facsimile was during the centennial of Lincoln's birth in February, 1909, when it was reproduced in *Putnam's Magazine*. The accompanying article was written by James Grant Wilson, a friend of the President, who provided this descriptive line for the illustration: "Facsimile of Abraham Lincoln's first copy of the Gettysburg Address *as actually delivered*, made for John Hay on the President's return from the dedicatory exercises, and now for the first time photographed and engraved."

This statement contradicted the Hay letter to Gilder in two or three instances, and made some assumptions that cannot be supported. The affirmation "as actually delivered" is placed in italics. However, Hay specifically states there were variations. The time of the writing is placed after, instead of before, its delivery, which is in error. Hay affirms that it was written in preparation for the address Wilson alleges that it was written afterwards, at the request of Mr. Hay. These discrepancies must have been called to Wilson's attention, as he contributed to the New York *Times* on June 29, 1913, the statement: "The first two (Hay and Nicolay) he prepared in the White House before going to Gettysburg and afterwards gave one to Nicolay and one to Hay."

60. p. 88 / See end sheet A / *161*. Feb. 1909

This acknowledgement reversed his former statement with reference to the time the Hay address was written. Wilson introduced another tradition for which he gives no authority, but there is available no positive evidence to disprove it. He affirms that upon leaving Washington, the President inadvertently left the Hay copy at the executive mansion. Upon his return, it was found and presented to Hay.

The author of a Gettysburg book, Orton H. Carmichael, inquired of Clarence Hay, son of the deceased Secretary of State, about the origin of his father's copy of the address and received this reply: "I have spoken with Miss Nicolay and Robert Lincoln and it is fairly certain, that the copy was made after Mr. Lincoln's return from Gettysburg." Regardless of these affirmations, they are in disagreement with John Hay's own statement that the address was "reduced to writing, before it was delivered." Apparently at this time Robert Lincoln was under the impression that the manuscript was written out at the request of Hay and presented to him. Later on, Mr. Carmichael stated that both the Hay and Nicolay copies "were given by Lincoln to John Hay." According to Henry Cabot Lodge, Hay was in possession of still a third copy, "on slips of small note paper size, written he would say, in pencil," which Lodge saw Hay present to Theodore Roosevelt at the White House, on March 4, 1905, just before leaving for the inaugural. Lodge later concluded he might have been mistaken, as the Roosevelt family was unable to find it.

NICOLAY'S DELETED FRAGMENTS

The earliest significant contribution which John Nicolay made to the printed story of Abraham Lincoln, was a biographical sketch prepared in 1882, for the ninth edition of the Encyclopaedia Britannica. He mentioned the dedication at Gettysburg and wrote: "President Lincoln made the following oration which has taken permanent place as a classic in American literature." Then followed the Bliss, or Baltimore version of the address.

138. June 29, 1913 / *36.* p. 91, 128. p. 14 / *69.* XVI, 703–712

The editor of the *Century Magazine* received a letter from David Wills of Gettysburg, dated September 10, 1885, inquiring if an article on Abraham Lincoln, writing his address at the Wills' home the night before the dedication, would be of interest. The letter was sent immediately to John Nicolay who advised Gilder that Mr. Wills had little new to offer, and commented: "It is true that Mr. Lincoln wrote the Gettysburg Address (but in part only) in his house. The original manuscript is now before my eyes." As far as we know, this is the first evidence, but of a confidential nature, that a preliminary copy of the address had been preserved.

Nicolay and Hay began their month by month "History of Abraham Lincoln" in the November, 1886 issue of the *Century Magazine*, and the last installment appeared in February, 1890. This long series of articles was prepared to serve as an introduction to their ten-volume, *Abraham Lincoln: A History*, which came from the press after the conclusion of the magazine series. While they were working on the *History*, Hay wrote, chiding Nicolay for giving a whole chapter to "The Gettysburg Address," stating that he had thought of "tacking Lincoln's speech on to the end of the battle chapter." Whether or not Nicolay intended to tell his story of the writing of the address at this time is not known, but if he did, the rebuff of Hay changed his mind. He allowed the chapter caption to stand, however, and used eleven of his thirteen pages to review Everett's oration, reserving but two pages for Lincoln's address. No mention was made of Nicolay's own copy, but the Baltimore holograph was reproduced in facsimile.

Upon completion of their ten-volume *History*, Nicolay and Hay brought out in 1894, a two-volume publication entitled, *Abraham Lincoln: Complete Works*. Strangely, this did not contain either the Hay or Nicolay version. Instead, the authors deliberately continued to use a facsimile of the Baltimore copy. To give this new enterprise some publicity, Nicolay prepared a monograph for the February, 1894 issue of *Century Magazine* entitled, "The

41. Sept. 10, 1885 / 41. Nov. 1886, *181*. II, 33–36

Gettysburg Address," using the same caption appearing in the *History* chapter. It was illustrated by a facsimile copy of the two Nicolay fragments of the address with this descriptive line: "The original autograph MS. draft, written by Mr. Lincoln partly at Washington and partly at Gettysburg."

This article has become the primary source of information for students writing about the address. Nicolay made no comment about having personally observed its preparation in Washington, but clearly implies that his information about the composition at the executive mansion, came from a statement made by James Speed, several years after the address was delivered. Speed first is reported to have said in an interview: "He wrote it before he left Washington and finished it up after arriving at Gettysburg." A second version was: "The day before he left Washington he found time to write about half of his speech."

Nicolay, still ignorant of the copy in possession of Hay, assumed that Speed was making reference to the two sheets, one in ink and another in pencil, which were in his custody. He built his *Century Magazine* story around the writing of the pencil fragment at Gettysburg: "Mr. Lincoln carried in his pocket the autographed copy of so much of his address as he had written the day before. . . . It fills one page of letter-paper at that time habitually used in the executive mansion. . . . It concludes with the statement: 'It is rather for us the living etc.' " Nicolay then observed: "From the fact that this sentence is incomplete, we may infer that at the time of writing it in Washington, the remainder of the sentence was written in ink on another piece of paper." This was a reasonable deduction but it furthermore conceded a finished ink copy was written in Washington as "the remainder of the sentence," actually completed the address.

The page in ink appears to have started out as a final transcript. It is written on executive mansion stationery with meticulous care, without a correction in it, as if it were copied from another manuscript. All the changes which Lincoln had made in the

143. II, 439, *41*. Feb. 1894 / *136*. II, 51 / End Sheets B, *41*. Feb. 1894

original Hay copy, were adopted without a single exception. He also made other grammatical improvements. The capital "L" in Liberty was put in lower case, and the phrase, all men are created equal, was placed in quotations. He removed the word "here" after "we are met." Two or three other phrases in the Hay copy were shortened. Lincoln also made a much better paragraph division than was used in the Hay copy, starting the third paragraph at the place where the thought changes: "It is rather for us, the living. . . ."

Already it has been noted that Lincoln did not appear to be satisfied with his effort, informing Brooks in Washington, that it was written "but not finished." Also he told Seward on the way to the dedication that he was not pleased with it. He had corrected a redundance, when he changed the second "We are met" to "We have come." There is evidence that he was again trying to avoid redundance in the use of "It is for us, the living, rather to be dedicated," appearing in consecutive sentences. Precisely at this point, he began a new sheet written in pencil, and encountered some difficulty with the transition. In joining the ink and pencil copies he left out this entire sentence: "It is, for us, the living, rather to be dedicated here to the unfinished work which they have thus far so nobly advanced." Apparently he united the ink and pencil copies at the wrong place. At best, the Hay copy wound up as two separate fragments of a deleted manuscript.

David Wills had Lincoln writing for more than an hour on the address Wednesday night; and Nicolay states that on Thursday morning, the time spent in completing the task, covered another hour. All there is to show for this labor is ten lines in pencil, minus three lines of omitted copy, or a net gain of seven lines. Certainly he would not have turned over to Gilbert, of the Associated Press, the fragmentary Nicolay copy. There may have been a complete transcript made that was handed to the reporters and, as it passed among them, became lost. If so, his secretary did not know of it.

One reaction to the basic article in the *Century Magazine*, was a

41. Feb. 1894 / End Shets B / *136*. II, 49, *41*. Feb. 1894

query from James Grant Wilson which caused Nicolay to reply on July 19, 1895: "The original Gettysburg is in my custody." On April 7, 1900, in answer to another letter from Mr. Wilson with respect to the Second Inaugural Address, Nicolay wrote: "Col. Hay possesses the original manuscript and I have the Gettysburg Address." John Nicolay passed away seventeen months later on September 27, 1901. It is doubtful that he knew—at anytime—that John Hay was in possession of a copy of the speech.

Helen Nicolay received a letter from Mr. Wilson dated October 31, 1908, in which he inquired: "Who is the fortunate possessor of the precious original manuscript of the Gettysburg Address at present, I understand in your keeping?" Miss Nicolay replied: "I very much wish I could answer your question. . . . It was given by Mr. Lincoln to my father and should now belong to me as his heir." About a week later, she received a letter from Robert Lincoln, also asking where the address might be located. Miss Nicolay replied: "As you are aware, the Lincoln MMS. were in my father's custody at the time of his death. As soon as possible thereafter I turned them over to Sec. Hay to be restored to you. . . . Mr. Hay told me shortly after the transfer was made— that your father gave my father the original MS. of the Gettysburg Address—and that it was therefore his private property." Miss Nicolay, later on, feared she might have misunderstood Mr. Hay.

Robert again wrote to Miss Nicolay stating that he presumed the address had been given to her father and also commented: "I did not wish of course in any way to obtain it for myself, but I thought it might be an interesting object in the temporary exhibition which is to be made in New York City." At a later date, he wrote: "I am told that the paper is certainly not among those which came to me from the state department." Mr. Hay was Secretary of State from 1898, until the time of his death in 1905. It is doubtful that during Secretary Hay's lifetime, Robert Lincoln ever knew that a copy of the Gettysburg manuscript was in his

109. No. 1438 / 109. Nos. 1437, 1438

possession. Robert would have been just as anxious to borrow it, as he was the Nicolay copy for the centennial exhibit in New York had he known one was in the Hay family.

When Miss Nicolay discovered the letter to Wilson, in which her father stated that the Gettysburg Address was in "his custody," she expressed a doubt that it had been his personal property. However, the search for it, actually, was never abandoned. It was not until 1916, when Miss Nicolay and Mrs. Wardsworth, Mr. Hay's daughter, were leafing through the late John Hay's papers, that the Nicolay copy of the Gettysburg Address—missing for the fifteen years since her father's death eventually came to light. The Hay and Nicolay copies were found bound together in a volume of John Hay's rare manuscripts. Hay must have secured the Nicolay copy sometime between April 7, 1900, when Nicolay last mentioned it was in his possession, and the date of his own death in 1905.

The discovery of these two copies of the address, as well as the Second Inaugural which was endorsed in Lincoln's hand: "Original manuscript of second Inaugeral presented to Major John Hay. A. Lincoln, April 10, 1865," prompted the Hay children to give them to the Library of Congress on April 11, 1916. Miss Nicolay also made a gift to the Library of the Lincoln memorandum which had come to her from Mrs. Hay. This caused Herbert Putnam, the librarian, to write to Miss Nicolay: "Your presentation . . . coincident with the presentation by Mr. Hay and his sisters, of the two drafts of the Gettysburg Address and the original draft of the second inaugural, groups into one occasion . . . the most precious individual documents that have been entrusted to me since I took office seventeen years ago."

109. Nos. 1437, 1438 / ibid / *161*. Feb. 1909, *109*. No. 1438

CHAPTER 17

Subsequent Holographs

ONLY ONE of the three remaining copies of the Gettysburg Address which were written out by request several weeks after the President's return from the dedication, is of special historical importance. The first of these subsequent holographs is of some interest because of its association with Edward Everett. The second one, although prepared for George Bancroft, contributes little to a study of the context. But the last one which came into the hands of Alexander Bliss, and often called the Bliss-Baltimore version is by far the most significant of all five transcriptions.

The day before the President started for Gettysburg, he presented to Attorney General Edward Bates, an elastic pen holder. Upon reaching his desk, after trying out the new instrument, Bates wrote a note of thanks stating, that it "fitted" his "rough hand exactly." He reciprocated by sending Mr. Lincoln a pen of historical significance made from a quill of a bald eagle. It had been presented to Mr. Bates in 1860, by Lieutenant J. E. B. Stuart who became the Confederate General Jeb Stuart, of Gettysburg prominence. The attorney general expressed the hope: "That you may find occasion to use it, during your present term in signing your name to some historic document." If the

109. No. 1128

President penned with it the Bliss-Baltimore copy of the Gettysburg Address, Mr. Blair would have had his wish fulfilled.

Shortly before the President was invited to make the address at the dedication, it was requested that he present the final Emancipation Proclamation to the Sanitary Fair in Chicago. Isaac N. Arnold followed the request with this telegram: "I am desired by the ladies . . . to remind you of it, & beg you will send the original proclamation of freedom if possible." Lincoln replied on October 26: "I had some desire to retain the paper; but if it shall contribute to the relief or comfort of the soldiers that will be better." The original copy of his epochal Thanksgiving Proclamation of October 3, is not known to exist, and there is evidence that it, too, was solicited for a sanitary fair.

With other historical manuscripts badgered away from him, one would assume he would like to have kept a copy of his remarks to preserve along with the complimentary letter from Everett. However, just four days after the Gettysburg program, David Wills sent to the President this blunt and demanding requisition: "On behalf of the states interested in the National Cemetery here, I request of you the original manuscript of the Dedicatory Remarks delivered by you here last Thursday. We desire them to be placed with correspondence and other papers connected with the project. (Please append your certificate to them.)" No statement was made that it was wanted for any purpose other than filing. The President had but two copies, the Hay trial writing with the many corrections, and the fragmentary Nicolay transcript, neither of which was suitable for presentation. There is no evidence that Mr. Lincoln granted this request of Mr. Wills, but considerable information exists to prove that no copy was forwarded.

On September 10, 1885, Wills wrote to Gilder: "I have a facsimile of the copy of the speech which he afterwards made." Upon seeing Wills' letter, Nicolay wrote to Gilder: "The copy

111. Wells to Lincoln, Nov. 17, 1863 / *1.* VI, 540, 539 / *111.* Wells to Lincoln, Nov. 23, 1863

which Mr. Wills has is one of several of the revision which Mr. Lincoln made after his return to Washington." Later, Major Lambert received a letter from Mr. Wills which admitted: "I did not make a copy of my report of President Lincoln's speech at Gettysburg from a transcript from the original, but from one of the press reports. I have since always used the revised copy furnished the Baltimore fair, of which I have a facsimile." While Mr. Wills makes it quite clear that he had never had an original copy of the address, there has been a vigorous search made for what has been known as the "Lost Copy." An all-out attempt to discover any such hidden treasure was made by the Blumhaven Library of Philadelphia, which offered $5,000, "to any person who will produce the document for unrestricted examination." The offer expired on December 31, 1953, with the premium unclaimed.

When John Nicolay and David Wills were engaged in controversy over the writing of the address at the Wills' home, Nicolay made this interesting observation: "My twenty years experience of somewhat minute examination and criticism of war history, has deeply impressed upon me the conviction how liable we all are to error in our recollections of detailed incidences which occurred thirty years ago." At the time Nicolay prepared his basic Gettysburg article for *Century Magazine* in 1894, coincidently, it had been just thirty years since the dedication and its aftermath. Yet, the "detailed incidences" he recalled have gone unchallenged, primarily because he was the President's secretary. One of Nicolay's several statements which lack supporting evidence, is the time element in the President's preparation for the revision, brought about by Mr. Wills' appeal.

According to Mr. Nicolay: "To comply with his (Mr. Wills') request, the President re-examined his original draft, and the version which had appeared in the newspapers, and saw that, because of variations between them, the first seemed incomplete and the others imperfect. By his direction, therefore, his secre-

109. No. 1436, *151*. October, 1909 / *109*. No. 1437, *109*. No. 1436

taries made copies of the Associated Press report as it was printed in several prominent papers. Comparing these with his original draft, and with his own fresh recollections of the form in which he delivered it, he made a new autograph copy.—A careful and deliberate revision, which has become the standard and authentic text." In this statement, Nicolay again refers to the fragmentary copy in his possession as the original draft—with no mention of the Hay transcript.

Mr. Wills' letter, written on November 23, probably was not in the hands of Mr. Lincoln before November 25. It will be recalled that when the President reached Washington, early on the morning of November 20, he was ill and grew steadily worse, on November 25, his minimum daily correspondence stopped altogether. From then, until December 2, there is no record of any of his writings published in the *Collected Works*. However, this brief note has been discovered dated November 27, 1863: "Hon. Secy. of State, I am improving but I cannot meet the cabinet today. A. Lincoln." Incapacitated for much writing, and avoiding conferences, when the Wills' letter arrived, he would not have delegated his secretaries to undertake the relatively unimportant task of gathering data, as Nicolay says he did. After December 2, all the time available would be needed by the President to prepare his message to Congress for presentation on December 8.

EVERETT'S REVISED MANUSCRIPT (See endsheet C.)

We shall have to look for some other occasion when need for revision of the address seems to be more urgent. On January 30, 1864, Edward Everett wrote to the President: "I have promised to give the Manuscript of my address to Mrs. Governor (Hamilton) Fish of New York, who is the head of the Ladies Committee of the Metropolitan fair. It would add very greatly to its value, if I could bind up with it the manuscript of your dedication Remarks, if you happen to have preserved them." At the same time this letter was sent, Mr. Everett forwarded to Mr. Lincoln by express, a printed

41. Feb. 1894 / *136.* IV, 41

copy of the proceedings of the dedicatory exercises at Gettysburg published by Little, Brown, and Company of Boston, which appeared "owing to unavoidable delays only yesterday."

About the same time the request came from Everett, Julia K. Fish, by order of the board of the fair, wrote this letter to the President: "The managers of the Metropolitan Fair about to be held in New York for the benefit of the sick and wounded of the army and navy of the United States respectively: ask that your excellency will bestow upon them the manuscript of the Gettysburg Address. Those noble words spoken at the grave yard of the heroes of the memorable days of July, will be ever precious to the soldiers and citizens of this country. The managers trust that your Excellency will think the Metropolitan Fair worthy of being entrusted with his valuable document for the benefit of those who have suffered in the service of their country."

Here were two simultaneous appeals which could not be laid aside. They prompted the President to make the revision which Nicolay mentions in the *Century* article, but fully six weeks later than the original date he recalled. Upon receiving from Everett the Little-Brown publication, containing both Mr. Everett's oration and his own remarks at the dedication. Mr. Lincoln would have immediately checked the report of what he said. For the sake of continuity, at least, he would not depart from it to any marked degree. There was also available for checking, the original copies he had made, and his own good memory.

In comparing the Associated Press report of the speech published in the Little-Brown brochure, without considering punctuation marks, these corrections were made in the copy prepared for Mr. Everett: "are met" to "have come," "of it" to "that field," "the" to "a," "power" to "poor power," "that" to "which," "carried on" to "nobly advanced," "the" to "this," "shall, under God, have" to "under God, shall have," respectively. There are fewer variations between the corrected Hay copy and the Everett transcript: "are met here" to "are met," "carried on" to "advanced," "nation

---

1. VII, 168, *171* / *111.* Fish to Lincoln, Feb. 1864 / *41.* Feb. 1894

Photo by Brown Brothers

Early drawing with Evergreen Cemetery gatehouse and Everett's tent in background

Photo by Fredrick Tilberg

Gettysburg Speech Memorial near south entrance to Soldiers' National Cemetery

BLISS STANDARD VERSION

An act of Congress approved February 11, 1895, directed the secretary of war: "To cause a suitable bronze tablet, containing on it the address delivered November 19, 1863 . . ." to be erected at Gettysburg. Robert S. Olliver, assistant secretary, selected the Bliss or Baltimore copy to become: "The standard version of the Lincoln Gettysburg Address," for use on all tablets in national cemeteries and parks.

> Address delivered at the dedication of the Cemetery at Gettysburg.
>
> Four score and seven years ago our fathers brought forth on this continent, a new nation, conceived in Liberty, and dedicated to the proposition that all men are created equal.
>
> Now we are engaged in a great civil war, testing whether that nation, or any nation so conceived and so dedicated, can long endure. We are met on a great battle-field of that war. We have come to dedicate a portion of that field, as a final resting place for those who here gave their lives that that nation might live. It is altogether fitting and proper that we should do this.
>
> But, in a larger sense, we can not dedi=

Page one

cate — we can not consecrate — we can not hallow — this ground. The brave men, living and dead, who struggled here, have consecrated it, far above our poor power to add or detract. The world will little note, nor long remember what we say here, but it can never forget what they did here. It is for us the living, rather, to be dedicated here to the unfinished work which they who fought here have thus far so nobly advanced. It is rather for us to be here dedicated to the great task remaining before us — that from these honored dead we take increased devotion to that cause for which they gave the last full measure of devotion — that we here highly resolve that these dead shall not have died in vain — that this nation, under God, shall have a new birth of freedom — and that government of the people,

by the people, for the people, shall not perish from the earth.

Abraham Lincoln.

November 19, 1863.

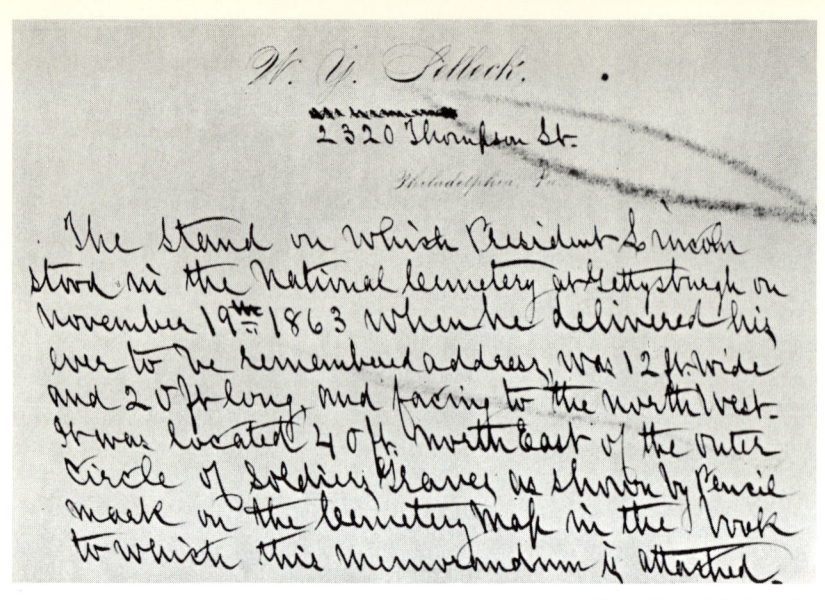

Lincoln National Life Foundation

Memorandum by W. Y. Selleck, secretary of Soldiers' National Cemetery Commission. See marked plat below.

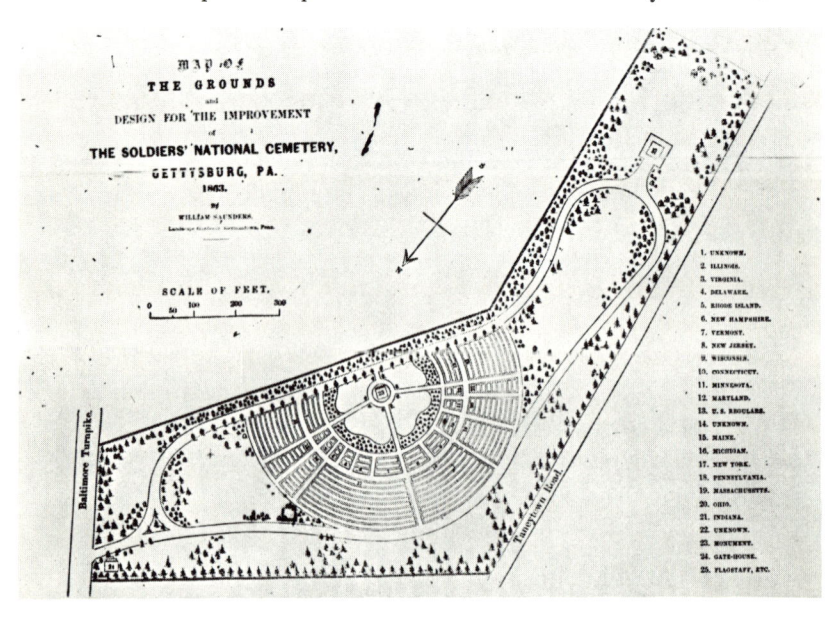

Published in printed report of Soldiers' National Cemetery Commission

shall have" to "nation, under God, shall have," "that government" to "that this government." Mr. Everett had made some corrections in his address before printing, and he called the copy used in the Little-Brown publication the "Authorized Edition." Lincoln would have had no scruples in making the slight changes in the wording of his few simple sentences.

This letter was written to Mr. Everett on February 4: "Yours of Jan. 30th, was received four days ago; and since then the address mentioned has arrived. Thank you for it. I send herewith the manuscript of my remarks at Gettysburg, which, with my note to you of Nov. 20th. you are at liberty to use for the benefit of our soldiers as you have requested."

Mr. Everett acknowledged the President's letter on March 3 in these words: "I have this day received your letter of the fourth of February kindly transmitting the manuscript of your remarks at Gettysburg and also complying with my request relative to your obliging letter of the 20th of November. I feel very sensible your goodness in having found time amidst your necessary occupations and cares to attend so small a matter."

The purchaser of the manuscript for $1,000 at the Metropolitan Fair, was Carlos Pierce of Boston. In 1875, it was in possession of his wife. We have already noted that ten years later, it became the property of Mrs. Pierce's relatives, the Keyes family of Boston, as revealed in Bell F. Keyes correspondence with Robert Lincoln. Honorable Henry W. Keyes, Senator from New Hampshire, on February 12, 1920, read the Gettysburg Address from the original manuscript before the United States Senate. It was acquired from the Keyes family by autograph dealer Thomas A. Madigan, in February, 1930, and later sold to a Chicagoan for $150,000. While in his possession, at the request of his friend, Charles B. Pike, it was placed on exhibition at the Chicago Historical Society in February, 1935. On October 12, 1943, a campaign was inaugurated to raise $60,000 in pennies from Illinois school

---

1. VII, 167, 168, See End Sheet C, *3.* pp. 1–87 / *1.* VII, 167, 168 / *111.* Everett to Lincoln, Mar. 3, 1864

children for their part in purchasing the document. The amount was raised by March 21, 1944, and on that date a check for $60,000 was deposited with the Harris Trust and Savings Bank of Chicago, on consummation of the purchase. The following day it was received by the Illinois State Historical Library for permanent custody. The children of Illinois were aided in the purchase by a substantial gift from Marshall Field.

The February, 1962 issue of *Hobbies Magazine* contained a contribution by Foster Cannon of Washington, in which he states that the Everett copy was written in the Wills' house prior to the dedication, and was the identical transcript from which he read. Internal evidence appears to refute the claim.

BANCROFT'S HOLOGRAPH COPY (See endsheet D.)

It is a strange coincidence that on the same day, November 18, 1861, Abraham Lincoln should be answering correspondence from both Edward Everett and George Bancroft, and now in the month of February, 1864, should be sending to the very same men, copies of his Gettysburg Address. The closing paragraph in Bancroft's letter contained this word of encouragement: "Your administration has fallen upon times, which will be remembered as long as human events find a record. I certainly wish you the glory of perfect success."

George Bancroft, like Everett, was from Massachusetts, educated at Exeter, and was graduated from Harvard in 1817. He spent five years in European Universities and returned to Harvard, where, like Everett, he became a tutor of Greek. In 1834, he published volume number one of his exhaustive *History of the United States*. Entering politics, he became collector of the Port of Boston, Secretary of the Navy under President Polk, was instrumental in establishing the Naval Academy at Annapolis, and ordered the taking possession of fabulous California. From 1846 to 1849, he served as United States Minister to Great Britain, later, to Prussia, and then to Germany. Aside from the

138. Feb. 12, 1930, *136.* IV, 52–62 / *90.* Feb. 1962 / *1.* V, 25, 26

twelve-volume history begun in 1834, he was the author of many historical manuscripts. He was selected by Congress to give the "Memorial Address on the Life and Character of Abraham Lincoln," delivered before a joint assembly on February 12, 1866.

Bancroft's request for a copy of the Gettysburg Address probably was made verbally, as no correspondence from him with respect to it has been discovered. He made the appeal on behalf of the committee for the Maryland Soldiers' and Sailors' Fair to be held at Baltimore. On February 29, 1864, Lincoln forwarded the writing with this brief note: "Herewith is the copy of the manuscript which you did me the honor to request." It can be understood why Lincoln would consider this entreaty an honor, coming, as it did, from such a distinguished American.

Besides Lincoln's remarkable memory, it was probably the Hay copy he used in preparing the Bancroft version. Even so, it is almost identical with the Everett copy. Only one word was changed and this was in the very first sentence, where "upon" became "on" preceded by a comma. The other changes were in the removal of commas, one after "it" following the words "have consecrated it," another was dropped after "remember," and three in the clause beginning "who fought here" after the words "here," "have," and "far,".

It is generally assumed that being written on both sides of a single sheet of paper, was responsible for the address not measuring up to requirements for inclusion in a contemplated book; such was not the case. Other deficiencies made it unusable, but Mr. Bancroft was allowed to retain the copy. Upon his death in 1891, it passed on to his son, John C. Bancroft. The executors of the estate, Professor Wilbur D. Bancroft of Cornell University, and William Lowell Putnam of Boston, permitted photographed copies to be made for the Library of Congress. By April 18, 1935, it was acquired by Thomas F. Madigan, autograph dealer, and later came into the possession of Mrs. Nicholas H. Noyes of Indianapolis. She presented it, with other documents, in 1940 to

10. I, 154–156 / 1. VII, 212 / 1. VII, 21, 22

Cornell University, of which her husband was a graduate and trustee.

BLISS' STANDARD VERSION (See facsimile opposite page 164.

The most important holograph of the Lincoln speech which has been preserved, is known as the Bliss version so named for Alexander Bliss of Baltimore who came into possession of it. John Pendleton Kennedy, an active member of a committee selecting writings for publication in *Autograph Leaves of our Country's Authors*, wrote to the President on March 4, explaining that the copy replacing the one sent by Bancroft should have a title, date, and signature of the author. It will always be regretted, that in complying with this request, Mr. Lincoln did not at that time choose an appropriate heading embodying the nativity theme he employed—the theme with its striking "new birth" climax. If the epochal pronouncement in 1776 had been called the Philadelphia Declaration instead of the The Declaration of Independence, its inspirational value would have been impaired both then and now. Appearing under a title which featured a small Pennsylvania town, an early appreciation of Lincoln's Freedom Declaration was greatly delayed. Today, considering its tremendous impact on world civilization, the caption is even more inappropriate; Mr. Lincoln's final transcript, written on three sheets of paper, follows:

> Address delivered at the dedication of the Cemetery at Gettysburg.
>
> Four score and seven years ago our fathers brought forth on this continent, a new nation, conceived in Liberty, and dedicated to the proposition that all men are created equal.
>
> Now we are engaged in a great civil war, testing whether that nation, or any nation so conceived or so dedicated, can long endure. We are met on a great battle-field of that war. We have come to dedicate a portion of that field, as a final resting place for those who here gave their lives that that nation might live. It is altogether fitting and proper that we should do this.

1. VII, 22, *129.* p. 27, *109.* pp. 65, 66 / *15.* pp. 3–5 / *1.* VII, 22, *15.* pp. 3–5 / ibid

But, in a larger sense, we cannot dedicate—we cannot consecrate—we cannot hallow—this ground. The brave men, living and dead, who struggled here, have consecrated it, far above our poor power to add or detract. The world will little note, nor long remember what we say here, but it can never forget what they did here. It is for us the living, rather, to be dedicated here to the unfinished work which they who fought here have thus far so nobly advanced. It is rather for us to be here dedicated to the great task remaining before us—that from these honored dead we take increased devotion to that cause for which they gave the last full measure of devotion—that we highly resolve that these dead shall not have died in vain—that this nation, under God, shall have a new birth of freedom—and that government of the people, by the people, for the people, shall not perish from the earth.

Abraham Lincoln

November 19, 1863

No forwarding letter has been discovered, but Secretary Nicolay states that it was sent "to the committee on March 11, 1864." The President took more pains with his handwriting than in the former copy and did not crowd his words at the end of the lines, as he often did. Although there are six more lines than he used in the previous writing, the wordage is identical except for one omission, "here" in the clause "they here gave the last full measure." Two commas were dropped, one after "conceived," the other after "lives." A comma was added after the close of the expression, "have consecrated it." Excepting the inclusion of the words, "under God," there was no significant change made from the time Lincoln corrected his working copy given to John Hay, and its final composition as presented above.

A contributor to *Nation Magazine* in 1889, observed: "What promises to be the most classic and most enduring of American orations ought to be as carefully preserved without alteration or abridgement as a standard of weight and measure." An act of Congress in 1895, made it necessary to cite an exact wording of the address. Robert Lincoln submitted this statement for the consideration of the committee: "The Baltimore fair version repre-

15. pp. 3–5 / ibid

sents my father's last and best thought as to the address and the corrections in it were legitimate for an author, and I think there is no doubt they improve upon the version as written out for Col. Hay." Secretary Oliver was given final jurisdiction in the controversy. He favored the last copy the President is known to have made. The Bliss-Baltimore copy was thereby made "the standard version" of the address for use on, "all tablets to be erected in national cemeteries and parks."

After Lincoln's holograph of the Gettysburg Address—as well as other documents—had been used to make the plates for the autograph book, no buyers for the original manuscripts appeared. The writings became the property of Alexander Bliss and upon his death passed to his son, Dr. William J. A. Bliss. Later, his widow and Miss Eleanor Bliss, trustees under a deed of trustees of the late Dr. Bliss, came into possession. After more than eighty-five years in Baltimore, the manuscript was offered for sale through the Parke-Bernet auction galleries in New York on April 27, 1949. It was purchased for $54,000 by Oscar B. Cintas of Havana, Cuba, a former ambassador to the United States. Mr. Cintas, in his will, bequeathed the document to the United States of America with the understanding that it be placed in the White House, where it now reposes.

41. Feb. 1894 / *136.* IV, 72–74, *136.* IV, 80

CHAPTER 18

Increasing Respect

THE INCREASING RESPECT in which the Lincoln address is held, in both America and throughout the world, is best set forth by Lord Curzon, Earl of Kedleston, Chancellor of the University of Oxford. On November 6, 1913, he delivered an address on "Modern Parliamentary Eloquence" before the students of the University of Cambridge, in which he opened his remarks with this timely introduction: "Just as the oratory of the Georgian era was attuned to an aristocratic age and that of the Victorian epoch in the middle-class ascendancy, so does it seem to me likely that democracy will produce an eloquence, even an oratory of its own. Should a man arise from the ranks of the people, as Abraham Lincoln from the back-woods of America, a man gifted with real oratorical power, and commanding genius, I can see no reason why he should not revive in England the glories of a Chatham or a Gratton."

This comment on the brief remarks of Lincoln at Gettysburg then follows: "The Gettysburg Address is far more than a pleasing piece of occasional oratory. It is a marvelous piece of English composition. It is a pure well of English undefiled. . . . The more closely the address is analyzed the more one must confess astonishment at the choice of words, the precision of the

20. pp. 127–129

thought, its simplicity, directness and effectiveness. . . . Above all it was a declaration of America's fundamental principles. . . . The long, hard fought battle for the liberation of humanity has been a struggle for the rights and welfare of humanity."

In closing his address which surveyed the history of British parliamentary oratory, Lord Curzon said that he presumed he would be expected to select the supreme masterpiece in the field of eloquence he has been covering. "Three," he said, "are preeminent, much as the 'Funeral Oration of Pericles' was generally allowed to be the masterpiece of the ancient world. . . . The toast of William Pitt after the victory of Trafalgar and two of Lincoln's speeches: The Gettysburg Address and the Second Inaugural." Curzon then continued: "I escape the task of deciding which is the masterpiece of modern English eloquence by awarding the prize to an American."

The compilation of testimonials which follow, with the dates on which they were presented, will allow one to observe the increasing respect which the address has enjoyed.

ADAMS, CHARLES FRANCIS, 1865—The railsplitter is one of the wonders of the day. Once at Gettysburg and now on a greater occasion (Second Inaugural), he has shown his capacity for rising to the need of the hour.

ARNOLD, ISAAC N., 1866—For appropriateness, comprehension, grasp of thought, brevity, beauty, the sublime in sentiment and expression, has scarcely its equal in English or American literature.

AUSTIN, GEORGE LOWELL, 1885—He simply read the touching speech which is already placed among the classics of our language.

BOUTELL, GEORGE S., 1885—Is there any composition more certain of destiny than Lincoln's oration?

BROOKS, NOAH, 1888—Public opinion seized upon it and glorified it as one of the few masterpieces of oratory the world has received . . . these pregnant sentences have become classic, and generations yet unborn may wonder why they did not at once arouse great enthusiasm.

BROWNE, FRANCIS FISHER, 1886—The simple and sublime words

---

20. pp. 127–129 / ibid / *109*. No. 1152 / *12*. p. 423 / *21*. Aug. 1885, p. 132 / *165*. p. 132 / *30*. p. 398

shook the hearts of the listeners. Before the first sentence was ended, they were under the spell of the mighty magician.

BRYAN, WILLIAM JENNINGS, 1909—Not surpassed, if equaled, in beauty, simplicity, force and appropriateness by any speech of the same length of any language. It is the world's model in eloquence, elegance and condensation. He might safely rest his reputation as an orator on that speech alone.

BRYCE, JAMES, 1903—It is wonderfully terse in expression. . . . Alike in thought and in language it is simple, plain, direct. . . . One feels as if those truths could have been conveyed in no other words.

CAINE, SIR HALL, 1926—In nobility of spirit and majesty of phrase, it is unequaled by any modern utterance.

CHARNWOOD, LORD, 1916—They were such as perhaps sank deep, but left his audience unaware that a classic had been spoken which would endure with the English language.

CONWAY, MONCURE D., 1865—For terse, well pronounced clear speech, for a careful easy reflection of the fit word for the right place, for perfect tones, for quiet chaste and dignified manner,—it would be hard to find the late President's superior.

CURTIS, WILLIAM ELEROY, 1901—No orator of ancient or modern times produced purer rhetoric, more beautiful sentiment, or elegant diction.

DUSERGIER DE HAURANNE, M. E., 1866—I do not believe that modern speech has ever produced anything that will excel his eloquent discourse over the graves of the dead soldiers at Gettysburg.

ELIOT, CHARLES W., 1922—The finest piece of English ever written, matchless in dignity, justness and fitness.

EMERSON, RALPH WALDO, 1864—One of the "two best specimens of eloquence we have had in this century."

FISH, JOHN, 1894—For its quiet depth of feeling and solemn beauty of expression this speech is rightly regarded as one of the greatest masterpieces of English prose.

GRAHAM, GEORGE M., 1913—It is necessary to go to the Ten Commandments, the Lord's Prayer, the Sermon on the Mount, or the Creation of the World, as told in the first chapter of Genesis, to find so much told in so small a compass.

GREELEY, HORACE, 1863—The finest gem in American literature.

32. p. 605 / *63.* Feb. 12, 1809 / *120.* Ex. No. 125 / *136.* III, 118 / *43.* p. 363 / *72.* May, 1865 / *60.* p. 86 / *109.* No. 343 / *135.* July, 1922 / *136.* I, 31 / *136.* III, 118 / *136.* V, 24 / *136.* III, 118

GREEN, DR. SAMUEL A., 1901—For simplicity and strength of style it is unsurpassed, and it has already taken high rank among the finest specimens of choice diction. . . . His words were so plain that they were understood by all, and his ideas so grand and lofty that they reached the heart of the English-speaking world.

HANLEY, J. FRANK, 1913—Our hearts today will melt with profound admiration, as we meditate upon the greatest speech that ever fell from human lips.

HAYES, RUTHERFORD B., 1878—He, by his immortal words spoken here, has indissolubly linked his name, fame and memory with the battle of Gettysburg.

HIGGINSON, THOMAS WENTWORTH, 1895—The high-water mark of American oratory.

HILLIS, NEWELL DWIGHT, 1913—Great as the influence of the battle of Gettysburg, it may be doubted whether in the long run the influence of Abraham's speech will not prove an equally effective force upon democracy and liberty and the destiny of the human race.

HOOVER, HERBERT, 1930—No monument has been or can be erected here so noble and enduring as that simple address which has become a part of this place. Greater than the tribute of granite or bronze remains that memorable message to the American people.

INGERSOLL, ROBERT G., 1880—The oration of Lincoln will never be forgotten. It will live until languages are dead and lips are dust.

IRELAN, JOHN ROBERT, M.D., 1888—This simple and beautiful speech touched the sympathetic chord . . . it will live in the literary history of this country when the lofty periods of the Massachusetts scholar and orator shall be lost.

LAMBROS, PETER S., 1922—Neither America, nor England, nor the whole world has furnished a lamentation its equal in thought, sympathy, language, and literature. It was a masterpiece in eloquence that no man in the past ever did equal.

LONGFELLOW, HENRY W., 1863—Seems to me, admirable.

LUDLOW, JOHN MALCOLM, 1866—Simply one of the noblest extant specimens of human eloquence.

McCULLOCH, HUGH, 1895—Where in the English language can be found eloquence of higher tone or more magnetic power?

NEWTON, JOSEPH FORT, 1913—There is in it no trace of rancor, no lack of faith in God and man, no boast, no gleam of selfish pride

122. May, 1901 / 76. Nov. 26, 1913 / 136. I, 44 / 145. p. 67 / 136. V, 20 / 136. V, 33 / 100. p. 93 / 101. II, 488 / 46. Feb. 11, 1923 / 136. III, 118 / 118. p. 149 / 145. p. 72

in power, more wonder still, there is no word of rebuke for the men who fought against him: who else in all history save Him who walked in Galilee, could have spoken on that field amid those newly made graves, and uttered no word of reproach.

NICOLAY, JOHN G., 1886—So pertinent, so brief yet so comprehensive, so terse yet so eloquent, linking the deeds of the present to the thoughts of the future, with simple words, in such living, original, yet exquisitely moulded maxime-like phrases that the best critics have awarded it an unquestioned rank as one of the world's masterpieces in rhetorical art.

PARKER, COURTLAND, 1874—It ought to be remembered as long as the language lasts in which it was spoken.

PURVIS, SAMUEL W., 1927—Besides the Sermon on the Mount, in human appreciation, has been placed Lincoln's speech at Gettysburg.

ROOSEVELT, FRANKLIN D., 1938—Immortal deeds and immortal words have created here at Gettysburg a shrine of American patriotism. We are compassed by "the last full measure of devotion" of many men and by the words in which Abraham Lincoln expressed the simple faith for which they died.

ROOSEVELT, THEODORE, 1909—His Gettysburg speech and his Second Inaugural are two of the half dozen greatest speeches ever made.—I am tempted to call them the two greatest ever made. . . . They are great in their wisdom and dignity and earnestness, and in a loftiness of thought and expression which makes them akin to the utterances of the prophets of the Old Testament.

SMITH, GOLDWIN, 1865—Not a sovereign of Europe, however trained from the cradle for state pomps, and however prompted by statesman and courtier, could have uttered himself more regally.

SUMNER, CHARLES, 1865—Every word was appropriate, none could be omitted and none added, and none changed.

TUMULTY, JOSEPH P., 1917—No more perfectly phrased or eternally truthful utterance has come from the lips of man.

WATTERSON, HENRY, 1922—He was master of English prose . . . there need be no further proof, that the man who could scribble such a composition . . . was equal to any man who ever wrote the mother tongue.

WHEELER, ANDREW C., 1912—It is the noblest condensation

136. III, 118 / *142.* VIII, 201, 202 / *197.* Jan., 1874 / *153.* Nov. 19, 1927 / *136.* III, 118 / *163.* Jan. 1, 1909 / *123.* Feb. 1863 / *16.* II, 208 / *136.* III, 115 / *99.* July 23, 1922

into the fittest words of all the emotions, aspirations and sentiments that millions of mute people wanted at that moment to utter.

WILSON, JAMES GRANT, 1913—It may be doubted if Webster or Burke, Bright or Gladstone could have found equally beautiful and pure language to express the broad philosophy and the exquisite pathos of the Gettysburg Address.

A Philadelphia woman, visiting in Athens shortly after the centennial of Lincoln's birth, relates that coming to the Acropolis, a brilliant and learned professor of Greek, "delivered Pericles Funeral Oration," then a superb looking Kentucky Colonel "recited Paul's sermon delivered on the very heights where we stood." Following the Kentuckian, a lawyer from Illinois, "standing on a block of marble, impressively and lovingly repeated Lincoln's address at Gettysburg." The narrator of the story concluded: "We began to understand how that one simple speech was the utterance of a lofty theme for all climes and all ages."

After reading these spontaneous and laudatory comments by eminent persons, well qualified to speak with discernment, there should be universal acceptance of Lord Curzon's observations. He ascribed to Lincoln, not only one, but two of the masterpieces of modern English eloquence, and expressed his surprise, "nothing short of wonder," at Lincoln's oratorical ability. This book will have failed in its purpose, if it has not, to some extent, answered the question raised by Lord Curzon: "How knoweth this man his letters?" Anyone who is familiar with the authoritative story of Abraham Lincoln's childhood in Kentucky, his formative years in Indiana, and his phenomenal development in Illinois, will have little difficulty in understanding his mastery of words and his eloquent manner of expression.

136. III, 24 / *98.* Apr. 24, 1913 / *201.* Nov. 19, 1914 / *20.* pp. 127, 129

CHAPTER 19

In Memoriam

SECRETARY OF WAR STANTON, reading the Gettysburg Address, prophesied: "It will be remembered as long as anybody's speeches are remembered who speaks the English language;" thereby prefacing his more familiar tribute at the moment of Lincoln's death: "Now he belongs to the ages!" Many of the testimonials complimenting the masterpiece, express or imply the sentiment of perpetuity, supplement Lincoln's closing thought that the people's government "shall not perish from the earth."

The memorializing of Abraham Lincoln's dedicatory remarks has brought forth many unique and diversified creations. In fact, there are such a great number of objects, in every conceivable form and material, associated with the speech, that a compilation of descriptive monographs about them would fill a volume. Just a few are noted: commemorative stamps, covers and post cards, murals, oil paintings, cartoons by the hundreds, beautifully illuminated lithographs, specimens of fine printing on numerous broadsides, translations of the speech in nearly every language, as well as in braille, scores of paraphrasings, some satirical, some constructive, such as the full page in *Webster's Collegiate Dictionary* illustrating proof-reading. There exists innumerable souvenirs, ranging from microscopic engravings of the speech to

201. Nov. 19, 1914, 142. X, 302

reproductions on medals, medallions and plaques. Even the day of its delivery, November 19, has been set aside as Dedication Day. Only those memorials located in the Gettysburg environs and associated with the address, will be given attention here.

On the day before the anniversary of Lincoln's birth in 1895, the government, by an Act of Congress, acquired from the Gettysburg Battlefield Memorial Association, a tract of land embracing about 800 acres and all the improvements thereon. Section six, in the document of acquisition, charged the Secretary of War with "the custody, preservation, and care of the monuments now erected on which may be hereafter erected within the limits of said National Military Park."

Section eight specified: "That the Secretary of War is hereby authorized and directed to cause to be made a suitable bronze tablet, containing on it the address delivered by Abraham Lincoln, President of the United States, at Gettysburg on the nineteenth day of November, eighteen hundred and sixty-three, on the occasion of the dedication of the national cemetery at that place, and such tablet having on it besides the address a medallion likeness of President Lincoln, shall be erected on the most suitable site within the limits of said park; which address was in the following words: . . ." (The Bliss-Baltimore version of the address was approved except for the use of the word 'upon' for 'on.')

The enactment continues: "And the sum of five thousand dollars, or so much thereof as may be necessary, is hereby appropriated out of any money in the treasury not otherwise appropriated, to pay the cost of said tablet and medallion and pedestal." A sundry civil act, approved May 27, 1908, appropriated $3,000 for "placing iron tablets containing the address of Abraham Lincoln in the other seventy-five national cemeteries." A long delay was experienced in an attempt to decide the exact wording of the address.

Assistant Secretary Oliver was given jurisdiction in the selec-

---

109. No. 1008, 1327, *136.* I, 54, *109.* No. 1412, *136.* VI, 57–62, *136.* I, 32, 34, 48, 90–101 / *136.* IV, 73 / ibid / ibid

tion of the version of the address to be used. He stated: "It is proposed to place the latter tablet (bronze) as near as possible to the exact spot where the martyred President stood when he delivered the address." The memorial was dedicated on January 22, 1912. It consists of a low semi-circular bay of white marble, with a taller section in the center, in front of which is a pedestal with a bronze bust of Lincoln by Henry K. Bush-Brown.

The bust is flanked on its left by the address on a bronze tablet, and on its right, by a similar tablet depicting, the invitation to the President to participate. Below the invitation, this note follows: "Abraham Lincoln, near this place delivered the address at the dedication of the cemetery." However, an information tablet close by informs the visitor that "The address was delivered about 300 yards from the spot upon the upper cemetery drive. . . ."

The Lincoln bust on the exedra is not the only bronze likeness of the President in the cemetery. A favorite pose in which the many sculptors have created Lincoln, presents him delivering his most famous oration. Such an heroic, full length bronze statue, by J. Otto Schweizer, appears on the Pennsylvania state monument (see frontispiece.), and it has caused visitors to wonder if it might not occupy the site where the oration was delivered.

The most general use of the Lincoln oration in the field of art, is in its reproduction on buildings and monuments. The inscription on the interior wall of the Lincoln Memorial in Washington, and another on the mammoth slabs of stone, forming a background for the statue at Lincoln, Nebraska, are excellent examples. More numerous and nationwide are the instances where timely excerpts from the address have been used to embellish memorials. Apparently, the earliest such inscription is found on the Soldiers' National Monument.

As soon as hostilities ceased, the citizens of Gettysburg began to advocate the erection of a monument to the memory of the soldiers who fell there. Subscriptions of $1.00 were solicited for that purpose, and the project soon became nationwide. Five days

136. IV, 73 / ibid, VI, 108 / *124.* pp. 157, 177 / *136.* VI, 100, *109.* No. 1030

after the dedication of the cemetery, the Adams *Sentinel* announced that a publication "embodying the exercises at the commemoration of the National Cemetery," would be placed on sale, the proceeds to go toward the monument fund. William Saunders had a memorial in mind when he drew the plans for the cemetery. He specified that a round plot of ground from which the semi-circular arrangement of graves radiated, should be preserved for a monument.

J. B. Batterson of Hartford, Connecticut, designed the monument, patterned after The Immaculate Conception in Rome and the monument erected to Columbus at Genoa, Italy. Randolph Rogers was the sculptor engaged to do the statuary. Upon completion, it was pronounced the most beautiful monument in America. It stands sixty feet tall, crowned with "The Genius of Liberty," on a three-quarter globe. The Goddess holds in her right hand a victor's laurel wreath and in her left hand, the folds of the national flag. On the pedestal are four allegorical figures representing war, history, peace, and plenty. In a rectangular panel on the front of the monument, there is inscribed "Gettysburg, July 1, 2, 3, 1863." In the corresponding position on the back, there is carved the conclusion of Lincoln's address beginning with the sentence: "It is rather for us the living . . ."

The appearance on the monument of a fragment of the Lincoln address, may have contributed to the tradition that it was delivered there. Such has been the general belief through the years. Clark E. Carr, whose faulty memory, when attempting to recreate the Gettysburg scene, has so often led Lincoln students astray, seems to have been the earliest author to sponsor this supposition. In 1906, he wrote: "It was upon the ground in the center reserved for the monument that the platform upon which the addresses were delivered was placed."

Orton H. Carmichael, in his Gettysburg book published in 1917, notes the same location. F. Lauriston Bullard in his 1944 volume, states in a caption over the picture of the monument:

136. V, 14, 2. Nov. 24, 1863 / *76.* Nov. 20, 1913 / *38.* p. 16

"Marking the spot where Lincoln delivered his immortal address." N. C. Melegakes, in his book published in 1950, notes that the soldiers' monument was "erected on the spot where the address was delivered."

Even today, the visitors to Gettysburg are advised in many ways that the Soldiers' National Monument marks the place of Lincoln's address. In the National Park Gettysburg Center the film presented in the auditorium affirms that the speech was delivered from a platform where the soldiers' monument stands. Besides the exedra already mentioned, an information sign advises that the address was given "at the site of the Soldiers' National Monument." Close by the monument, is an information tablet stating: "Abraham Lincoln delivered his address on this spot Nov. 19, 1863. . . ." The press account of the centennial exercises in 1964, agree with this conclusion.

Possibly, the primary source for this almost unanimous opinion can be found in the November 24, 1863, issue of the Adams *Sentinel*. It reported that by the time the parade "entered the Cemetery grounds the stand erected in the center of the same, was surrounded by at least 20,000 citizens, several thousand of whom were congregated immediately in front of the stand." Apparently, the word "center" was associated with the point which served as the apex of the semi-circular arrangement of graves, where later the Soldiers' Monument was constructed. The place designated on the original burial ground plat for the erection of a monument, is literally surrounded with graves. On three sides, the soldiers are interred and the area directly behind, is Evergreen Cemetery, the public burial ground. There would have been no room for a large assembly to extend in any direction from the monument site without trampling the sacred mounds of the dead.

Furthermore, the marshal's printed directions for the parade's line of march, specified that it should move out Baltimore Street to the Emmitsville Road, over which it would proceed to the

36. p. 12, *33.* p. 28, *124.* pp. 157, 177 / *74.* p. 15, *136.* VI, 107, 109, *79.* Nov. 19, 1963 / *2.* Nov. 23, 1863

Taneytown Road, thence to the place of the ceremonies. If the program had been presented at the site of the Soldiers' Monument, the parade would have continued out Baltimore Street. It is difficult to understand how the monument site could be accepted almost unanimously as the place of the speakers' stand, when there is such an array of facts to disprove it—and overwhelming evidence to the contrary.

Recently there has been discovered documentary evidence of the exact site where the speakers' stand was constructed, its dimensions and the direction it faced. A second edition of the *Revised Report of the Select Committee of the Soldiers' National Cemetery* was published in 1865. The chairman of the committee, David Wills, presented an autograph copy of this issue to the secretary of the committee, W. Y. Selleck, who inscribed his own signature in the book. Secretary Selleck prepared a holograph writing which he pasted in this copy opposite the plat of the cemetery. On the map, he designated with a small rectangle, the exact position where the platform was located. This marked copy of the volume is in the library of the Lincoln National Life Foundation in Fort Wayne. A verbatim copy of the important memorandum is presented.

"The stand on which President Lincoln stood in the National Cemetery at Gettysburg on Nov. 19th 1863 when he delivered his ever to be remembered address, was 12 ft. wide and 20 ft. long, and facing to the North West. It was located 40 ft. North East of the outer circle of Soldiers Graves as shown by pencil mark on the Cemetery Map in the book to which this memorandum is attached."

Mr. Selleck's diagram places the platform location about 350 feet almost due north of the Soldiers' National Monument, and forty feet from a point in the outer circle of lots where the Michigan and New York sections are separated by a path. With this arrangement, the soldiers' graves would be at the rear of the platform, thereby protecting the burial area from trespassers

136. VI, 107, 109, *173.* p. 193 / *172.* p. 152 / ibid

during the exercises. The thousands of visitors stood in the open space which gradually sloped away from the front of the speakers' stand.

Many statesmen have suggested that the central figure in the Gettysburg pageantry is Lincoln, and that his immortal words "dominate the scene." However, in the area containing 800 monuments and over a 1,000 tablets, the Lincoln Speech Exedra becomes a rather unimpressive memorial for such an enduring declaration.

There is adjacent to the place where the original platform stood, a cleared enclosure of about five acres recently presented by The Bethlehem Steel Company to the National Park System. Here a large segment of the people witnessed the dedicatory program. A talented and discerning sculptor may some day be commissioned to fashion a colossal statue depicting Lincoln standing on the site where, one hundred years ago, he spoke his immortal words. Possibly some skillful and appreciative landscape architect may be engaged to transform the barren and unused field into an impressive and quiet retreat, inviting meditation and reflection. Here, on the hour, from sunrise to sunset, there might be heard by those in the immediate vicinity of the statue, the recorded voice of a carefully selected orator presenting the three-minute Gettysburg masterpiece. Such a presentation in an appropriate environment, would give a new emphasis to the significant address. Hearing it would become a visitor's most inspirational experience at the battlefield.

A century has passed since Abraham Lincoln's few words, couched in simple language, and comprising but ten sentences, were spoken at the dedicatory services on November 19, 1863. Properly evaluated, the address becomes an enduring state paper, an epilogue to the initial avowal of independence, a document to be read and accentuated when the liberties of the people are denied, or the rights of the minorities challenged—a declaration of "A new birth of freedom."

172. p. 152 / *136.* I, 50 / *79.* Nov. 20, 1963, p. 1 / *109*

Appendix

Oration of Edward Everett
Gettysburg, Pennsylvania, November 19, 1863

Authorized Edition

"Standing beneath this serene sky, overlooking these broad fields now reposing from the labors of the waning year, the mighty Alleghenies dimly towering before us, the graves of our brethren beneath our feet, it is with hesitation that I raise my poor voice to break the eloquent silence of God and Nature. But the duty to which you have called me must be performed;—grant me, I pray you, your indulgence and your sympathy.

"It was appointed by law in Athens, that the obsequies of the citizens who fell in battle should be performed at the public expense, and in the most honorable manner. Their bones were carefully gathered up from the funeral pyre, where their bodies were consumed, and brought home to the city. There, for three days before the interment, they lay in state, beneath tents of honor, to receive the votive offerings of friends and relatives,—flowers, weapons, precious ornaments, painted vases, (wonders of art, which after two thousand years adorn the museums of modern Europe,)—the last tributes of surviving affection. Ten coffins of funeral cypress received the honorable deposit, one for each of the tribes of the city, and an eleventh in memory of the unrecognized, but not therefore unhonored, dead, and of those whose remains could not be recovered. On the fourth day the mournful procession was formed; mothers, wives, sisters, daughters led the way, and to them it was permitted by the simplicity of ancient manners to utter aloud their lamentations for the beloved and the lost; the male relatives and friends of the deceased followed; citizens and strangers closed the train, thus marshalled, they moved to the place of interment in that famous Ceramicus, the most beautiful suburb of Athens, which had been adorned by Cimon, the son of Miltiades, with walks and fountains and columns,—whose groves were filled with altars, shrines, and temples,—whose gardens were kept forever green by the streams from the neighboring hills, and shaded with the trees sacred to Minerva and coeval with the foundation of the city,—whose circuit enclosed

> " 'the olive Grove of Academe,
> Plato's retirement, where the Attic bird
> Trilled his thick-warbled note the summer long;'

whose pathways gleamed with the monuments of the illustrious dead, the work of the most consummate masters that ever gave life to marble. There, beneath the over-arching plane-trees, upon a lofty stage erected for the purpose, it was ordained that a funeral oration should be pronounced by some citizen of Athens, in the presence of the assembled multitude.

"Such were the tokens of respect required to be paid at Athens to the memory of those who had fallen in the cause of their country. For those alone who fell at Marathon a special honor was reserved. As the battle fought upon that immortal field was distinguished from all others in Grecian history for its influence over the fortunes of Hellas,—as it depended upon the event of that day whether Greece should live, a glory and a light to all coming time, or should expire like the meteor of a moment; so the honors awarded to its martyr-heroes were such as were bestowed by Athens on no other occasion. They alone of all her sons were entombed upon the spot which they had forever rendered famous. Their names were inscribed upon ten pillars, erected upon the monumental tumulus which covered their ashes, (where after six hundred years, they were read by the traveler Pausanias,) and although the columns beneath the hand of time and barbaric violence, have long since disappeared, the venerable mound still marks the spot where they fought and fell,—

> " 'That battle-field where Persia's victim horde
> First bowed beneath the brunt of Hellas' sword.'

"And shall I, fellow citizens, who, after an interval of twenty-three centuries, a youthful pilgrim from the world unknown to ancient Greece, have wandered over that illustrious plain, ready to put off the shoes from off my feet, as one that stands on holy ground,—who have gazed with respectful emotion on the mound which still protects the dust of those who rolled back the tide of Persian invasion, and rescued the land of popular liberty, of letters, and of arts, from the ruthless foe,—stand unmoved over the graves of our dear brethren, who so lately, on three of those all-important days which decide a nation's history,—days on whose issue it depended whether this august republican Union, founded by some of the wisest statesmen that ever lived, cemented with the blood of some of the purest patriots that ever died, should perish or endure,—rolled back the tide of an invasion, not less unprovoked, not less ruthless, than that which came to plant the dark banner of Asiatic despotism and slavery on the free soil of Greece? Heaven forbid! And could I prove so insensible to every prompting of patriotic duty and affection, not only would you, fellow citizens, gathered, many of you from distant States, who have come to take part in these pious offices of gratitude—you, respected fathers, brethren, matrons, sisters, who surround me—cry out for shame, but the forms of brave and patriotic men who fill these honored graves would heave with indignation beneath the sod.

"We have assembled, friends, fellow citizens, at the invitation of the Executive of the great central State of Pennsylvania, seconded by the Governors of seventeen other loyal States of the Union, to pay the last tribute of respect to the brave men, who, in the hard fought battles of the first, second and third days of July last, laid down their lives for the country on these hill sides and the plains before us, and whose remains have been gathered into the Cemetery which we consecrate this day. As my eye ranges over the fields whose sods were so lately moistened by the blood of gallant and loyal men, I feel, as never before, how truly it was said of old, that it is sweet and becoming to die for one's country. I feel as never before, how justly, from the dawn of history to the present time, men have paid the homage of their gratitude and admiration to the memory of those who nobly sacrificed their lives, that their fellow men may live in safety and in honor. And if this tribute were ever due, when, to whom, could it be more justly paid than to those whose last resting place we this day commend to the blessing of Heaven and of men?

"For consider, my friends, what would have been the consequences to the country, to yourselves, and to all you hold dear, if those who sleep beneath our feet, and their gallant comrades who survive to serve their country on other fields of danger, had failed in their duty on those memorable days. Consider what, at this moment, would be the condition of the United States, if that noble Army of the Potomac, instead of gallantly and for the second time beating back the tide of invasion from Maryland and Pennsylvania, had been itself driven from these well contested heights, thrown back in confusion on Baltimore, or trampled down, discomfited, scattered to the four winds. What, in that sad event, would have been the fate of the Monumental city, of Harrisburg, of Philadelphia, of Washington, the capital of the Union, each and every one of which would have lain at the mercy of the enemy, accordingly as it might have pleased him, spurred by passion, flushed with victory, and confident of continued success, to direct his course?

"For this we must bear in mind, it is one of the great lessons of the war, indeed of every war, that it is impossible for a people without military organization, inhabiting the cities, towns, and villages of an open country, including, of course, the natural proportion of non-combatants of either sex, and of every age, to withstand the inroad of a veteran army. What defence can be made by the inhabitants of villages mostly built of wood, of cities unprotected by walls, nay, by a population of men, however high-toned and resolute, whose aged parents demand their care, whose wives and children are clustering about them, against the charge of the war-horse whose neck is clothed with thunder—against flying artillery and batteries of rifled cannon planted on every commanding eminence—against the onset of trained veterans led by skilful chiefs? No, my friends, army must be met by army, battery by battery, squadron by squadron; and the shock of organized thousands must be encountered by the firm breasts and valiant arms of other thousands, as well organized and as skilfully led. It is no reproach, therefore, to the unarmed population of the country to say, that we owe it to the brave men who sleep in their beds of honor before us, and to their gallant surviving associates, not merely that your fertile fields, my friends of Pennsylvania and Maryland, were redeemed from the presence of the invader, but that your capitals were not given up to threatened plunder, perhaps laid in ashes, Washington seized by the enemy, and a blow struck at the heart of the nation.

"Who that hears me has forgotten the thrill of joy that ran through the country on the 4th of July—auspicious day for the glorious tidings, and rendered still more so by the simultaneous fall of Vicksburg—when the telegraph flashed through the land the assurance from the President of the United States that the army of the Potomac, under General Meade, had again smitten the invader? Sure I am, that with the ascriptions of praise that rose to Heaven from twenty millions of freemen, with the acknowledgments that breathed from patriotic lips throughout the length and breadth of America, to the surviving officers and men who had rendered the country this inestimable service, there beat in every loyal bosom a throb of tender and sorrowful gratitude to the martyrs who had fallen on the sternly contested field. Let a nation's fervent thanks make some amends for the toils and sufferings of those who survive. Would that the heartfelt tribute could penetrate these honored graves!

"In order that we may comprehend, to their full extent, our obligations to the martyrs and surviving heroes of the army of the Potomac, let us contemplate for a few moments the train of events, which culminated in the battles of the first days of July. Of this stupendous rebellion, planned as its originators boast, more than thirty years ago, matured and prepared for during an entire generation, finally commenced because, for the first time since the adoption of the Constitution, an election of President had been effected without the votes of the South, (which retained, however, the control of the two other branches of the government,) the occupation of the national capital, with the seizure of the public archives and of the treaties with foreign powers, was an essential feature. This was, in substance, within my personal knowledge, admitted in the winter of 1860–61, by one of the most influential leaders of the rebellion; and it was fondly thought that this object could be effected by a bold and sudden movement on the 4th of March, 1861. There is abundant proof, also, that a darker project was contemplated, if not by the responsible chiefs of the rebellion, yet by nameless ruffians, willing to play a subsidiary and murderous part in the treasonable drama. It was accordingly maintained by the Rebel emissaries in England, in the circles to which they found access, that the new American Minister ought not, when he arrived, to be received as the envoy of the United States, inasmuch as before that time Washington would be captured, and the capital of the nation and the archives and muniments of the government would be in the possession of the Confederates. In full accordance also with this threat, it was declared, by the Rebel Secretary of War, at Montgomery, in the presence of his Chiefs and of his colleagues, and of five thousand hearers, while the tidings of the assault on Sumter were traveling over the wires on that fatal 12th of April, 1861, that before the end of May 'the flag which then flaunted the breeze,' as he expressed it, 'would float over the dome of the Capitol at Washington.'

"At the time this threat was made, the rebellion was confined to the cotton-growing States, and it was well understood by them, that the only hope of drawing any of the other slaveholding States into the conspiracy, was in bringing about a conflict of arms, and 'firing the heart of the South' by the effusion of blood. This was declared by the Charleston press, to be the object for which Sumter was to be assaulted; and the emissaries sent from Richmond, to urge on the unhallowed work, gave the promise, that, with the first drop of blood that should be shed, Virginia would place herself by the side of South Carolina.

"In pursuance of this original plan of the leaders of the rebellion, the capture of Washington has been continually in view, not merely for the sake of its public buildings, as the capital of the Confederacy, but as the necessary preliminary to the absorption of the border States, and for the moral effect in the eyes of Europe of possessing the metropolis of the Union.

"I allude to these facts, not perhaps enough borne in mind, as a sufficient refutation of the pretence, on the part of the Rebels, that the war is one of self-defence, waged for the right of self-government. It is in reality, a war originally levied by ambitious men in the cotton-growing States, for the purpose of drawing the slaveholding border States into the vortex of the conspiracy, first by sympathy—which, in the case of South-Eastern Virginia, North Carolina, part of Tennessee and Arkansas, succeeded—and then by force and for the purpose of subjugating Maryland, Western Virginia, Kentucky, Eastern Tennessee and Missouri; and it is a most extraordinary fact, considering the clamors of the Rebel chiefs on the subject of invasion, that not a soldier of the United States has entered the States last named, except to defend their Union-loving inhabitants from the armies and guerillas of the Rebels.

"In conformity with these designs on the city of Washington, and notwithstanding the disastrous results of the invasion of 1862, it was determined by the Rebel Government last summer to resume the offensive in that direction. Unable to force the passage of the Rappahannock, where General Hooker, notwithstanding the reverse at Chancellorsville, in May, was strongly posted, the Confederate general resorted to strategy. He had two objects in view. The first was by a rapid movement northward, and by manoeuvring with a portion of his army on the east side of the Blue Ridge, to tempt Hooker from his base of operations, thus leading him to uncover the approaches to Washington, to throw it open to a raid by Stuart's cavalry, and to enable Lee himself to cross the Potomac in the Neighborhood of Poolesville and thus fall upon the capital. This plan of operations was wholly frustrated. The design of the Rebel general was promptly discovered by General Hooker, and, moving with great rapidity from Fredericksburg, he preserved unbroken the inner line, and stationed the various corps of his army at all the points protecting the approach to Washington, from Centreville up to Leesburg. From this vantage-ground the Rebel general in vain attempted to draw him. In the mean time, by the vigorous operations of Pleasanton's cavalry, the cavalry of Stuart, though greatly superior in numbers, was so crippled as to be disabled from performing the part assigned it in the campaign. In this manner, General Lee's first object, namely, the defeat of Hooker's army on the south of the Potomac and a direct march on Washington, was baffled.

"The second part of the Confederate plan, which is supposed to have been undertaken in opposition to the views of General Lee, was to turn the demonstration northward into a real invasion of Maryland and Pennsylvania, in the hope, that, in this way, General Hooker would be drawn to a distance from the capital, and that some opportunity would occur of taking him at disadvantage, and, after defeating his army, of making a descent upon Baltimore and Washington. This part of General Lee's plan, which was substantially the repetition of that of 1862, was not less signally defeated, with what honor to the arms of the Union the heights on which we are this day assembled will forever attest.

"Much time had been uselessly consumed by the Rebel general in his unavailing attempts to out-manoeuvre General Hooker. Although General Lee broke up from Fredericksburg on the 3d of June, it was not till the 24th that the main body of his army entered Maryland. Instead of crossing the Potomac, as he had intended, east of the Blue Ridge, he was compelled to do it at Shepherdstown and Williamsport, thus materially deranging his entire plan of campaign north of the river. Stuart, who had been sent with his cavalry to the east of the Blue Ridge, to guard the passes of the mountains, to mask the movements of Lee, and to harass the Union general in crossing the river, having been severely handled by Pleasanton at Beverly Ford, Aldie, and Upperville, instead of being able to retard General Hooker's advance, was driven himself away from his connection with the army of Lee, and cut off for a fortnight from all communication with it—a circumstance to which General Lee, in his report, alludes more than once, with evident displeasure. Let us now rapidly glance at the incidents of the eventful campaign.

"A detachment from Ewell's corps, under Jenkins, had penetrated, on the 15th of June, as far as Chambersburg. This movement was intended at first merely as a demonstration, and as a marauding expedition for supplies. It had, however, the salutary effect of alarming the country; and vigorous preparations were made, not only by the General Government, but here in Pennsylvania and in the sister States, to repel the inroad. After two days passed at Chambersburg, Jenkins, anxious for his communications with Ewell, fell back with his plunder to Hagerstown. Here he remained for several days, and then having swept the recesses of the Cumberland valley, came down upon the eastern flank of the South mountain, and pushed his marauding parties as far as Waynesboro. On the 22nd, the remainder of Ewell's corps crossed the river and moved up the valley. They were followed on the 24th by Longstreet and Hill, who crossed at Williamsport and Shepherdstown, and pushing up the valley, encamped at Chambersburg on the 27th. In this way the whole rebel army, estimated at 90,000 infantry, upwards of 10,000 cavalry, and 4,000 or 5,000 artillery, making a total of 105,000 of all arms, was concentrated in Pennsylvania.

"Up to this time no report of Hooker's movements had been received by General Lee, who, having been deprived of his cavalry, had no means of obtaining information. Rightly judging, however, that no time would be lost by the Union army in pursuit, in order to detain it on the eastern side of the mountains in Maryland and Pennsylvania, and thus preserve his communications by the way of Williamsport, he had, before his own arrival at Chambersburg, directed Ewell to send detachments from his corps to Carlisle and York. The latter detachment, under Early, passed through this place on the 26th of June. You need not, fellow citizens of Gettysburg, that I should recall to you those moments of alarm and distress, precursors as they were of the more trying scenes which were so soon to follow.

"As soon as Gen. Hooker perceived that the advance of the Confederates into Cumberland valley was not a mere feint to draw him away from Washington, he moved rapidly in pursuit. Attempts, as we have seen, were made to harass and retard his passage across the Potomac. These attempts were not only altogether unsuccessful, but were so unskilfully made as to place the entire Federal army between the cavalry of Stuart and the army of Lee. While the latter was massed in the Cumberland valley, Stuart was east of the mountains, with Hooker's army between, and Gregg's cavalry in close pursuit. Stuart was accordingly compelled to force a march northward, which was destitute of strategical character, and which deprived his chief of all means of obtaining intelligence.

"Not a moment had been lost by General Hooker in the pursuit of Lee. The day after the Rebel army entered Maryland, the Union army crossed the Potomac at Edward's Ferry, and by the 28th of June lay between Harper's Ferry and Frederick. The force of the enemy on that day was partly at Chambersburg, and partly moving on the Cashtown road in the direction of Gettysburg, while the detachments from Ewell's corps, of which mention has been made, had reached the Susquehanna opposite Harrisburg and Columbia. That a great battle must soon be fought, no one could doubt; but in the apparent and perhaps real absence of plan on the part of Lee, it was impossible to foretell the precise scene of the encounter. Wherever fought, consequences the most momentous hung upon the result.

"In this critical and anxious state of affairs, General Hooker was relieved, and General Meade was summoned to the chief command of the army. It appears to my unmilitary judgment to reflect the highest credit upon him, upon his predecessor, and upon the corps commanders of the army of the Potomac, that a change could take place in the chief command of so large a force on the eve of a general battle—the various corps necessarily moving on lines somewhat divergent, and all in ignorance of the enemy's intended point of concentration—and that not an hour's hesitation should ensue in the advance of any portion of the entire army.

"Having assumed the chief command on the 28th, General Meade directed his left wing, under Reynolds, upon Emmitsburg, and his right upon New Windsor, leaving General French with 11,000 men to protect the Baltimore and Ohio railroad, and convoy the public property from Harper's Ferry to Washington. Buford's cavalry was then at this place, and Kilpatrick's at Hanover, where he encountered and defeated the rear of Stuart's cavalry, who was roving the country in search of the main army of Lee. On the Rebel side, Hill had reached Fayetteville on the Cashtown road on the 28th, and was followed on the same road by Longstreet on the 29th. The eastern side of the mountain, as seen from Gettysburg, was lighted up at night by the camp-fires of the enemy's advance, and the country swarmed with his foraging parties. It was now too evident to be questioned, that the thunder-cloud, so long gathering blackness, would soon burst on some part of the devoted vicinity of Gettysburg.

"The 30th of June was a day of important preparation. At half-past eleven o'clock in the morning, General Buford passed through Gettysburg, upon a reconnaissance in force, with his cavalry, upon the Chambersburg road. The information obtained by him was immediately communicated to General Reynolds, who was, in consequence, directed to occupy Gettysburg. That gallant officer accordingly, with the First Corps, marched from Emmitsburg to within six or seven miles of this place, and encamped on the right bank of Marsh's creek. Our right wing, meantime, was moved to Manchester. On the same day the corps of Hill and Longstreet were pushed still further forward on the Chambersburg road, and distributed in the vicinity of Marsh's creek, while a reconnaissance was made by the Confederate General Pettigrew up to a very short distance from this place.—Thus at nightfall, on the 30th of June, the greater part of the Rebel force was concentrated in the immediate vicinity of two corps of the Union army, the former refreshed by two days passed in comparative repose and deliberate preparation for the encounter, the latter separated by a march of one or two days from their supporting corps, and doubtful at what precise point they were to expect an attack.

"And now the momentous day, a day to be forever remembered in the annals of the country, arrived. Early in the morning, on the 1st of July, the conflict began. I need not say that it would be impossible for me to comprise, within the limits of the hour, such a narrative as would do anything like full justice to the all-important events of these three great days, or to the merit of the brave officers and men, of every rank, of every arm of the service, and of every loyal State, who bore their part in the tremendous struggle—alike those who nobly sacrificed their lives for their country, and those who survive, many of them scarred with honorable wounds, the objects of our admiration and gratitude. The astonishingly minute, accurate, and graphic accounts contained in the journals of the day, prepared from personal observation by reporters who witnessed the scenes, and often shared the perils which they describe, and the highly valuable "notes" of Professor Jacobs, of the University in this place, to which I am greatly indebted, will abundantly supply the deficiency of my necessarily too condensed statement.

"General Reynolds, on arriving at Gettysburg, in the morning of the 1st, found Buford with his cavalry warmly engaged with the enemy, whom he held most gallantly in check. Hastening himself to the front, General Reynolds directed his men to be moved over the fields from the Emmitsburg road, in front of M'Millan's and Dr. Schmucker's, under cover of the Seminary Ridge. Without a moment's hesitation, he attacked the enemy, at the same time sending orders to the Eleventh Corps (General Howard's) to advance as promptly as possible. General Reynolds immediately found himself engaged with a force which greatly outnumbered his own, and had scarcely made his dispositions for the action when he fell, mortally wounded, at the head of his advance. The command of the First Corps devolved on General Doubleday, and that of the field on General Howard, who arrived at 11:30, with Schurz's and Barlow's divisions of the Eleventh Corps, the latter of whom received a severe wound. Thus strengthened, the advantage of the battle was for some time on our side. The attacks of the Rebels were vigorously repulsed by Wadsworth's division of the First Corps, and a large number of prisoners, including General Archer, were captured. At length, however, the continued reinforcement of the Confederates from the main body in the neighborhood, and by the divisions of Rodes and Early, coming down by separate lines from Heidlersberg and taking post on our extreme right, turned the fortunes of the day. Our army, after contesting the ground for five hours, was obliged to yield to the enemy, whose force outnumbered them two to one; and toward the close of the afternoon General Howard deemed it prudent to withdraw the two corps to the heights where we are now assembled. The great part of the First Corps passed through the outskirts of the town, and reached the hill without serious loss or molestation. The Eleventh Corps and portions of the First, not being aware that the enemy had already entered the town from the north, attempted to force their way through Washington and Baltimore streets, which, in the crowd and confusion of the scene, they did with a heavy loss in prisoners.

"General Howard was not unprepared for this turn in the fortunes of the day. He had, in the course of the morning, caused Cemetery Hill to be occupied by General Steinwehr, with the second division of the Eleventh Corps. About the time of the withdrawal of our troops to the hill, General Hancock arrived, having been sent by General Meade, on hearing of the death of Reynolds, to assume the command of the field till he himself could reach the front. In conjunction with General Howard, General Hancock immediately proceeded to post troops and to repel an attack on our right flank. This attack was feebly made and promptly repulsed. At nightfall, our troops on the hill, who had so gallantly sustained themselves during the toil and peril of the day, were cheered by the arrival of General Slocum with the Twelfth Corps and of General Sickles with a part of the Third.

"Such was the fortunes of the first day, commencing with decided success to our arms, followed by a check, but ending in the occupation of this all-important position. To you, fellow citizens of Gettysburg, I need not attempt to portray the anxieties of the ensuing night. Witnessing, as you had done with sorrow, the withdrawal of our army through your streets, with a considerable loss of prisoners—mourning as you did over the brave men who had fallen—shocked with the wide-spread desolation around you, of which the wanton burning of the Harman House had given the signal—ignorant of the near approach of General Meade, you passed the weary hours of the night in painful expectation.

"Long before the dawn of the 2d of July, the new Commander-in-Chief had reached the ever-memorable field of service and glory. Having received intelligence of the events in progress, and informed by the reports of Generals Hancock and Howard of the favorable character of the positions, he determined to give battle to the enemy at this point. He accordingly directed the remaining corps of the army to concentrate at Gettysburg with all possible expedition, and breaking up his head-quarters at Taneytown at ten p.m., he arrived at the front at one o'clock in the morning of the 2d of July. Few were the moments given to sleep, during the rapid watches of that brief midsummer's night, by officers or men, though half of our troops were exhausted by the conflict of the day and the residue wearied by the forced marches which had brought them to the rescue. The full moon, veiled by thin clouds, shone down that night on a strangely unwonted scene. The silence of the grave-yard was broken by the heavy tramp of armed men, by the neigh of the war-horse, the harsh rattle of the wheels of artillery hurrying to their stations, and all the indescribable tumult of preparation. The various corps of the army, as they arrived, were moved to their positions, on the spot where we are assembled and the ridges that extend south-east and south-west; batteries were planted and breastworks thrown up. The Second and Fifth Corps, with the rest of the Third, had reached the ground by seven o'clock, a.m.; but it was not till two o'clock in the afternoon that Sedgwick arrived with the Sixth Corps. He had marched thirty-four miles since nine o'clock on the evening before. It was only on his arrival that the Union army approached in equality of numbers with that of the Rebels, who were posted upon the opposite and parallel ridge, distant from a mile to a mile and a half, overlapping our position on either wing, and probably exceeding by ten thousand the army of General Meade.

"And here I cannot but remark on the providential inaction of the Rebel army. Had the contest been renewed by it at daylight on the 2d of July, with the First and Eleventh Corps exhausted by the battle and the retreat, the Third and Twelfth weary from their forced march, and the Second, Fifth and Sixth not yet arrived, nothing but a miracle could have saved the army from a great disaster. Instead of this, the day dawned, the sun rose, the cool hours of the morning passed, the forenoon and a considerable part of the afternoon wore away, without the slightest aggressive movement on the part of the enemy. Thus time was given for half of our forces to arrive and take their places in the lines, while the rest of the army enjoyed a much needed half day's repose.

"At length, between three and four o'clock in the afternoon, the work of death began. A signal gun from the hostile batteries was followed by a tremendous cannonade along the Rebel lines, and this by a heavy advance of infantry, brigade after brigade, commencing on the enemy's right against the left of our army, and so onward to the left center. A forward movement of General Sickles, to gain a commanding position from which to repel the Rebel attack, drew upon him a destructive fire from the enemy's batteries, and a furious assault from Longstreet's and Hill's advancing troops. After a brave resistance on the part of his corps, he was forced back, himself falling severely wounded. This was the critical moment of the second day, but the Fifth and part of the Sixth Corps, with portions of the First and Second, were promptly brought to the support of the Third. The struggle was fierce and murderous, but by sunset our success was decisive, and the enemy was driven back in confusion. The most important service was rendered towards the close of the day, in the memorable advance between Round Top and Little Round Top, by General Crawford's division of the Fifth Corps, consisting of two brigades of the Pennsylvania Reserves, of which one company was from this town and neighborhood. The Rebel force was driven back with great loss in killed and prisoners. At eight o'clock in the evening a desperate attempt was made by the enemy to storm the position of the Eleventh Corps on Cemetery Hill; but here, too, after a terrible conflict, he was repulsed with immense loss. Ewell, on our extreme right, which had been weakened by the withdrawal of the troops sent over to support our left, had succeeded in gaining a foothold within a portion of our lines, near Spangler's spring. This was the only advantage obtained by the rebels to compensate them for the disasters of the day, and of this, as we shall see, they were soon deprived.

"Such was the result of the second act of this eventful drama,—a day hard fought, and at one moment anxious, but, with the exception of the slight reverse just named, crowned with dearly earned but uniform success to our arms, auspicious of a glorious termination of the final struggle. On these good omens the night fell.

"In the course of the night, General Geary returned to his position on the right, from which he had hastened the day before to strengthen the Third Corps. He immediately engaged the enemy, and after a sharp and decisive action, drove them out of our lines, recovering the ground which had been lost on the preceding day. A spirited contest was kept up all the morning on this part of the line; but General Geary, reinforced by Wheaton's brigade of the Sixth Corps, maintained his position, and inflicted very severe losses on the Rebels.

"Such was the cheering commencement of the third day's work, and with it ended all serious attempts of the enemy on our right. As on the preceding day, his efforts were now mainly directed against our left centre and left wing. From eleven till half-past one o'clock, all was still—a solemn pause of preparation, as if both armies were nerving themselves for the supreme effort. At length the awful silence, more terrible than the wildest tumult of battle, was broken by the roar of two hundred and fifty pieces of artillery from the opposite ridges, joining in a cannonade of unsurpassed violence—the Rebel batteries along two thirds of their line pouring their fire upon Cemetery Hill, and the centre and left wing of our army. Having attempted in this way for two hours, but without success, to shake the steadiness of our lines, the enemy rallied his forces for a last grand assault. Their attack was principally directed against the position of our Second Corps. Successive lines of Rebel infantry moved forward with equal spirit and steadiness from their cover on the wooded crest of Seminary Ridge, crossing the intervening plain, and, supported right and left by their choicest brigades, charged furiously up to our batteries. Our own brave troops of the Second Corps, supported by Doubleday's division and Stannard's brigade of the First, received the shock with firmness; the ground on both sides was long and fiercely contested, and was covered with the killed and the wounded; the tide of battle flowed and ebbed across the plain, till, after 'a determined and gallant struggle,' as it is pronounced by General Lee, the Rebel advance, consisting of two-thirds of Hill's corps and the whole of Longstreet's—including Pickett's division, the élite of his corps, which had not yet been under fire, and was now depended upon to decide the fortune of this last eventful day—was driven back with prodigious slaughter, discomfited and broken. While these events were in progress at our left centre, the enemy was driven, with a considerable loss of prisoners, from a strong position on our extreme left, from which he was annoying our force on Little Round Top. In the terrific assault on our centre, Generals Hancock and Gibbon were wounded. In the Rebel army, Generals Armistead, Kemper, Pettigrew and Trimble were wounded, the first named mortally, the latter also made prisoner, General Garnett was killed, and thirty-five hundred officers and men made prisoners.

"These were the expiring agonies of the three days' conflict, and with them the battle ceased. It was fought by the Union army with courage and skill, from the first cavalry skirmish on Wednesday morning to the fearful route of the enemy on Friday afternoon, by every arm and every rank of service, by officers and men, by cavalry, artillery, and infantry. The superiority of numbers was with the enemy, who were led by the ablest commanders in their service; and if the Union force had the advantage of a strong position, the Confederates had that of choosing time and place, the prestige of former victories over the army of the Potomac, and of the success of the first day. Victory does not always fall to the lot of those who deserve it; but that so decisive a triumph, under circumstances like these, was gained by our troops, I would ascribe, under Providence, to the spirit of exalted patriotism that animated them, and the consciousness that they were fighting in a righteous cause.

"All hope of defeating our army, and securing what General Lee calls 'the valuable results' of such an achievement, having vanished, he thought only of rescuing from destruction the remains of his shattered forces. In killed, wounded and missing, he had, as far as can be ascertained, suffered a loss of about 37,000 men—rather more than a third of the army with which he is supposed to have marched into Pennsylvania. Perceiving that his only safety was in rapid retreat, he commenced withdrawing his troops at daybreak on the 4th, throwing up field works in front of our left, which, assuming the appearance of a new position, were intended probably to protect the rear of his army in retreat. That day—sad celebration of the 4th of July for an army of Americans—was passed by him in hurrying off his trains. By nightfall, the main army was in full retreat upon the Cashtown and Fairfield roads, and it moved with such precipitation, that, short as the nights were, by day-light the following morning, notwithstanding a heavy rain, the rear guard had left its position. The struggle of the last two days resembled, in many respects, the battle of Waterloo; and if, in the evening of the third day, General Meade, like the Duke of Wellington, had had the assistance of a powerful auxiliary army to take up the pursuit, the route of the Rebels would have been as complete as that of Napoleon.

"Owing to the circumstances just named, the intentions of the enemy were not apparent on the 4th. The moment his retreat was discovered, the following morning, he was pursued by our cavalry on the Cashtown road and through the Emmitsburg and Monterey passes, and by Sedgwick's corps on the Fairfield road. His rear guard was briskly attacked at Fairfield; a great number of wagons and ambulances were captured in the passes of the mountains; the country swarmed with his stragglers, and his wounded were literally emptied from the vehicles containing them into the farm houses on the road. General Lee, in his report, makes repeated mention of the Union prisoners whom he conveyed into Virginia, somewhat overstating their number. He states, also, that 'such of his wounded as were in a condition to be removed' were forwarded to Williamsport. He does not mention that the number of his wounded *not* removed, and left to the Christian care of the victors, was 7,540, not one of whom failed of any attention which it was possible, under the circumstances of the case, to afford them, not one of whom, certainly, has been put upon Libby prison fare—lingering death by starvation. Heaven forbid, however, that we should claim any merit for the exercise of common humanity.

"Under the protection of the mountain ridge, whose narrow passes are easily held even by a retreating army, General Lee reached Williamsport in safety, and took up a strong position opposite to that place. General Meade necessarily pursued with the main army by a flank movement through Middletown, Turner's Pass having been secured by General French. Passing through the South mountain, the Union army came up with that of the Rebels on the 12th, and found it securely posted on the heights of Marsh run. The position was reconnoitred, and preparations made for an attack on the 13th. The depth of the river, swollen by the recent rains, authorized the expectation that the enemy would be brought to a general engagement the following day. An advance was accordingly made by General Meade on the morning of the 14th; but it was soon found that the

Rebels had escaped in the night, with such haste that Ewell's corps forded the river where the water was breast-high. The cavalry, which had rendered the most important services during the three days, and in harassing the enemy's retreat, was now sent in pursuit, and captured two guns and a large number of prisoners. In an action which took place at Falling Waters, General Pettigrew was mortally wounded. General Meade, in further pursuit of the Rebels, crossed the Potomac at Berlin. Thus again covering the approaches to Washington, he compelled the enemy to pass the Blue Ridge at one of the upper gaps; and in about six weeks from the commencement of the campaign, General Lee found himself on the south side of the Rappahannock, with the probable loss of about a third part of his army.

"Such, most inadequately recounted, is the history of the ever-memorable three days, and of the events immediately preceding and following. It has been pretended, in order to diminish the magnitude of this disaster to the Rebel cause, that it was merely the repulse of an attack on a strongly defended position. The tremendous losses on both sides are a sufficient answer to this misrepresentation, and attest the courage and obstinacy with which the three days' battle was waged. Few of the great conflicts of modern times have cost victors and vanquished so great a sacrifice. On the Union side there fell, in the whole campaign, of generals killed, Reynolds, Weed and Zook, and wounded, Barlow, Barnes, Butterfield, Doubleday, Gibbon, Graham, Hancock, Sickles and Warren; while of officers below the rank of General, and men, there were 2,834 killed, 13,709 wounded, and 6,643 missing. On the Confederate side, there were killed on the field or mortally wounded, Generals Armistead, Barksdale, Garnett, Pender, Pettigrew and Semmes, and wounded, Heth, Hood, Johnson, Kemper, Kimball and Trimble. Of officers below the rank of general, and men, there were taken prisoners, including the wounded, 13,621, an amount ascertained officially. Of the wounded in a condition to be removed, of the killed and the missing, the enemy has made no report. They are estimated, from the best data which the nature of the case admits, at 23,000. General Meade also captured 3 cannon, and 41 standards; and 24,978 small arms were collected on the battle-field.

"I must leave to others, who can do it from personal observation, to describe the mournful spectacle presented by these hill-sides and plains at the close of the terrible conflict. It was a saying of the Duke of Wellington, that next to a defeat, the saddest thing was a victory. The horrors of the battlefield, after the contest is over, the sights and sounds of woe,—let me throw a pall over the scene, which no words can adequately depict to those who have not witnessed it, on which no one who has witnessed it, and who has a heart in his bosom, can bear to dwell. One drop of balm alone, one drop of heavenly, life-giving balm, mingles in this bitter cup of misery. Scarcely has the cannon ceased to roar, when the brethren and sisters of Christian benevolence, ministers of compassion, angels of pity, hasten to the field and the hospital, to moisten the parched tongue, to bind the ghastly wounds, to soothe the parting agonies alike of friend and foe, and to catch the last whispered messages of love from dying lips. 'Carry this miniature back to my dear wife, but do not take it from my bosom till I am gone.' 'Tell my little sister not to grieve for me; I am willing to die for my country.' 'Oh, that my mother were here!' When, since Aaron stood between the living and the dead, was there ever so gracious a ministry as this? It has been said that it is characteristic of Americans to treat women with a deference not paid to them in any other country. I will not undertake to say whether this is so; but I will say, that, since this terrible war has been waged, the women of the loyal States, if never before, have entitled themselves to our highest admiration and gratitude,—alike those who at home, often with fingers unused to the toil, often bowed beneath their own domestic cares, have performed an amount of daily labor not exceeded by those who work for their daily bread, and those who, in the hospital and the tents of the Sanitary and Christian Commissions, have rendered services which millions could not buy. Happily, the labor and the service are their own reward. Thousands of matrons and thousands of maidens have experienced a delight in these homely toils and services, compared with which the pleasures of the ball room and the opera house are tame and unsatisfactory. This, on earth, is reward enough, but a richer is in store for them. Yes, brothers, sisters of charity, while you bind up the wounds of the poor sufferers—the humblest, perhaps, that have shed their blood for the country,—forget not Who it is that will hereafter say to you, 'Inasmuch as ye have done it unto one of the least of these my brethren, ye have done it unto me.'

"And now, friends, fellow citizens, as we stand among these honored graves, the momentous question presents itself: Which of the two parties to the war is responsible for all this suffering, for this dreadful sacrifice of life, the lawful and constitutional government of the United States, or the ambitious men who have rebelled against it? I say 'rebelled' against it, although Earl Russell, the British Secretary of State for Foreign Affairs, in his recent temperate and conciliatory speech in Scotland, seems to intimate that no prejudice ought to attach to that word, inasmuch as our English forefathers rebelled against Charles I. and James II., and our American fathers rebelled against George III. These, certainly, are venerable precedents, but they prove only that it is just and proper to rebel against oppressive governments. They do not prove that it was just and proper for the son of James II. to rebel against George I., or his grandson Charles Edward to rebel against George II.; nor, as it seems to me, ought these dynastic struggles, little better than family quarrels, to be compared with this monstrous conspiracy against the American Union. These precedents do not prove that it was just and proper for the 'disappointed great men' of the cotton-growing States to rebel against 'the most beneficent government of which history gives us any account,' as the Vice President of the Confederacy, in November, 1860, charged them with doing. They do not create a presumption even in favor of the disloyal slaveholders of the South, who, living under a government of which Mr. Jefferson Davis, in the session of 1860–61, said that it 'was the best government ever instituted by man, unexceptionably administered, and under which the people have been prosperous beyond comparison with any other people whose career has been recorded in history,' rebelled against it because their aspiring politicians, himself among the rest, were in danger of losing their monopoly of its offices. —What would have been thought by an impartial posterity of the American rebellion against George III., if the colonists had at all times been more than equally represented in parliament, and James Otis, and Patrick Henry, and Washington, and Franklin, and the Adamses, and Hancock, and Jefferson, and men of their stamp, had for two generations enjoyed the confidence of the sovereign and administered the government of the empire? What would have been thought of the rebellion against Charles I., if Cromwell, and the men of his school, had been the responsible advisers of that prince from his accession to the throne, and then, on account of a partial change in the ministry, had brought his head to the block, and involved the country in a desolating war, for the sake of dismembering it and establishing a new government south of the Trent? What would have been thought of the Whigs of 1688, if they had themselves composed the cabinet of James II., and been the advisers of the measures and the promoters of the policy which drove him into exile? The Puritans of 1640, and the Whigs of 1688, rebelled against arbitrary power in order to establish constitutional liberty. If they had risen against Charles and James because those monarchs favored equal rights, and in order themselves, 'for the first time in the history of the world,' to establish an oligarchy 'founded on the corner-stone of slavery,' they would truly have furnished a precedent for the Rebels of the South, but their cause would not have been sustained by the eloquence of Pym, or of Somers, nor sealed with the blood of Hampden or Russell.

"I call the war which the Confederates are waging against the Union a 'rebellion,' because it is one, and in grave matters it is best to call things by their right names. I speak of it as a crime, because the Constitution of the United States so regards it, and puts 'rebellion' on a par with 'invasion.' The Constitution and law not only of England, but of every civilized country, regard them in the same light; or rather they consider the rebel in arms as far worse than the alien enemy. To levy war against the United States is the constitutional definition of treason, and that crime is by every civilized government regarded as the highest which citizen or subject can commit. Not content with the sanctions of human justice, of all the crimes against the law of the land it is singled out for the denunciations of religion. The litanies of every church in Christendom whose ritual embraces that office, as far as I am aware, from the metropolitan cathedrals of Europe to the humblest missionary chapel in the islands of the sea, concur with the Church of England in imploring the Sovereign of the Universe, by the most awful adjurations which the heart of man can conceive or his tongue utter, to deliver us from 'sedition, privy conspiracy and rebellion.' And reason good; for while a rebellion against tyranny—a rebellion designed, after prostrating arbitrary power, to establish free government on the basis of justice and truth—is an enterprise on which good men and angels may look with complacency, an unprovoked rebellion of ambitious men against a beneficent government, for the purpose—the avowed purpose—of establishing, extending and perpetuating any form of injustice and wrong, is an imitation on earth of that first foul revolt of 'the Infernal Serpent,' against which the Supreme Majesty sent forth the armed myriads of his angels, and clothed the right arm of his Son with the three-bolted thunders of omnipotence.

"Lord Bacon, in 'the true marshalling of the sovereign degrees of honor,' assigns the first place to 'the *Conditores Imperiorum*, founders of States and Commonwealths;' and, truly, to build up from the discordant elements of our nature, the passions, the interests and the opinions of the individual man, the rivalries of family, clan and tribe, the influences of climate and geographical position, the accidents of peace and war accumulated for ages—to build up from these oftentimes warring elements a well-compacted, prosperous and powerful State, if it were to be accomplished by one effort or in one generation, would require a more than mortal skill. To contribute in some notable degree to this, the greatest work of man, by wise and patriotic council in peace and loyal heroism in war, is as high as human merit can well rise, and far more than to any of those to whom Bacon assigns this highest place of honor, whose names can hardly be repeated without a wondering smile—Romulus, Cyrus, Caesar, Ottoman, Ismael—is it due to our Washington, as the founder of the American Union. But if to achieve or help to achieve this greatest work of man's wisdom and virtue gives title to a place among the chief benefactors, rightful heirs of the benedictions, of mankind, by equal reason shall the bold, bad men who seek to undo the noble work, *Eversores Imperiorum*, destroyers of States, who for base and selfish ends rebel against beneficent governments, seek to overturn wise constitutions, to lay powerful republican Unions at the foot of foreign thrones, to bring on civil and foreign war, anarchy at home, dictation abroad, desolation, ruin—by equal reason, I say, yes, a thousandfold stronger shall they inherit the execrations of the ages.

"But to hide the deformity of the crime under the cloak of that sophistry which strives to make the worse appear the better reason, we are told by the leaders of the Rebellion that in our complex system of government the separate States are 'sovereigns,' and that the central power is only an 'agency' established by these sovereigns to manage certain little affairs—such, forsooth, as Peace, War, Army, Navy, Finance, Territory, and Relations with the native tribes—which they could not so conveniently administer themselves. It happens, unfortunately for this theory, that the Federal Constitution (which has been adopted by the people of every State of the Union as much as their own State constitutions have been adopted, and is declared to be paramount to them) nowhere recognizes the States as 'sovereigns'—in fact, that, by their names, it does not recognize them at all; while the authority established by that instrument is recognized, in its text, not as an 'agency,' but as 'the Government of the United States.' By that Constitution, moreover, which purports in its preamble to be ordained and established by 'the People of the United States,' it is expressly provided, that 'the members of the State legislatures, and all executive and judicial officers, shall be bound by oath or affirmation to support the Constitution.' Now it is a common thing, under all governments, for an agent to be bound by oath to be faithful to his sovereign; but I never heard before of sovereigns being bound by oath to be faithful to their agency.

"Certainly I do not deny that the separate States are clothed with sovereign powers for the administration of local affairs. It is one of the most beautiful features of our mixed system of government; but it is equally true, that, in adopting the Federal Constitution, the States abdicated, by express renunciation, all the most important functions of national sovereignty, and, by one comprehensive, self-denying clause, gave up all right to contravene the Constitution of the United States. Specifically, and by enumeration, they renounced all the most important prerogatives of independent States for peace and for war,— the right to keep troops or ships of war in time of peace, or to engage in war unless actually invaded; to enter into compact with another State or a foreign power; to lay any duty on tonnage, or any impost on exports or imports, without the consent of Congress; to enter into any treaty, alliance, or confederation; to grant letters of marque and reprisal, and to emit bills of credit—while all these powers and many others are expressly vested in the General Government. To ascribe to political communities, thus limited in their jurisdiction—who cannot even establish a post office on their own soil—the character of independent sovereignty, and to reduce a national organization, clothed with all the transcendent powers of government, to the name and condition of an 'agency' of the States, proves nothing but that the logic of secession is on a par with its loyalty and patriotism.

"Oh, but 'the reserved rights!' and what of the reserved rights? The tenth amendment of the Constitution, supposed to provide for 'reserved rights,' is constantly misquoted. By that amendment, 'the *powers* not delegated to the United States by the Constitution, nor prohibited by it to the States, are reserved to the States respectively, or to the people.' The 'powers' reserved must of course be such as could have been, but were not delegated to the United States,—could have been, but were not prohibited to the States; but to speak of the *right* of an *individual* State to secede, as a *power* that could have been, though it was not delegated to the *United States*, is simple nonsense.

"But waiving this obvious absurdity, can it need a serious argument to prove that there can be no State right to enter into a new confederation reserved under a constitution which expressly prohibits a State to 'enter into any treaty, alliance, or confederation,' or any 'agreement or compact with another State or a foreign power?' To say that the State may, by enacting the preliminary farce of secession, acquire the right to do the prohibited things—to say, for instance, that though the States, in forming the Constitution, delegated to the United States and prohibited to themselves the power of declaring war, there was by implication reserved to each State the right of seceding and then declaring war; that, though they expressly prohibited to the States and delegated to the United States the entire treaty-making power, they reserved by implication (for an express reservation is not pretended) to the individual States, to Florida, for instance, the right to secede, and then to make a treaty with Spain retroceding that Spanish colony, and thus surrendering to a foreign power the key to the Gulf of Mexico,—to maintain propositions like these, with whatever affected seriousness it is done, appears to me egregious trifling.

"Pardon me, my friends, for dwelling on these wretched sophistries. But it is these which conducted the armed hosts of rebellion to your doors on the terrible and glorious days of July, and which have brought upon the whole land the scourge of an aggressive and wicked war—a war which can have no other termination compatible with the permanent safety and welfare of the country but the complete destruction of the military power of the enemy. I have, on other occasions, attempted to show that to yield to his demands and acknowledge his independence, thus resolving the Union at once into two hostile governments, with a certainty of further disintegration, would annihilate the strength and the influence of the country as a member of the family of nations; afford to foreign powers the opportunity and the temptation for humiliating and disastrous interference in our affairs; wrest from the Middle and Western States some of their great natural outlets to the sea and of their most important lines of internal communication; deprive the commerce and navigation of the country of two-thirds of our sea coast and of the fortresses which protect it; not only so, but would enable each individual State—some of them with a white population equal to a good sized Northern county—or rather the dominant party in each State, to cede its territory, its harbors, its fortresses, the mouths of its rivers to any foreign power. It cannot be that the people of the loyal States—that, twenty-two millions of brave and prosperous freemen—will, for the temptation of a brief truce in an eternal border war, consent to this hideous national suicide.

"Do not think that I exaggerate the consequences of yielding to the demands of the leaders of the rebellion. I understate them. They require of us not only all the sacrifices I have named, not only the cession to them, a foreign and hostile power, of all the territory of the United States at present occupied by the Rebel forces, but the abandonment to them of the vast regions we have rescued from their grasp—of Maryland, of a part of Eastern Virginia and the whole of Western Virginia; the sea coast of North and South Carolina, Georgia, and Florida; Kentucky, Tennessee, and Missouri; Arkansas, and the larger portion of Mississippi, Louisiana, and Texas—in most of which, with the exception of lawless guerillas, there is not a Rebel in arms, in all of which the great majority of the people are loyal to the Union. We must give back, too, the helpless colored population, thousands of whom are perilling their lives in the ranks of our armies, to a bondage rendered ten-fold more bitter by the momentary enjoyment of freedom. Finally we must surrender every man in the Southern country, white or black, who has moved a finger or spoken a word for the restoration of the Union, to a reign of terror as remorseless as that of Robespierre, which has been the chief instrument by which the Rebellion has been organized and sustained, and which has already filled the prisons of the South with noble men, whose only crime is that they are not the worst of criminals. The South is full of such men. I do not believe there has been a day since the election of President Lincoln, when, if an ordinance of secession could have been fairly submitted, after a free discussion, to the mass of the people in any single Southern State, a majority of ballots would have been given in its favor. No, not in South Carolina. It is not possible that the majority of the people, even of that State, if permitted, without fear or favor, to give a ballot on the question, would have abandoned a leader like Petigru, and all the memories of the Gadsdens, the Rutledges, and the Cotesworth Pinckneys of the revolutionary and constitutional age, to follow the agitators of the present day.

"Nor must we be deterred from the vigorous prosecution of the war by the suggestion, continually thrown out by the Rebels and those who sympathize with them, that, however it might have been at an earlier stage, there has been engendered by the operations of the war a state of exasperation and bitterness which, independent of all reference to the original nature of the matters in controversy, will forever prevent the restoration of the Union, and the return of harmony between the two great sections of the country. This opinion I take to be entirely without foundation.

"No man can deplore more than I do the miseries of every kind unavoidably incident to war. Who could stand on this spot and call to mind the scenes of the first days of July with any other feeling? A sad foreboding of what would ensue, if war should break out between North and South, has haunted me through life, and led me, perhaps too long, to tread in the path of hopeless compromise, in the fond endeavor to conciliate those who were predetermined not to be conciliated. But it is not true, as is pretended by the Rebels and their sympathizers, that the war has been carried on by the United States without entire regard to those temperaments which are enjoined by the law of nations, by our modern civilization, and by the spirit of Christianity. It would be quite easy to point out, in the recent military history of the leading European powers, acts of violence and cruelty, in the prosecution of their wars, to which no parallel can be found among us. In fact, when we consider the peculiar bitterness with which civil wars are almost invariably waged, we may justly boast of the manner in which the United States have carried on the contest. It is of course impossible to prevent the lawless acts of stragglers and deserters, or the occasional unwarrantable proceedings of subordinates on distant stations; but I do not believe there is, in all history, the record of a civil war of such gigantic dimensions where so little has been done in the spirit of vindictiveness as in this war, by the Government and commanders of the United States; and this notwithstanding the provocation given by the Rebel Government by assuming the responsibility of wretches like Quantrell, refusing to quarter colored troops and scourging and selling into slavery free colored men from the North who fall into their hands, by covering the sea with pirates, refusing a just exchange of prisoners, while they crowd their armies with paroled prisoners not exchanged, and starving prisoners of war to death.

"In the next place, if there are any present who believe that, in addition to the effect of the military operations of the war, the confiscation acts and emancipation proclamations have embittered the Rebels beyond the possibility of reconciliation, I would request them to reflect that the tone of the Rebel leaders and Rebel press was just as bitter in the first months of the war, nay, before a gun was fired, as it is now. There were speeches made in Congress in the very last session before the outbreak of the Rebellion, so ferocious as to show that their authors were under the influence of a real frenzy. At the present day, if there is any discrimination made by the Confederate press in the affected scorn, hatred and contumely with which every shade of opinion and sentiment in the loyal States is treated, the bitterest contempt is bestowed upon those at the North who still speak the language of compromise, and who condemn those measures of the administration which are alleged to have rendered the return of peace hopeless.

"No, my friends, that gracious Providence which over-rules all things for the best, 'from seeming evil still educing good,' has so constituted our natures, that the violent excitement of the passions in one direction is generally followed by a reaction in an opposite direction, and the sooner for the violence. If it were not so—if injuries inflicted and retaliated of necessity led to new retaliations, with forever accumulating compound interest of revenge, then the world, thousands of years ago, would have been turned into an earthly hell, and the nations of the earth would have been resolved into clans of furies and demons, each forever warring with his neighbor. But it is not so; all history teaches a different lesson. The Wars of the Roses in England lasted an entire generation, from the battle of St. Albans in 1455 to that of Bosworth Field in 1485. Speaking of the former, Hume says; 'This was the first blood spilt in that fatal quarrel, which was not finished in less than a course of thirty years; which was signalized by twelve pitched battles; which opened a scene of extraordinary fierceness and cruelty; is computed to have cost the lives of eighty princes of the blood; and almost entirely annihilated the ancient nobility of England. The strong attachments which, at that time, men of the same kindred bore to each other, and the vindictive spirit which was considered a point of honor, rendered the great families implacable in their resentment, and widened every moment the breach between the parties.' Such was the state of things in England under which an entire generation grew up; but when Henry VII., in whom the titles of the two Houses were united, went up to London after the battle of Bosworth Field, to mount the throne, he was everywhere received with joyous acclamations, 'as one ordained and sent from heaven to put an end to the dissensions' which had so long afflicted the country.

"The great rebellion of England of the seventeenth century, after long and angry premonitions, may be said to have begun with the calling of the Long Parliament in 1640—and to have ended with the return of Charles II., in 1660—twenty years of discord, conflict and civil war; of confiscation, plunder, havoc; a proud hereditary peerage trampled in the dust; a national church overturned, its clergy beggared, its most eminent prelate put to death; a military despotism established on the ruins of a monarchy which had subsisted seven hundred years, and the legitimate sovereign brought to the block; the great families which adhered to the king proscribed, impoverished, ruined; prisoners of war—a fate worse than starvation in Libby—sold to slavery in the West Indies; in a word, everything that can embitter and madden contending factions. Such was the state of things for twenty years; and yet, by no gentle transition, but suddenly, and 'when the restoration of affairs appeared most hopeless,' the son of the beheaded sovereign was brought back to his father's blood-stained throne, with such 'unexpressible and universal joy' as led the merry monarch to exclaim 'he doubted it had been his own fault he had been absent so long, for he saw nobody who did not protest he had ever wished for his return.' 'In this wonderful manner,' says Clarendon, 'and with this incredible expedition did God put an end to a rebellion that had raged near twenty years, and had been carried on with all the horrid circumstances of murder, devastation and parracide that fire and sword, in the hands of the most wicked men in the world,' (it is a royalist that is speaking,) 'could be instruments of, almost to the desolation of two kingdoms, and the exceeding defacing and deforming of the third. . . . By these remarkable steps did the merciful hand of God, in this short space of time, not only bind up and heal all those wounds, but even made the scar as undiscernable as, in respect of the deepness, was possible, which was a glorious addition to the deliverance.'

"In Germany, the wars of the Reformation and of Charles V., in the sixteenth century, the Thirty Years' war in the seventeenth century, the Seven Years' war in the eighteenth century, not to speak of other less celebrated contests, entailed upon that country all the miseries of intestine strife for more than three centuries. At the close of the last named war—which was the shortest of all, and waged in the most civilized age—'an officer,' says Archenholz, 'rode through seven villages in Hesse, and found in them but one human being.' More than three hundred principalities, comprehended in the Empire, fermented with the fierce passions of proud and petty States; at the commencement of this period the castles of robber counts frowned upon every hilltop; a dreadful secret tribunal, whose seat no one knew, whose power none could escape, froze the hearts of men with terror throughout the land; religious hatred mingled its bitter poison in the seething caldron of provincial animosity; but of all these deadly enmities between the States of Germany scarcely the memory remains. There are controversies in that country, at the present day, but they grow mainly out of the rivalry of the two leading powers. There is no country in the world in which the sentiment of national brotherhood is stronger.

"In Italy, on the breaking up of the Roman Empire, society might be said to be resolved into its original elements—into hostile atoms, whose only movement was that of mutual repulsion. Ruthless barbarians had destroyed the old organizations, and covered the land with a merciless feudalism. As the new civilization grew up, under the wing of the church, the noble families and the walled towns fell madly into conflict with each other; the secular feud of Pope and Emperor scourged the land; province against province, city against city, street against street, waged remorseless war with each other from father to son, till Dante was able to fill his imaginary hell with the real demons of Italian history. So ferocious had the factions become, that the great poet-exile himself, the glory of his native city and of his native language, was, by a decree of the municipality, condemned to be burned alive if found in the city of Florence. But these deadly feuds and hatred yielded to political influences, as the hostile cities were grouped into States under stable governments; the lingering traditions of the ancient animosities gradually died away, and now Tuscan and Lombard, Sardinian and Neapolitan, as if to shame the degenerate sons of America, are joining in one cry for a united Italy.

"In France, not to go back to the civil wars of the League, in the sixteenth century, and of the Fronde, in the seventeenth; not to speak of the dreadful scenes throughout the kingdom, which followed the revocation of the edict of Nantes; we have, in the great revolution which commenced at the close of the last century, seen the bloodhounds of civil strife let loose as rarely before in the history of the world. The reign of terror established at Paris stretched its bloody Briarean arms to every city and village in the land, and if the most deadly feuds which ever divided a people had the power to cause permanent alienation and hatred, this surely was the occasion. But far otherwise the fact. In seven years from the fall of Robespierre, the strong arm of the youthful conqueror brought order out of this chaos of crime and woe; Jacobins whose hands were scarcely cleansed from the best blood of France met the returning emigrants, whose estates they had confiscated and whose kindred they had dragged to the guillotine, in the Imperial antechambers; and when, after another turn of the wheel of fortune, Louis XVIII. was restored to his throne, he took the regicide Fouche, who had voted for his brother's death, to his cabinet and confidence.

"The people of loyal America will never ask you, sir, to take to your confidence or admit again to a share in the government the hardhearted men whose cruel lust of power has brought this desolating war upon the land, but there is no personal bitterness felt even against them. They may live, if they can bear to live after wantonly causing the death of so many thousands of their fellow-men; they may live in safe obscurity beneath the shelter of the government they have sought to overthrow, or they may fly to the protection of the governments of Europe—some of them are already there, seeking, happily in vain, to obtain the aid of foreign powers in furtherance of their own treason. There let them stay. The humblest dead soldier, that lies cold and stiff in his grave before us, is an object of envy beneath the clods that cover him, in comparison with the living man, I care not with what trumpery credentials he may be furnished, who is willing to grovel at the foot of a foreign throne for assistance in compassing the ruin of his country.

"But the hour is coming and now is, when the power of the leaders of the Rebellion to delude and inflame must cease. There is no bitterness on the part of the masses. The people of the South are not going to wage an eternal war, for the wretched pretext by which this Rebellion is sought to be justified. The bonds that unite us as one people—a substantial community of origin, language, belief, and law, (the four great ties that hold the societies of men together;) common national and political interests; a common history; a common pride in a glorious ancestry; a common interest in this great heritage of blessings; the very geographical features of the country; the mighty rivers that cross the lines of climate and thus facilitate the interchange of natural and industrial products, while the wonder-working arm of the engineer has leveled the mountain-walls which separate the East and West, compelling your own Alleghenies, my Maryland and Pennsylvania friends, to open wide their everlasting doors to the chariot-wheels of traffic and travel; these bonds of union are of perennial force and energy, while the causes of alienation are imaginary, factitious and transient. The heart of the people, North and South, is for the Union. Indications, too plain to be mistaken, announce the fact, both in the East and the West of the States in rebellion. In North Carolina and Arkansas the fatal charm at length is broken. At Raleigh and Little Rock the lips of honest and brave men are unsealed, and an independent press is unlimbering its artillery. When its rifled cannon shall begin to roar, the hosts of treasonable sophistry—the mad delusions of the day—will fly like the Rebel army through the passes of yonder mountain. The weary masses of the people are yearning to see the dear old flag again floating upon their capitols, and they sigh for the return of the peace, prosperity, and happiness, which they enjoyed under a government whose power was felt only in its blessings.

"And now, friends, fellow citizens of Gettysburg and Pennsylvania, and you from remoter States, let me again, as we part, invoke your benediction on these honored graves. You feel, though the occasion is mournful, that it is good to be here. You feel that it was greatly auspicious for the cause of the country, that the men of the East and men of the West, the men of nineteen sister States, stood side by side, on the perilous ridges of the battle. You now feel it a new bond of union, that they shall lie side by side, till the clarion, louder than that which marshalled them to the combat, shall awake their slumbers. God bless the Union; it is dearer to us for the blood of brave men which has been shed in its defence. The spots on which they stood and fell; these pleasant heights; the fertile plain beneath them; the thriving village whose streets so lately rang with the strange din of war; the fields beyond the ridge, where the noble Reynolds held the advancing foe at bay, and, while he gave up his own life, assured by his forethought and self-sacrifice the triumph of the two succeeding days; the little streams which wind through the hills, on whose banks in aftertimes the wondering ploughman will turn up, with the rude weapons of savage warfare, the fearful missiles of modern artillery; Seminary Ridge, the Peach Orchard, Cemetery, Culp, and Wolf Hill, Round Top, Little Round Top, humble names, henceforward dear and famous—no lapse of time, no distance of space, shall cause you to be forgotten. 'The whole earth,' said Pericles, as he stood over the remains of his fellow citizens, who had fallen in the first year of the Peloponnesian war, 'the whole earth is the sepulchre of illustrious men.' All time, he might have added, is the millennium of their glory. Surely I would do no injustice to the other noble achievements of the war, which have reflected such honor on both arms of the service, and have entitled the armies and the navy of the United States, their officers and men, to the warmest thanks and the richest rewards which a grateful people can pay. But they, I am sure, will join us in saying, as we bid farewell to the dust of these martyr-heroes, that wheresoever throughout the civilized world the accounts of this great warfare are read, and down to the latest period of recorded time, in the glorious annals of our common country, there will be no brighter page than that which relates The Battles of Gettysburg."

Sources

This combined bibliography and reference compilation is arranged to relieve the text from the use of superior letters or numerals, and the footnotes from constant repetition of titles. The numbers in italics find their counterparts in the lines at the bottom of each page. One or more references are provided for every paragraph with this symbol (/) marking the divisions. All sources, in the original or in duplicate, are available in the library of the Lincoln National Life Foundation.

1. Abraham Lincoln Association, *The Collected Works of Abraham Lincoln* (8 volumes plus index, Rutger's University Press, New Brunswick, N. J., 1952–1955).
2. Adams (Gettysburg) *Sentinel.*
3. *Address of Hon. Edward Everett at the consecration of the National Cemetery at Gettysburg* . . . (Boston, 1864).
4. Albany *Evening Journal.*
5. *American Druggist* (New York).
6. Anderson, Charles, *The Cause of the War* . . . (1906).
7. Andrew, John A., *Address of His Excellency John A. Andrew to the Legislature of Massachusetts* . . . *January, 1864* (Boston, 1864).
8. Andrews, Mary Shipman Raymond, *The Perfect Tribute* (Charles Scribner's Sons, New York, 1906).
9. *An Oration delivered on the Battlefield of Gettysburg (November 19, 1863) at the consecration of the Cemetery* . . . (New York, 1863).
10. *Appleton's Cyclopaedia of American Biography* (6 volumes, New York, 1888–1889).
11. *Army and Navy Journal* (Washington, D. C.).
12. Arnold, Isaac N., *The History of Abraham Lincoln and the Overthrow of Slavery* (Chicago, 1866).
13. Arnold, Isaac N., *The Life of Abraham Lincoln* (Chicago, 1885).
14. Atlanta (Ga.) *Constitution.*

15. *Autograph Leaves of the Country's Authors* (Baltimore, 1864).
16. Barrett, Joseph H., *Abraham Lincoln and his Presidency* (2 volumes, Cincinnati, 1904).
17. Barrett, Joseph H., *Life of Abraham Lincoln* (New York, 1888).
18. Bartlett, John, *Familiar Quotations* (Boston, 1911).
19. Bartlett, John Russell, *Catalogue of the Books and Pamphlets Relating to the Civil War* (Boston, 1866).
20. Barton, William E., *Lincoln at Gettysburg* (Bobbs-Merrill Company, Indianapolis, 1930).
21. *Bay State Monthly* (Boston).
22. Bicknell, Albion H., *Lincoln at Gettysburg* (Boston, 1879).
23. Bridwell, Elizabeth R., *Why Abraham Lincoln went to Gettysburg* (Buffalo, 1928).
24. Boston *Atlas*.
25. (Boston) *City Document-106 . . . Burial of Massachusetts Dead at Gettysburg* (Boston, 1863).
26. Boston *Daily Advertiser*.
27. Boston *Journal*.
28. Boston *Transcript*.
29. Brooklyn *Eagle*.
30. Brooks, Noah, *A Biography for Young People* (New York, 1888).
31. Brooks, Noah, *Washington in Lincoln's Time* (New York, 1895).
32. Browne, Francis F., *The Every-Day Life of Abraham Lincoln* (New York and St Louis, 1886).
33. Bullard, F. Lauriston, "*A Few Appropriate Remarks*" (Harrogate, Tenn., 1944).
34. Burrage, Henry Sweetser, *Gettysburg and Lincoln* (New York and London, 1906).
35. Cambridge (Ohio) *Jeffersonian*.
36. Carmichael, Orton H., *Lincoln's Gettysburg Address* (New York, Cincinnati, 1937).
37. Carpenter, Francis B., *Six Months at the White House* (New York, 1866).
38. Carr, Clark E., *Lincoln at Gettysburg* (Chicago, 1906).
39. *Case and Comment* (Rochester, N. Y.).
40. Cazeau, Theodore C., *Why Lincoln went to Gettysburg* (Cincinnati, 1931).
41. *Century Magazine* (New York).
42. Charleston *Journal Post*.

43. Charnwood, Godfrey Rathbone Benson, Lord, *Makers of the Nineteenth Century* (London, 1916).
44. Chicago *Daily Journal.*
45. Chicago *Daily News.*
46. Chicago *Herald Tribune and Examiner.*
47. Chicago *Journal of Commerce.*
48. Chicago *Times.*
49. Chicago *Tribune.*
50. *Christian Science Monitor* (Boston).
51. Chittenden, L. E., *Abraham Lincoln's Speeches* (New York, 1895).
52. Cincinnati *Daily Commercial.*
53. Cincinnati *Enquirer.*
54. Cleveland *Plain Dealer.*
55. *Congressional Record* (Washington, D. C.).
56. Conway, Moncure D., *Autobiography, Memoirs, and Experiences of Moncure D. Conway* (Boston, 1904).
57. *Coronet.*
58. Corson, Oscar Taylor, *Abraham Lincoln His Words and Deeds* (Danville, N. Y., 1927).
59. Cross, Andrew B., *The War, Battle of Gettysburg and the Christian Commission* (1865).
60. Curtis, William Eleroy, *Abraham Lincoln* (Philadelphia and London, 1902).
61. Daugherty, James, *Lincoln's Gettysburg Address* (Chicago, 1947).
62. Dearborn (Mich.) *Independent.*
63. Denver *Daily News.*
64. Dennett, Tyler, *Lincoln and the Civil War* . . . (New York, 1939).
65. Detroit *Advertiser and Tribune.*
66. *Dial, The* (Chicago and New York).
67. Doll and Richards, *Albert H. Bicknell Painting* (Boston, 1879).
68. Eggleston, Percy, *Lincoln in New England* (New York, 1922).
69. *Encyclopaedia Britannica, The* (26 volumes, New York, 1910).
70. *Epworth Herald* (Cincinnati).
71. *Forney's War Press* (Philadelphia).
72. *Fortnightly Review, The* (London).
73. *Forward* (Philadelphia).
74. Fortenbaugh, Robert, *Lincoln and Gettysburg* (Gettysburg, 1957).

75. Frothingham, Paul Revere, *Edward Everett* (1925).
76. Gettysburg *Compiler.*
77. *Gettysburg Solemnities, Dedication of the National Cemetery at Gettysburg* . . . (Washington, 1863).
78. Gettysburg *Star and Sentinel.*
79. Gettysburg *Times.*
80. Gotwald, Frederick G., *Gettysburg, Lincoln's Address and Our Educational Institutions.* (York, Pa., 1907).
81. Hanover (Pa.) *Weekly Spectator.*
82. Haney, John L., "*Of the People, By the People, For the People,*" (1944).
83. *Harper's New Monthly Magazine* (New York).
84. *Harper's Weekly* (New York).
85. Harrisburg (Pa.) *Patriot and Union.*
86. Harrisburg (Pa.) *Telegraph.*
87. Hastings (Minn.) *Conservator.*
88. Hay, John, *Letters of John Hay and Extracts from Diary* (3 volumes, Washington, 1908).
89. Hertz, Emanuel, *As Lincoln said at Gettysburg* (Washington, 1939).
90. *Hobbies Magazine* (Chicago).
91. Holland, Josiah G., *The Life of Abraham Lincoln* (Springfield, Mass., 1866).
92. *Holy Bible* (King James Version).
93. Howe, Beverly, *Two Hours and Two Minutes* (1937).
94. Howells, William Dean, *Life of Abraham Lincoln* (Bloomington, Ind., 1960).
95. Illinois State Historical Society, *Journal* (Springfield).
96. Illinois State Historical Society, *Transactions* (Springfield).
97. Illinois *State Journal* (Springfield).
98. *Independent, The* (New York).
99. Indianapolis *Star.*
100. Ingersoll, Robert G., *Abraham Lincoln* (Chicago, 1880).
101. Irelan, John Robert, *History of the Life, Administration and Times of Abraham Lincoln* (2 volumes, Chicago, 1888).
102. Jacobs, Henry Eyster, *Lincoln's Gettysburg World Message* (Philadelphia, 1919).
103. Jacobs, Warren, *Lincoln on the New Haven and the Boston & Albany Railroads* (Boston, 1934).
104. Kansas City (Mo.) *Times.*

Sources 219

105. Lambert, William H., *Versions of the Gettysburg Address* (Philadelphia, 1909).
106. Lamon, Ward H., *Recollections of Abraham Lincoln, 1847–1865* (Chicago, 1911).
107. Liberty Magazine (New York).
108. Lincoln Herald (Harrogate, Tenn.).
109. Lincoln Lore (Fort Wayne).
110. Lincoln National Life Foundation, Manuscripts (Fort Wayne).
111. Lincoln, Robert Todd, Papers (Library of Congress).
112. Lincoln Sesquicentennial Commission, *Lincoln Day by Day* (3 volumes, Washington, 1960).
113. Literary Digest (New York).
114. Locomotive Fireman's Magazine (Cincinnati).
115. London *Star.*
116. Louisville *Commercial.*
117. Louisville *Courier Journal.*
118. Ludlow, John Malcolm, *President Lincoln Self Portrayed* (London, 1866).
119. Luhrs, Henry E., *Lincoln at the Wills' Home and the Gettysburg Address* (Shippensburg, Pa., 1938).
120. Magazine of History with Notes and Queries (Extra Numbers) (Tarrytown, N. Y., 1926,7).
121. Massachusetts Historical Society, *Edward Everett at Gettysburg* (Boston, 1963).
122. Massachusetts Historical Society, *Proceedings, March, April, May, 1901* (Boston, 1901).
123. Macmillan's Magazine (London).
124. Meligakes, N. A., *The Spirit of Gettysburg* (Gettysburg, 1915).
125. Mentor, The (New York).
126. Military Order of the Loyal Legion . . . February 13, 1907 (1907).
127. Milwaukee *Evening Wisconsin.*
128. Moore, Charles, *Lincoln's Gettysburg Address and Second Inaugural* (Boston and New York, 1927).
129. Moores, Charles W., *Lincoln's Addresses and Letters* (Cincinnati, Chicago, 1914).
130. Murray, Lindley, *The English Reader* (New York, 1815).
131. Nason, Elias, *Eulogy on Abraham Lincoln* (Boston, 1865).
132. Nation, The (New York).

133. *National Granite Monthly* (Concord, N. H.).
134. *National Republic, The* (Washington, D. C.).
135. *New England Historical and Genealogical Register* (Boston, Mass.).
136. Newspaper Clippings on Gettysburg Address, Lincoln National Life Foundation (6 Volumes, Fort Wayne, 1863–1963).
137. New York *Herald*.
138. New York *Times*.
139. New York *Tribune*.
140. New York *World*.
141. *New Yorker, The* (New York).
142. Nicolay, John G., and Hay, John, *Abraham Lincoln: A History* (10 volumes, New York, 1890).
143. Nicolay, John G., and Hay, John, *Abraham Lincoln: Complete Works* (2 volumes, New York, 1894).
144. Ohio *State Journal* (Columbus).
145. Oldroyd, Osborn H., *Words of Lincoln* (Washington, D. C., 1895).
146. Oskaloosa *Daily Herald* (Iowa).
147. Ottawa *Journal* (Canada).
148. *Outlook, The* (New York).
149. Page, Edwin L., *Abraham Lincoln in New Hampshire* (Boston and New York, 1929).
150. Parke-Bernet Galleries, *Catalogue, April 7, 1944* (New York, 1944).
151. *Pennsylvania Magazine of History and Biography, The* (Philadelphia).
152. Peoria (Ill.) *Star*.
153. Philadelphia *Bulletin*.
154. Philadelphia *Inquirer*.
155. Portland *Oregonian*.
156. *Potomac Edison News* (Hagerstown, Md.)
157. *Prairie Farmer* (Chicago).
158. *Presbyterian Banner* (Pittsburg).
159. *President's Words, The* (Boston, 1865).
160. Providence *Daily Journal*.
161. *Putnam's Magazine* (New York).
162. *Religious Telescope* (Dayton, Ohio).
163. *Review of Reviews* (New York).
164. *Review of Two Worlds*.

165. Rice, Charles Allen Thorndike, *Reminiscences of Abraham Lincoln by Distinguished Men of His Time* (New York, 1888).
166. Roberts, Kate L., *Hoyt's Encyclopaedia of Practical Quotations* (New York, 1940).
167. *Rotarian, The* (Chicago).
168. Scott, William, *Lessons in Elocution . . .* (Philadelphia, 1801).
169. *Scribner's Magazine* (New York).
170. Scripps, John Locke, *The First Published Life of Abraham Lincoln* (Detroit, 1900).
171. Soldiers' National Cemetery Commission, *Report of Select Committee Relative to the Soldiers' National Cemetery* (Boston, 1864).
172. Soldiers' National Cemetery Commission, *Revised Report made to The Legislature of Pennsylvania* (Harrisburg, 1865).
173. Soldiers' National Cemetery Commission, *Revised Report made to The Legislature of Pennsylvania* (Harrisburg, 1867).
174. Souder, Mrs. Edmund A., *Leaves from the Battlefield of Gettysburg* (Philadelphia, 1864).
175. Spencer, J. H., *A History of Kentucky Baptists from 1796 to 1885 . . .* (2 volumes, Cincinnati, 1885).
176. Springfield (Mass.) *Republican.*
177. St. Louis *Republican.*
178. Stoddard, William O., *Abraham Lincoln: The True Story of a Great Life* (Philadelphia, 1884).
179. Sweet, Forrest H., *Autograph List No. 142* (Battle Creek).
180. Tausek, Joseph, *True Story of the Gettysburg Address* (New York, 1933).
181. Thayer, William E., *The Life and Letters of John Hay* (2 volumes, Boston, 1915).
182. United States Adjutant General's Office. Records for 1861.
183. United States, *Revised U.S. Army Regulations* (Washington, 1861,62,63).
184. United States, *General Orders, Volunteer Forces* (Washington, 1861,62,63).
185. United States, *War of the Rebellion: A Compilation of the Official Records* (4 series, 70 volumes, Washington, 1880–1901).
186. Vicksburg (Miss.) *Daily Citizen.*
187. Wanamaker, R. N., *The Voice of Lincoln* (New York, 1915).

188. Warren, Louis A., *Lincoln's Parentage and Childhood* (New York, 1926).
189. Warren, Louis A., *Lincoln's Youth: Indiana Years* (New York, 1959).
190. Warren, Louis A., *The Slavery Atmosphere of Lincoln's Youth* (Fort Wayne, 1933).
191. Washington *Chronicle*.
192. Watterson, Henry, *Abraham Lincoln, an Oration* (Chicago, 1900).
193. Weems, Mason L., *The Life of George Washington . . .* (Philadelphia, 1809).
194. Welles, Gideon, *Diary of Gideon Welles* (3 Volumes).
195. *Wesleyan Alumnus* (Middletown, Conn.).
196. *Westminster Review* (New York).
197. *Wood's Household Magazine*.
198. Worcester (Mass.) *Spy*.
199. Youngstown (Ohio) *Vindicator*.
200. Young, Robert, *Analytical Concordance of the Bible* (New York, 1920).
201. *Youth's Companion* (New York).

Index

Abraham Lincoln: A History, 155
Abraham Lincoln: Complete Works, 155
Acropolis, 176
Adams, Charles Francis, 172
Adams, John, 23, 203
Adams, John Quincy, 203
Adams County, Pa., 19, 74, 119
Adams Express Company, 28
Adams *Sentinel*, 20, 28, 29, 31, 36, 130, 133, 135–136, 137, 148, 180, 181
Albany *Evening Journal*, 67, 75, 134
Aldie, Va., 191
Allegheny County, Pa., 124, 149
Allegheny Mountains, 213
Alleman, M. J., 60
Allerman, H. C., 30
Alton, Ill., 14
American House, Gettysburg, 75
American Revolution, 3, 25, 26, 68
Anderson, Charles, 59, 85, 137
Anderson, Robert, 137
Andrew, John A., 32, 97, 109, 143
Andrews, Mary Raymond Shipman, *The Perfect Tribute*, XVIII, 61, 62, 63, 126, 127
Andrews, Paul, 62
Angell, James Burrill, 144
Annapolis, 166
Anthony, Henry B., 144
Archenholz, Johann, 211
Archer, James J., 195
Arkansas, 190, 208, 213
Armistead, L. A., 199, 201
Army and Navy Journal, 145
Army of the Potomac, 20, 187
Arnold, Isaac, N., 21, 60, 115, 124, 161, 172

Associated Press, 139, 140–142, 157, 163, 164
Atchison, Kan., 6
Athens, 176, 185, 186
Atherton, Peter, 11
Atlanta *Constitution*, 146
Attendance, 75
Attic bird, 186
Austin, George Lowell, 172
Austria, 51
Autograph Leaves of Our Country's Authors, 168

Bacon, Francis, 204, 205
Baker & Goodwin, 143
Baltimore, 19, 28, 56, 58, 79, 119, 167, 188
Baltimore Fire Department, 28
Baltimore Glee Club, 82
Baltimore & Ohio Railroad, 57
Bancroft, George, 150, 160, 166, 167
Bancroft, John C., 167
Bancroft, Wilbur D., 167
Banks, Nathanial P., 50
Banners, 80, 134
Baptist Churches, 11
Barclay, Clement C., 59
Barclay, John M., 69
Barksdale, William, 201
Barlow, Francis C., 195, 200
Barnes, James, 201
Barrett, Nathan B., 69
Barton, William E., *Lincoln at Gettysburg*, XVIII, 42
Bates, Edward, 160
Batterson, James B., 122, 180
Baugher, Henry L., 85, 123, 130, 131
Beecher, Henry Ward, 100, 142

224 INDEX

Behan, W. M., 69
Bellefonte, Pa., 39
Beloit, Wis., 6
Benediction, 130, 132
Berlin, Md., 201
Berry, John S., 86
Bertinatti, Joseph, 57
Bethlehem, 105, 112
Bethlehem Steel Company, 183
Beverly Ford, Va., 191
Bible, 2
Bicknell, Albion H., 87
Bielheimen, T. C., 122
Bierbower, Austin, 121
Biersecker, F. W., 37
Bikle, Philip H., 120, 122
Bingham, H. P., 70, 71
Birgfeld's Band, 88
Black, Chauncey, 125
Blair, Montgomery, 57, 79
Bliss, Alexander, 150, 160, 168, 170
Bliss, Eleanor, 170
Bliss, W. J. A., 170
Blood, Captain, 81
Blue Ridge Mountain, 190, 191, 201
Blumhaven Library, 162
Bond, George W., 141
Border States, 15, 190
Boreman, Arthur I., 59, 85
Boston, 4, 40, 66, 147, 166
Boston City Document, 116, 145
Boston, *Commonwealth*, 6
Boston *Daily Advertiser*, 141
Boston *Daily Traveler*, 101
Boston *Journal*, 83, 101, 137, 147
Boston Whig Club, 4
Bosworth Field, 210
Boteler, C. B., 69
Boutwell, George S., 172
Bowles, Samuel, 172
Bradford, Augustus W., 85
Brastrow, George B., 69
Briggs, Russell M., 134
Bright, John, 176
Brookly, 142
Brooklyn *Daily Eagle*, XVI
Brooks, Noah; President's address written, 54, 55; makes few changes, 122, 157; remarks about Boston people, 128, 147; several trial sheets, 150; tribute to Lincoln, 172
Brooks, William, 69
Brough, John, 59, 85
Brown, L. W., 86
Browne, Francis Fisher, 172
Bruce, Robert, 132
Bryan, William Jennings, 173
Bryce, James, 173
Buford, John, 20, 193, 194
Bullard, F. Lauriston, *A Few Appropriate Remarks*, XVIII, 180
Bunker Hill, Va., 76
Burke, Edmund, 176
Burlingame, Anson, 62
Burlingame, Walter, 62, 63
Burns, John L., 135, 136
Burnside, Ambrose, 71
Burrage, Henry Sweetser, XVIII
Burton, Henry S., 79
Bush-Brown, Henry K., 179
Bust of Lincoln, 178
Butler, Benjamin, F., 87
Butterfield, Daniel, 201

Caesar, 205
Caine, Thomas Henry Hall, 173
California, 166
Calvert Street Station, 58
Cameron, Simon, 26, 39, 54, 55, 59, 85
Cannon, Foster, 166
Carlisle, Pa., 19, 192
Carmichael, Orton H., *Lincoln's Gettysburg Address*, XVIII, 154, 180
Carnegie, Andrew, 61
Carr, Clark E., his Gettysburg book widely accepted, 42; commissioner for Illinois, 42, 86; reminiscences for Chicago *Tribune*, 126, 127, 132; address before Illinois Historical Society, 43; states invitation to Lincoln "an afterthought," 43; responsible for sending it, 43; circulates many untenable traditions, 180; discrepancy in his memoirs,

INDEX

43, 75, 82, 96, 98, 99; both praises and ridicules Lincoln, 132, 133
Carrington, Edward C., 69
Casey, Joseph, 69
Casey, Silas, 86
Cashtown, Pa., 20, 193, 200
Cemetery, Commissioners, 86
Cemetery Hill, (Ridge), 31, 33, 74, 195, 197, 198, 214
Centreville, Va., 191
Century Magazine, XVII, 53, 61, 72, 155–156, 157, 162
Ceramicus, 165
Chambersburg, Pa., 190, 191, 192, 193, 194
Charles I, 203, 210
Charles V, 211
Charleston, S. C., 189
Charnwood, Godfrey R. B., 173
Chase, Salmon P., 87, 90
Chatham, William Pitt, 171
Chelsea, Mass., 4
Chicago, 15, 25, 49
Chicago Christians, 15
Chicago *Daily Journal*, Chicago Historical Society, XVIII, 53, 165
Chicago *Times*, 147, 148
Chicago *Tribune*, XVII, 43, 86, 106, 125, 126, 145
China, 144
Chipman, Norton Parker, 69
Chittenden, Lucius E., 6
Christian Commission, 28, 30, 202
Church, W. L., 68
Church of England, 203
Cimon, 186
Cincinnati, 6, 75, 114
Cincinnati *Daily Commercial*, 87, 122
Cincinnati *Gazette*, 86, 145
Cintas, Oscar B., 170
Civil War Centennial Commission, XVI
Claredon, Edward H., 211
Clark, Daniel, 135
Clay, Henry, 5, 6, 39, 49, 106, 108
Cleon, 116
Coburn, Abner, 85

Cochrane, Henry Clay, *With Lincoln at Gettysburg*, 55, 61, 79
Coit, Alfred, 86
Cole, Cornelius, 65, 73
Collected Works of Abraham Lincoln, The, 163
Columbia, Pa., 193
Columbus, 6
Columbus *State Journal*, 86, 145
Compensated Emancipation, 14
Concord, N. H., 6
Concord *Statesman*, 6
Confiscation Act, 15
Conkling, James C., 50, 93, 118
Connecticut, 38
Constitution, 205–206, 207
Constitutional-Union party, 94
Conway, Moncure D., 6, 173
Cook, Elenora, 86
Cook, Sarah, 86
Cooper, Lane, 105
Cooper, Thomas, 116
Cooper Union, 6, 14, 94
Cora, Lieutenant, 57
Cornell University, 167
Couch, Darius N., 77, 78, 86
Cowper, William, 12
"Cradle of Liberty," 18
Crawford, H. B., 81, 197
Crawford, Samuel W., 44
Cromwell, Oliver, 51, 203
Cross, Andrew B., 30, 31
Croton ice, 100
Culp's Hill, 35, 214
Cumberland Valley, 81, 192
Curtin, Andrew G., biographical sketch, 39; asks Lincoln's advice, 39, 40; visited by President-elect, 40, 110, 111; roll of host, 45–47, 85, 119, 120, 130; appoints David Wills his Gettysburg representative, 29, 30, 32, 33, 40, 69, 90; visits President at Washington, 44; late in reaching Gettysburg, 59, 60, 64; provides own accomodations, 69, 96; highly complimentary of President, 127; receives dedication visitors, 134
Curtis, William Eleroy, 152, 173

Curzon, George Nathaniel, 171, 172, 176
Cyrus, 205

Dante, 212
Danville, Ill., 76
Davis, Jefferson, 203
Dayton, 6
Debates, 5, 14
Decatur, Ill., 3
Declaration of Independence, 17, 25, 168
Dedication program, 41–43, 84, 92
Defrees, John D., 53–54, 55
Delaney, Alfred, 130
Dennison, William, 59, 85, 124
Depew, Chauncey M., 121
Detroit *Advertiser and Tribune*, 145
Dickinson College, 39
Dirge by French, 91, 92
Dirge by Percival, 130
District of Columbia, 13, 17
Doniphan, Kan., 6
Doubleday, Abner, 59, 79, 86, 195, 198, 200
Douglas, Stephen A., 5, 14, 68
Douglass, Frederick A., 87
Dover, N. H., 6
Dusergier, M. E., XVI, 173

Eagle Hotel, Gettysburg, 76
Early, Jubal A., 182, 195
Eckert, John, 59
Edward, Charles, 203
Edwards, Henry, 86, 141
Edward's Ferry, Va., 193
Egypt, 107
Eisendrath, Joseph L., Jr., 132
Elastic pen holder, 160
Eliot, Charles W., 173
Elwood, Kan., 6
Emancipation Church, 11
Emancipation Proclamation, XV, 15, 16
Emerson, Ralph Waldo, 173
Emmitsburg, Md., 19, 181, 194, 195, 200
Encyclopaedia Britannica, 154
England, 49, 94, 166, 171, 189

Euclid, Six Books of, 106
Europe, 93, 95, 140, 175
Evangelical Lutheran Church, 118
Evergreen Cemetery; town's burial grounds, 31; Union stronghold, 31; draws Confederate fire, 31, 33; meeting of directors, 31, 32; "a lovely spot, a noble resting place," 31; many soldiers buried here, 31; proposal for joint cemetery, 32; criticism by Mr. Wills, 32; Miss Wade's grave, 137; adjacent to Soldiers' National Cemetery, 181
Everett, Edward; birth and early life, 93; professor at Harvard, 93; political achievements, 94; outstanding orator, 94; Vice-Presidential nominee, 95; disparages Lincoln's ability, 95; first meets the President, 95; interviewed about speaking at Gettysburg, 40; receives official invitation, 41, 45; suggests change of date for dedication, 41, 42; manuscript printed in Boston, 129, 141; departure for and arrival at Gettysburg, 62, 96; entertained by Wills and accommodations, 64, 96; visits battlefield, 97; has tent erected at platform, 98; observes Lincoln at banquet, 96; reaches platform tent before parade, 97; erroneous tradition about being late, 97, 98; comments on program, 89, 92; escorted to platform, 98, 84; daughter present, 58; speaks for two hours, 99; complimented by the President, 99; traditional conversation on platform, 123–125; President's reaction to his letter, 126, 138; writes letter of congratulation to President, 126, 138; reaction to his oration, 100, 101, 110, 121, 141, 143; his own criticism of it, 102; authorized edition prepared, 102, 142; publication of address, 101; reproduced in appendix, 185, 214; requests MMS. of Lincoln's address, 163–167
Ewell, Richard S., 191–193, 201

INDEX

Fairfield, Pa., 200
Falling Waters, W. Va., 201
Farewell Address, 7
Farwell, J. E. & Co., 143
Farquhar, Arthur B., 86, 124
Fayetteville, Pa., 193
Ferry, Thomas F., 44
Fessenden, William P., 87
Field, Marshall, 166
Fifth New York Artillery, 77, 78
Fifth New York Artillery Band, 66
Fifth United States Regulars, Battery A., 78
First Inaugural Address, 8
Fish, Hamilton, 141
Fish, Mrs. Hamilton, 163, 164
Fish, John, 173
Fisher, George P., 86
Flags, 77
Flanagan, M. E., 69
Florence, Italy, 212
Florida, 207, 208
Forney, John W., 68, 85, 113
Forney's War Press, 86, 146
Fort Sumter, 114, 137, 188
Fouche, 212
Founding Fathers, 3, 18
Fourth of July, 17, 19, 22, 24, 25
France, 212
Frankfort, Ky., 10
Franklin, Benjamin, 203
Frazer, Allen, 134
Frederick, Md., 193
Fredericksburg, Va., 191
French, Benjamin B., 23, 69, 85, 86, 92, 121, 127, 128, 201
French, B. B., Jr., 69
French William H., 193
Fronde, 212
Fry, James B., 57, 58, 78

Gadsdens, 208
Galesburg *Register Mail*, 43
Garabaldi, 51
Garnett, Richard B., 199, 201
Geary, John W., 198
"Genius of Liberty, The," 180
Genoa, 180
George I, 203
George II, 203
George III, 203
Georgia, 208
Georgian era, 171
Germany, 166, 211
Getty, James, 19
Gettysburg, Pa.: founded in 1780, 19; county seat 1800, 19; hub of eleven roads, 19; carriage making industries, 19; educational institutions, 19, 136; on eve of battle, 20; after battle, 27, 28, 38; railroad, 56
Gettysburg battle: preliminaries, 190–193; eve of battle, 194, 195; first day, 195, 196; second day, 197, 198; third day, 198–200; summary, 200, 201
Gettysburg Battlefield Memorial Association, 178
Gettysburg College, 85
Gettysburg *Compiler*, 68, 134, 141
Gettysburg, *Sentinel*, 87
Gibbon, John, 79, 86, 199, 200
Gilbert, Joseph L., 112, 117, 127, 138, 140–142, 157, 161
Gilbert, The Misses, 86
Gilder, Richard Watson, 72, 152, 153, 155
Gilmer, Albert H., 43
Gladstone, William E., 176
Gordon, Percey, 69
Government an agency, 99, 205–207
Graham, George M., 173, 200
Grant, Ulysses S., 21, 22, 71, 87
Gratton, 171
Greece, 105, 186, 187
Greeley, Horace, 15, 87, 110, 113, 173
Green, John Richard, XVI
Green, Samuel A., 116, 174
Gregg, David McMurtrie, 192
Grove of Academe, 186
Gulf of Mexico, 207

Hagerstown, 19, 192
Hale, Charles, 86, 103, 128, 130, 131, 141, 142, 167
Hale, Edward Everett, 141

INDEX

Halleck, Henry W., 27, 107
Halloway, H. C., 120
Hamlin, Hannibal, 87
Hampden, John, 204
Hancock, Md., 20
Hancock, Winfield S., 195, 196, 199, 200, 203
Hanley, Frank J., 174
Hanover Junction, 60, 61
Hanover, Pa., 19, 60, 193
Hanover *Weekly Spectator*, 86, 145
Hanscomb, William L., 86
Hanson, S. P., 69
Hardin County, Ky., 11
Harman House, 196
Harper, Robert G., 67, 70, 75, 148
Harper's Ferry, 193
Harper's New Monthly Magazine, 145
Harper's Weekly, 101, 115, 146
Harris Trust & Savings Bank, 165
Harrisburg, 18, 19, 40, 110, 136, 188, 193
Harrisburg *Patriot and Union*, 148
Harrisburg *Telegraph*, 136
Harrison, William Henry, 39
Hartford, 6, 180
Harvard College, 83, 84, 166
Hastings *Conservator*, 116
Hay, Clarence, 154
Hay, John; assistant secretary to President, 150–159; accompanies Lincoln to Gettysburg, 57, 65, 79, 86, 123; gives account of evening speeches, 68, 79, 73; comments on Dr. Stockton's prayer, 89; receives copy of address from President, 153, 154; associated with Nicolay in Lincoln *History* and *Works*, 155; his copy of address kept secret, 153, 161, 168; acquisition of Nicolay's original copy, 159
Hay, Mrs. John, 152
Hayes, Rutherford, B., 174
Hayne, Robert Young, 1
Heidlersberg, Pa., 195
Hellas, 186
Hendricks, B. S., 69
Henry, Patrick, 116, 203

Henry VII, 207
Herod, 107
Hesse, Germany, 211
Heth, Henry, 201
Higginson, Thomas W., 174
Hill, Ambrose P., 192, 193, 194, 197, 199
Hillis, Newell Dwight, 103, 174
Hobbies Magazine, 166
Hodges, Albert G., 10
Holland, Josiah G., 143, 144
Hood, John B., 201
Hooker, Joseph, 190–193
Hoover, Herbert, XVI, 174
Horner, Charles, 75
Hospitals, 27, 28
House Divided Speech, 5
Howard, Oliver O., 110, 113, 119, 195, 196
Hughes, James, 86
Hume, David, 210
Hurlbut, Stephen A., 16
Huntertown, 19

Illinois, 3, 5, 12, 38
Illinois House of Representatives, 3, 13, 84
Illinois State Historical Society, 43, 165, 166
Illinois *State Journal*, 89, 95, 96, 116, 127
Immaculate Conception Statue, The, 180
Independence Day, 23, 25, 52
Independence Hall, 18, 32
Indiana, 12, 38, 172
"Infernal Serpent," 204
Ingersoll, Robert G., 174
Irelan, John Robert, 124
Irwin, W. W., 59
Ishmael, 205
Italy, 211

Jacob & Lydia of Ephrata, 87
Jacobins, 212
Jacobs, Henry, 122
Jacobs, Michael, 97, 194
James II, 203

INDEX 229

Janesville, Wis., 6
Jefferson, Thomas, 23, 203
Johnson, Andrew, 87
Johnson, Edward, 201
Johnston, William, 65

Kalamazoo, 5
Kansas, 6
Kearsarge, 66
Kemper, J. L., 199, 201
Kent, Charles, 86
Kent, Henry O., 69
Kentucky, 11, 12, 176, 190, 208
Kennedy, John Pendleton, 168
Keyes, Bell F., 61, 151
Keyes, Henry W., 165
Kilpatrick, Hugh, Jr., 60, 193
Kimball, Nathan, 201
King, Surgeon General, 57

Lambert, William H., 162
Lambros, Peter S., 174
Lammon, Robert, 69
Lamon, Dorothy, 126
Lamon, Ward H.; biographical sketch, 76; consults with President, 76; accepts appointment as Marshal, 76; visits Gettysburg Nov. 12 and 17, 76, 69, 91; address read to him by President, 54, 55; prepares for arrival of Mr. Lincoln, 65, 69, 76; calls meeting of marshals, 69; receives note from President, 76; an excellent horseman, 77; supervises parade, 79, 80; in charge of program, 84, 91; introduces President, 120; comment on the speech, 122, 125, 126; reminiscences for newspaper, XVII, 145; "wont scour" and "wet blanket" quotes, 125–127
Lancaster, Pa., 29, 68
Leavenworth, 6
Lee, Robert E.; crosses the Potomac, 190; plans attack on Washington, 191; cut off from his cavalry, 192, 193; pursued by Hooker, 193; "a determined and gallant struggle," 198; wins first day battle, 194, 195; avoids contest on July 4, 21, 22; reports on Union prisoners, 200; loses one-third of army, 201
Leesburg, Va., 191
Lexington, Ky., 62
Libby Prison, 69, 210
Library of Congress, 159
Lincoln, Abraham
 early environment: parents, 1, 2, 10–12; churches, 11; schools, 2, 3; books, 2, 3, 12
 training and oratory: youth, 2, 3; young adult, 3; politics, 3, 4; eulogies, 5; debates with Douglas, 5; appears in Ohio, Wisconsin, and Kansas, 6; New England itinerary, 6, 7; "Farewell Address," 7
 slavery influences: reaction as a child, 10, 11; removal to free state, 12; New Orleans auction block, 12; protest in legislature, 13; resolution in Congress, 13; morally wrong, 13, 14; discussed at Cooper Union, 14; constantly on mind, 16; letter to Greeley, 15; compensated emancipation, 15; Emancipation Proclamation, 16
 patriotic pronouncements: "burning fire crackers," 17; visit to Independence Hall, 18; political sentiments, 18; Independence Day, 22; annual July 4 celebration, 25
 invited to dedication: "afterthought," 43; oral, 44; written, 45, 47; acceptance, 46
 composing address: no amanuensis, 48; "a glorious theme," 23, 24, 49; Thanksgiving Proclamation, 24, 50, 52; Motley correspondence, 24, 51; Garabaldi letter, 51; first sentences, 53
 confidential readings: Defress, 53, 54; Brooks, 54; Lamon, 54, 55
 en route to dedication: revised arrangements, 56, 57; invited guests, 57, 78; Baltimore, 58, 59; Harrisburg special, 59, 60; Hanover comments, 60; traditional writings, 61,

62; *The Perfect Tribute*, 60–63; arrival, 65
accommodations at Gettysburg: Wills' invitation, 64, 65; evening meal, 66; serenade, 66, 67; impromptu speech, 67
traditional writings: Wills' testimony, 70; Bingham's observations, 70, 71; Nicolay's recollections, 72, 73; fantastic conclusions, 73, 74
an equestrian: traditional mounts for parade, 80; "horse play," 81; unfavorable comment, 81; at home in saddle, 82; towered above others, 83
platform appearance: arrived at 11:20, 84; salute by military, 84; conversation with Ohio governors, 85; seating arrangement, 85; chief executive chair, 87
address at Gettysburg
synopsis of remarks: Genesis, 104, 105; equality, 105, 106; criterion, 106, 107; dedication, 107, 108; propriety, 108, 109; futility, 109; consecration, 109; remembrance, 109; inspiration, 110, 111; devotion, 111; resolution, 111; incarnation, 111; declaration, 111–113; democracy, 114–117; perpetuity, 117, 118
presentation of address: quality of voice, 120, 121, 127; use of manuscript, 121–123
reaction to speech: applause, 126, 128; platform comments, 123–125, 138; Lamon's criticism, 125, 126, 128, 129, 133; Gettysburg newspapers, 148; individual tributes, 170–176
holograph copies extant: Hay's corrected writing, 152–154, 159; Nicolay's deleted fragment, 156–159; Everett's revised copy, 163–167; Bancroft's holograph manuscript, 167–168; Bliss' standard version, 168–170
contemporary press recordings:

Hale copy, 103, 104, 141, 142; Associated Press 139, 141; miscellaneous, 142, 161–163
Lincoln, Mrs. Abraham, (Mary Todd), 65, 85
Lincoln, F. W., 32, 40
Lincoln, G. B., 69
Lincoln, Robert Todd, 61, 65, 151, 158, 165, 169
Lincoln, Thomas (Tad), 65, 71, 138
Lincoln, Thomas, 1
Lincoln, Mrs. Thomas, (Nancy Hanks), 1
Lincoln Herald, 132
Lincoln Memorial (Washington), 179
Lincoln National Life Foundation, XIX, 182
Lincoln, Neb., 179
Lincoln Speech Exedra, 178, 179
Lincoln Parentage & Childhood, XIX
Lincoln's Youth, XIX
Little, Brown & Co., 143, 164, 165
Little Mount Separate Baptist Church, 11
Little Rock, Ark., 213
Little Round Top, 197, 199, 214
Lloyd, Thomas, 68
Lodge, Henry Cabot, 154
Lofland, Gordon, 86
Logan, Stephen T., 7, 53, 76
Lombard, 212
London, 210
London *Star*, XV, 51
London *Times*, 148
Long Parliament, 210
Longfellow, Henry W., 174
Longstreet, James, 192, 193, 194, 197, 199
Lost Speech, 5
Louisana, 208
Louis XVIII, 212
Louisville, 11
Louisville & Nashville Turnpike, 11
Low, Frederick F., 22
Lowell, Mass., 4
Loyal Men of Illinois, 95
Ludlow, John Malcolm, 174

INDEX

Lutheran Theological Seminary, 19, 27
Lytton, Edward Bulwer, XVI

MacFarlane, John J., 123
Macmillan's Magazine, 146
MacVeagh, Wayne, 58, 59, 68, 86, 89
McCanby, Hugh, 69
McClellan, George B., 87, 149
McClellan Hotel, Gettysburg, 75
McClure, A. K., 39
McConaughy, D., 3
McCrea, Clara, 82
McCulloch, Hugh, 174
McCurdy, Charles, 70
McDougall, William, 58, 71, 72, 86
McKnight, Harvey, W., 68, 86
McMurtry, R. Gerald, XIX
McPherson, Edward, 68, 86

Macaulay, Thomas, 101
Madigan, Thos. F., 57, 165, 167
Maine, 38, 85
Manchester, Md., 194
Marathon, 186
Marine Band, 78, 191
Marsh Creek, 20, 194, 200
Marshals' meeting, 68, 77, 86
Marshall, John, 116
Maryland, 38, 67, 68, 149, 188, 190–192, 208, 213
Maryland Soldiers and Sailors Fair, 167
Mason, L. B., 86
Mason and Dixon's Line, 19
Massachusetts, 2, 4, 37, 58, 94, 141, 166
Massachusetts Historical Society, 90, 116
Mattingly, John, 69
Maury, Matthew T., 116
Meade, George G., presented medal, 44; replaces Hooker, 193; directs attack, 195–197; victorious army, 22, 188, 201; pursues Lee, 200; wounded in my possession, 27, 201; invited to attend dedication, 46; regrets expressed, 46, 80, 87, 89; at Gettysburg, July 4, 1865, July 1, 1869, 119, 120
Melegakes, N. C., *The Spirit of Gettysburg*, 181
Memorials, 177–183
Mercier, Henri V., 57
Meridian, Conn., 7
Message to Congress, XV, 8, 14
Metro-Goldwyn-Mayer, 62
Metropolitan Fair, 164, 165
Mexican War, 26
Michigan, 38, 85, 182
Middle States, 207
Middletown, Md., 200
Milwaukee, 6
Minnesota, 38, 85
Mississippi, 208
Missouri, 138, 190, 208
Missouri Compromise, 13
Milroy, Robert H., 20
Miltiades, 186
Milton, John, 148
Minerva, 186
Monroe, James, 116
Monterey Pass, 200
Montgomery, 189
Morgan, George, 59
Morris, Charles, 128
Morrow, John, 116, 124
Motley, John Lathrop, 24, 51
Morton, Oliver P., 85, 120
Mt. Vernon Memorial Association, 94
Muhlenburg, Professor, 77
Mummasburg, Pa., 19
Murray, Lindley, 12
Murray, Robert, 78
Murray's English Reader, 12

Nantes, 212
Napoleon, 200
Nason, Elias, 2
Nashville, 11
Nation, The, 169
National Cemeteries, 26, 27
National Military Park, 178
National Park Gettysburg Center, 181

National Park System, 183
Neopolitan, 212
New England, 2, 6, 7, 85
New Hampshire, 6, 38, 165
New Haven, 7
New Jersey, 38
New Orleans, 12, 93
New Windsor, Md., 193
New York, 6, 7, 14, 38, 158, 163, 182
New York *Evening Post*, 70
New York *Herald*, 27, 100
New York *Times*, 68, 89, 100, 109, 110, 122, 126, 132, 137, 153
New York *Tribune*, 6, 15, 66, 67, 68, 113
New York *World*, 86, 100, 146
Newell, W. A., 69
Newton, Joseph Fort, 10, 174
Nickerson, A. H., 108, 122
Nicolay, Helen, 154, 158, 159
Nicolay, John; biographical, 150–152; Washington writing of address, 53; accompanies President to Gettysburg, 57, 60; observes no writing on train, 61, 156; takes part in evening celebration, 73; not on a binge, 73; reports to President, 72, 73; watched Lincoln write address, 72, 156; near President in parade, 79; comments on delivery of speech, 98, 123, 129; refers to revision of speech, 72; Lincoln sketch for *Encyclopaedia Britannica*, 154; Lincoln papers in his custody, 151; joins Hay in Lincoln *History*, 152; correspondence with Gilder, 152, 161, 162; publishes Lincoln's *Works*, 152, 153; magazine articles, 72, 155, 162; controversy with David Wills, 72, 155; Lincoln address in his custody, 151, 158, 159, 161; ignorant of Hay copy, 156, 163; revision of address, 162, 163; tribute, 175
Norris, B. W., 86
North America, 48
North Carolina, 208, 213

North Central Railroad, 58, 96
Noyes, Mrs. Nicholas, 169

Oglesby, Richard J., 114
Ohio *State Journal*, 81
Olin, Abram B., 69, 86
Oliver, Robert S., 170, 178
"One-Legged Brigade," 131
Otis, James, 203
Ottoman, 205
Owsley, Clifford P., 132

Painting by Bicknell, 87
Parade, 76, 83
Paris, 212
Park-Bernett Galleries, 179
Parker, Courtland, XVII, 175
Parker, Joel, 21, 85
Parker, Theodore, 116
Paul, the Apostle, 176
Pausanias, 186
Peach Orchard, 214
Peck, J. A., 23
Peirpoint, Francis H., 59
Peloponnesian dead, 146
Pemberton, John C., 21
Pender, William D., 201
Pennsylvania, 18, 20, 21, 24, 33, 38, 39, 187, 188, 191, 192, 213
Pennsylvania College, 19, 27, 29
Pennsylvania Legislature, 29
Pennsylvania Magazine of History and Biography, 122
Pennsylvania Reserve Corps., 44, 197
Pennsylvania Soldiers' Monument, 179
Peoria, 13
Perfect Tribute, The, XVIII, 62, 63
Pericles, 104, 105, 130, 146, 172, 176, 214
Persia, 186, 187
Pestilence feared, 28, 29
Peters, H. G., 86
Pettigrew, Johnston J., 194, 201, 208
Pettis, S. Newton, 69
Philadelphia, 5, 18, 19, 28, 52, 108, 112, 117, 176, 188
Philadelphia Athlete Club, 117

INDEX

Philadelphia *Bulletin*, XVI, 144
Philadelphia *Inquirer*, 116
Philadelphia *The Daily Age*, 100
Philadelphia *Press*, 86
Photographer, 120
Pickett, George E., 199
Pierce, Carlos, 165
Pierce, Mrs. Carlos, 165
Pike, Charles B., 165
Pilcher, Nathaniel, 116
Pinckney, C. Cotesworth, 208
Pitt, William, 172
Pittsburg, 19
Platform guests, 84, 87
Plato, 187
Pleasonton, Alfred V., 191
Political controversy in Pennsylvania, 38, 40
Pomeroy, John M., 39
Poolesville, Md., 190
Poore, Ben Perley, 61, 86
Porter, David D., 21
Potomac River, 20, 190–193, 201
Powers, Solomon, 25, 37, 134
Presbyterian Banner, 146
Presbyterian Church, Gettysburg, 136
Presidential salute, 131
Prescott, William, 101
Press Bohemians, 139, 140
Proclamation of Thanksgiving, 24, 50, 52, 106, 161
Providence, 6
Providence *Daily Journal*, 144
Provost, Charles M., 78
Prussia, 166
Puritans, 203
Purvis, Samuel W., 175
Putnam, Herbert, 159
Putnam, William Lowell, 167
Putnam's Magazine, 153
Pym, John, 204

Quantrell, W. C., 209
Quay, Matthew S., 59

Raleigh, 213
Raleston, J. H., 59
Ramsay, Alexander B., 44, 79

Rappahannock River, 190, 201
Rebert, James H., 76
Reformation, 211
Relics, 133, 134
Relief Corps of Iowa, 137
Remensnyder, J. B., 81
Republican Central Committee, 86
Republican Convention (1856), 5
Response to Serenade July 7, 1863, 23, 24
Review of Two Worlds, 146
Reynaud, Admiral, 57
Reynolds, John F., 59, 68, 193–195, 201, 214
Rhode Island, 38
Richmond, 189
Roberts, Joseph J., 59
Robespierre, 208
Rodes, Robert E., 195
Rogers, Randolph, 180
Roman Empire, 211
Rome, 180
Romulus, 205
Roosevelt, Franklin D., 175
Roosevelt, Theodore, 154, 175
Rosenburg, Lena Wolf, 81
Round Top, 35, 187, 214
Russell, Alexander L., 204
Russell, Earl, 202
Rutledges, 208

St. Albans, England, 216
Sales, Charles (Chick), 62
Sanitary Commission, 28, 202
Santayana, George, 117
Sardinian, 212
Saul of Tarsus, 83
Saunders, William, 34–36, 85, 108, 180
Scheetz, H. A., 69
Schenck, E. W., 72
Schenck, Robert C., 59, 78, 86
Schmutker, Doctor, 195
Schnyder, Benjamin, 86
Schurz, Carl, 195
Schweizer, J. Otto, 179
Scorey, Levi, 69, 86
Scott, William, 2
Scott, Winfield, 46, 90

INDEX

Scott's Lessons in Elocution, 2
Scribner's Magazine, 61
Second Inaugural Address, XVII
Second United States Artillery, 78
Sedgwick, John, 69, 200
Selleck, W. Yates, 69, 86, 89, 182
Seminary Ridge, 20, 195, 198, 214
Semmes, P. J., 201
Seven Years War, Germany, 211
Seward, William H.: at Boston with Lincoln, 4; named as President's amanuensis, 48; with Lincoln at dedication, 57; evening speech, 67–69, 149; contribution to Libby prisoners, 69; receives President at Harpers, 70, 71; in the parade, 79, 82; on platform, 85; comments on Lincoln's speech, 125, 126, 157; with John L. Burns, 135, 136; note from President, 163
Sewell, W. F., 79
Seymour, Horatio, 33, 59, 85, 134
Shannon, P. C., 68, 69
Shead School, 18
Shepherdstown, 191, 192
Sickles, Daniel E., 196, 197, 200
Sisters of Charity, 28
Site of speakers' platform, 180, 183
Slave markets, 12
Slocum, Henry W., 196
Smith, Goldwin, 175
Smith, J. O., 54
Smith, J. Preston, 56, 57
Snyder, B. P., 69
Soldiers' National Cemetery: Evergreen Cemetery projects, 32; proposals for a National Cemetery, 30, 32; selection of site, 30; purchase of grounds, 32, 34; plans by William Saunders, 34–36; promiscuous burials, 33, 34, 40, 42; burials by states, 33–35; contract for interments, 36, 38; identification of bodies, 35–38; states joining in memorial effort, 38; dedication plans, 41; government acquires cemetery, 178; custody of Secretary of War, 178

Soldiers' National Monument: local cemetery association takes initiative, 32; one dollar subscriptions, 179; Saunders selects exact site, 180; center of burial area, 180; proceeds from brochure, 180; designer and sculptor, 180; cornerstone laid, 119; description, 180; dedication, 120
Somers, John, 204
Souder, Mrs. Edmund, 28, 31
South Carolina, 190
South Mountain, 192, 200
Spain, 207
Spangler's Spring, 198
Speed, James, 138, 156
Speed, Joshua, 13
Sprengle, John A., 81, 123
Springfield, Ill., 3, 4, 7, 95
Springfield (Mass.) *Republican*, 143
Springfield (Ill.) *State Journal*, 146
Stahel, Julius H., 59, 78
Stahle, Henry J., 148, 149
Staley, Andrew B., 59
Stannard, George J., 198
Stanton, Edwin McMasters, 20, 56, 57, 71, 87, 177
Statue of Lincoln, 179
Steinwehr, Adolph, 195
Stephens, Alexander, 203
Stevens, Alex., 69
Stevens, Thad., 29
Stevenson, John G., 69, 86
Stickney, Colonel, 78
Stockton, T. H., 85, 88, 89, 97
Stoddard, William O., 14, 61
Stoneman, George, 59, 86
Stuart, Charles, 46
Stuart, J. E. B. (Jeb), 60, 160, 180, 191–193
Sullivan, Amos, 123
Sumner, Charles, XVI, 87, 106, 175
Susquehanna River, 193
Syracuse, 62

Tales of a Wayside Inn, 91
Taneytown, Md., 19, 186
Tappan, M. W., 69

INDEX

Taylor, Zachary, 5
Tennessee, 190, 208
Texas, 208
Thirty Years War, Germany, 211
Thomas, George H., 59
Tobias, John, 69
Tod, David, 59, 71, 85
To-Day, 141
Todd, Mary (See Lincoln)
Townsend, J. S., 35
Trafalgar, 172
Trent River, 203
Trenton, 105, 117
Trimble, Isaac R., 201
Trone, Daniel, 60
Troy, Greece, XVI
Troy, Kan., 6
Tumulty, Joseph P., 175
Turner's Pass, Md., 200
Tuscan, 212
Twentieth Pennsylvania Cavalry, 78
Tyng, Stephen H., 89

"under God," 111, 112
"under Providence," 199
Union League of Philadelphia, 18, 52, 88
Unitarian Church, Boston, 93
United States, 187, 189, 190, 204, 206, 207, 209
United States House of Representatives, 4, 13
University of Cambridge, 171
University of Michigan, 144
University of Oxford, XVII, 171
Upperville, Va., 191
Usher, John P., 57, 79

Valley Forge, 77
Van Resworth, John, 69
Vanderpoel, Aaron, 59
Vermont, 38
Vermont University, 144
Vicksburg, Miss., 17, 21–24, 188
Vicksburg *Daily Citizen*, 22, 142
Victorian epoch, 171
Vienna, 51
Virginia 20, 199, 208

Wade, Virginia, 136, 137
Wadsworth, James S., 195
Wadsworth, Mrs. James W., 159
War of 1812, 26
War of the Roses, 210
Warren, Gouverneur K., 200
Washington, D.C., 18, 19, 56, 91, 138, 188, 189, 190–192, 201
Washington, George, 51, 52, 112, 203, 205
Washington's Birthday, 18
Washington *Daily Morning Chronicle*, 35, 38, 58, 75, 86, 101, 127, 135, 146
Washington Hall, 4
Waterloo, 200
Watterson, Henry, 61, 175
Waynesboro, Pa., 192
Weaver, Samuel, 37, 38
Webster, Daniel, 1, 6, 116, 128, 176
Webster, Noah, 147, 177
Webster's Collegiate Dictionary, 177
Weed, Stephen H., 201
Weems, Mason, L., 2, 105, 108, 111–113, 117
Welles, Gideon, 20, 21, 22, 46, 87
Wellington, Duke of, 200, 201
Wesleyan College, 73
West Virginia, 38, 190
Western Maryland Railroad, 58
Westminster *Review*, 146
Wheaton, Frank, 198

Wheeler, Andrew C., 121, 175
Whigs, 40, 203
Whipple, Wayne, 87
White, A. H. S., 69
Williamsport, Md., 20, 191, 192, 200
Wills, David: biographical sketch, 29; directs removal of Pennsylvania dead, 29, 30; one of the advocates of the national cemetery, 31; Gov. Curtin's local representative, 29; insists on promiscuous burials, 33; opposed by Boston commission, 33; acquires land, 34; sets date for dedication, 40; writes Everett about address, 40; accepts proposal for change of date, 41–42; writ-

ten invitation to Lincoln, 45–47, 131–132; invites President to his home, 64; provides dinner for invited guests, 65–66; tradition about Lincoln's writing, 70, 71, 155, 157; commissioners associated with him, 86, 182; asks French to prepare poem, 91; not pleased with President's speech, 132, 133; dinner and reception at his home, 134; introduces John Burns to Lincoln, 135; requests copy of Lincoln's speech, 161; controversy with Nicolay, 162; traditional lost copy, 161–163

Wills, Mrs. David, 97

Wilson, Henry, 87, 116

Wilson, James Grant, 129, 153, 158, 159, 176

Winchester, Va., 20

Winslow, John A., 66

Wisconsin, 6, 38, 85, 98

Wise, H. A., 67, 86

Wise, Mrs. H. A., 57, 86,

Wolf Hill, 214

Women, Everett's tribute to, 99, 202

Worcester, 4

Worrall, James, 86

Wright, Joseph A., 59, 79, 85

Yingling, Colonel, 54

Young, John Russell, 86, 120, 129

Young Men's Lyceum, 3

York, 19, 192

Xenia, 137

Zook, Samuel K., 200